RECLAIMING THE FUTURE

D1231447

RECLAIMING THE FUTURE

Women's Strategies
for the 21st Century

Edited by
SOMER BRODRIBB

gynergy
books

0 420089748

Technical editing: Janice Weaver
Cover illustration (detail): © Diana Dabinett
Printed and bound in Canada

*gynergy books acknowledges the generous support of the Canada Council for the Arts
and the Department of Canadian Heritage.*
Canadä

Published by:
gynergy books
P.O. Box 2023
Charlottetown, PEI
Canada   C1A 7N7

"A Woman's Creed" is copyright © 1994 Robin Morgan and reprinted with
kind permission, from *Sisterhood is Global: The International Women's Movement Anthology*,
compiled and edited by Robin Morgan (New York: The Feminist Press at CUNY, 1996).

Canadian Cataloguing in Publication Data

Main entry under title:
Reclaiming the future

Includes bibliographical references.
ISBN 0-921881-51-7

1. Women — Social conditions — Forecasting.   2. Feminism — Forecasting.
3. Twenty-first century — Forecasts.   I Brodribb, Somer, 1954-

HQ1233.R42 1999   305.42'097'0905   C99-950168-2

ACKNOWLEDGEMENTS

I'm grateful to the more than 100 women who sent in abstracts, and those who gave encouragement, offered advice, recommended and contacted other writers, posted the call for papers on billboards, websites, conference tables, and published it in newsletters and magazines.

Thanks to the contributors who considered comments and made revisions with speed and grace.

I very much appreciate the careful and creative library work of Aleya Abdulla and Jennifer Spencer, summer research assistants. And I acknowledge the support of the Social Sciences and Humanities Council of Canada.

Sibyl Frei and Louise Fleming are ardent, committed feminist publishers — big ones. This project would not have taken form without their generous support. Special thanks to Sibyl, gynergy's managing editor, for her calm and skilful guidance along the way.

Janice Weaver's superb technical editing taught me more about the craft of words.

Fortune telling, another women's business. My line of women. My grandmother did it for us, her mother did it for a living. Make a wish, drain the cup and turn the handle three times ... read the shapes and now tell the story ...

Thanks for the readings, Mimi.

TABLE OF CONTENTS

PART FOUR: WOMEN IN CYBERSPACE

PART FIVE: KNOWLEDGE & POWER

PART SIX: THE FUTURE OF ACTIVISM

CONCLUSION

A WOMAN'S CREED

Declaration of the Woman's Global Strategies Meeting

Robin Morgan, in collaboration with Mahnaz Afkhami, Diane Faulkner, Perdita Huston, Corinne Kumar, Paola Melchiori, Sunetra Puri and Sima Wali

We are female human beings poised on the edge of the new millennium.

We are the majority of our species, yet we have dwelt in the shadows.

We are the invisible, the illiterate, the labourers, the refugees, the poor. And we vow: *No more*.

We are the women who hunger — for rice, home, freedom, each other, ourselves.

We are the women who thirst — or clean water and laughter, literacy, love.

We have existed at all times, in every society. We have survived femicide.

We have rebelled — and left clues.

We are continuity, weaving future from past, logic with lyric.

We are the women who stand in our sense and shout *Yes*.

We are the women who wear broken bones, voices, minds, hearts — but we are the women who dare whisper *No*.

We are the women whose souls no fundamentalist cage can contain.

We are the women who refuse to permit the sowing of death in our gardens, air, rivers, seas.

We are each precious, unique, necessary. We are strengthened and blessed and relieved at not having to be all the same. We are the daughters of longing. We are the mothers in labour to birth the politics of the 21st century.

We are the women men warned us about.

We are the women who know that all issues are ours, who will reclaim our wisdom, reinvent our tomorrow, question and redefine everything, including power.

We have worked now for decades to name the details of our need, rage, hope, vision. We have broken our silence, exhausted our patience. We are weary of listing refrains on our suffering — to entertain or be simply ignored. We are done with vague words and real waiting; famished for action, dignity, joy. We intend to do more than merely endure and survive.

They have tried to deny us, define us, defuse us, denounce us; to jail, enslave, exile, gas, rape, beat, burn, bury — and bore us. Yet nothing, not even the offer to save their failed system, can grasp us.

For thousands of years, women have had responsibility without power — while men have had power without responsibility. We offer those men who risk being brothers a balance, a future, a hand. But with or without them, we will go on.

For we are the Old Ones, the New Breed, the Natives who came first but lasted, indigenous to an utterly different dimension. We are the girlchild in Zambia, the grandmother in Burma, the woman in El Salvador and Afghanistan, Finland and Fiji. We are whale-song and rainforest; the depth-wave rising huge to shatter glass power on the shore; the lost and despised who, weeping, stagger into the light.

All this we are. We are intensity, energy, the people speaking — who no longer will wait and who cannot be stopped.

We are poised on the edge of the millennium — ruin behind us, no map before us, the taste of fear sharp on our tongues.

Yet we will leap.

The exercise of imagining is an act of creaion.

The act of creation is an exercise of will.

All this is political. And possible.

Bread. A clean sky. Active peace. A woman's voice singing somewhere, melody drifting like smoke from the cookfires. The army disbanded, the harvest abundant. The wound healed, the child wanted, the prisoner freed, the body's integrity honoured, the lover returned. The magical skill that reads marks into meaning. The labour equal, fair, and valued. Delight in the challenge for consensus to solve problems. No hand raised in any gesture but greeting. Secure interiors — of heart, home, land — so firm as to make secure borders irrelevant at last. And everywhere laughter, care, celebration, dancing, contentment. A humble, early paradise, in the now.

We will make it real, make it our own, make policy, history, peace, make it available, make mischief, a difference, love, the connections, the miracle, ready.

Believe it.

We are the women who will transform the world.

ENDNOTES

WRITTEN BY ROBIN MORGAN, in collaboration with Mahnaz Afkhami, Diane Faulkner, Perdita Huston, Corinne Kumar, Paola Melchiori, Sunetra Puri and Sima Wali, at the Women's Global Strategy Meeting, November 1994, sponsored by the Women's Environment and Development Organization (WEDO). "A Woman's Creed" is also available in Arabic, Chinese, French, Italian, Persian, Portuguese, Sanskrit, Spanish and Russian. To obtain copies in other languages, or for permission to reprint or translate the "Creed" into additional languages, contact Robin Morgan, c/o Edite Kroll Literary Agency, 12 Grayhurst Park, Portland, Maine 04102, USA; fax 207-773-3936; e-mail: ekroll@cre8v.com.

INTRODUCTION

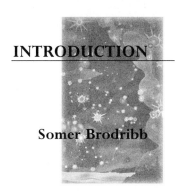

Somer Brodribb

"Black women, be ready. White women, get ready. Red women, stay ready, for this is our time and all must realize it."[1] This is a call to action by Honey, the Phoenix Radio disc jockey in Lizzie Borden's 1983 film *Born in Flames*. The film's themes of violence, poverty, patriarchy, racism, heterosexism, the media and feminist politics and organization are also the themes of *Reclaiming the Future: Women's Strategies for the 21st Century*. The film is set in a parallel universe and near-future New York City ten years after a successful social-democratic revolution. *Born in Flames* is a speculative and political film that focuses on feminist issues, strategies and goals. It speaks to an audience of women in formation, in movement, who are in different locations but who need one another to live. After the revolution, women are still exploited in the home and the workplace, violence against women still exists and homosexuality is punished. The governing Social Democratic Party has reverted to the patriarchal disregard for "women's issues" of work, violence and poverty. As Honey says on Phoenix Radio, "the rich get richer and the poor just wait on their dreams."[2]

Dissatisfied with the opportunism of the government and the "ordinary" oppression of women, community activists resist and take direct action in the film. A women's army organizes bicycle brigades, intervening in sexual assaults and harassments on the streets and in the subways, and protesting sexist and racist job segregation. Various communities of women (Black women, Latinas, single mothers, socialist intellectuals, punk performers) eventually organize to take over a television station, create mobile, free radio stations and blow up the transmission tower of the World Trade Center. Media, communication and organization are among the film's major concerns. The women have been subjected to FBI surveillance technologies, cultural propaganda and disinformation campaigns.

Reclaiming the Future forecasts a challenging new space for communication, freedom and movement that will grow from the collective action and analysis of women. I hope this is a book that makes what women are trying to do seem essential and possible, and that gives us hope, as Black feminist and lesbian activist and writer Barbara Smith says.[3] Through creative and critical work, manifesto, poetry, analyses and plans of action, this collection offers innovative and resourceful critiques of the future from the politics of feminism at the present. Positive and realistic, with a view of the past and a vision of the future, it explores, within the framework of women's lives, some of the questions feminists are considering at the turn of the millennium. How are we forming the future? What space will women have? What directions will our collective action and analysis take? How will feminist changes materialize? What will the issues of sex, race, class, nation, identity and history mean in the next century? What borders will there be, both in cyberspace and in the material, social and economic worlds around us?

This is strategy and speculation, grounded in the contexts of women's lives and the analyses from women's movements. Women's strategies are more than instants of political timing when endurance itself is a form of resistance, as Paula Gunn Allen points out in her closing poem. Strategic speculation uses the political imagination: rebellion takes place against oppression, yet even during times of resistance, new forms of domination are being forged which may not be obvious. But we can set our analyses and imaginations to work. There is a strong relationship between imagination and memory. Memories are political and full of significance for a sense of the future. Interlocking oppressions involving class, race and sexuality take women's time and try to restrict what can be imagined as well as remembered. For those times when women are told they have no future, I hope this book will fuel them to bring about change.

Mainstream millennium countdowns and threats about the "Y2K bug" are dire warnings, staged shivers to make the dominant more comfortable in their dominance. These glories and warnings function to forebode the status quo and to forbid liberation at a time when radicals have become complacent "progressives." Could an apocalypse disturb their tranquillity?

This book takes a completely different direction from millennial conceits and erasures. It is about women on the brink of a new century, contesting a future engineered to be a deadline.

The millennial countdown promotes the Christian world as though it were at the very centre of time and history. However, the year 2000 will be the year 5760 according to the Jewish calendar, 1420 according to the Moslem calendar, and 2544 according to the Buddhist calendar. Y2K will also be the year 6236 according to the first Egyptian calendar, 5119 in the current Maya great cycle, and 208 according to the calendar of the French revolution.[4]

Getting oriented and creating the future are related to how we count up and measure the days. Merlin Stone, who has written extensively on women, spirituality and symbols, argues that we are in a time warp. We are toeing the date line of a patriarchal civilization through daily orientations to the Christian Anno Domini. Stone suggests we re-count, call this the year 9999 and take as a point of origin women's central role in the birth of agriculture, which provided the foundation for neolithic communities and reliable subsistence thousands and thousands of years ago.[5] Women have been keeping time for at least 27,000 years — one of the first calendars was the 27,000-year-old "Earth Mother of Laussel," a carving of a pregnant woman holding a horn marked with 13 notches that may symbolize a lunar year[6] — so this could be the year 27,001.

Like the past, the future is not what it used to be — and it used to be either the Apocalypse or the Jetsons. Our itinerary in this book draws on feminist theories of time, space and energy — *Born in Flames*, for example. I hope this book shows us the politics in women's lives and demonstrates the reality of feminist politics. The writing in *Reclaiming the Future* is made from wisdom, insight, reconsiderations and assessments of politics and communication, place and economy that feminists and social critics want to read about.

The authors have come into the present through different routes, but all the writing is committed to justice and freedom for women. Wise and imaginative, the authors demonstrate alternatives to the crisis of the status quo, and they challenge the reader to rethink and change the present. Their frameworks encompass elements of race, class, nation, gender and sexuality. Broadly, subjects include women's consciousness, creativity and communication; women's collective action, analysis and alternatives. Topics range across cyberspace, utopian and science fiction, the body, virtual reality, violence, poverty, colonial legacies, globalization, the media and democratic solidarity.

The first section, on "Cities of Tomorrow," looks at capital and class:

homelessness in cities today and fantasy visions of the future. Mary Ann Beavis reads feminist utopian literature by authors such as Ursula Le Guin, Marion Zimmer Bradley and Starhawk, as well as feminist urban planning, to speculate about cities of women in the future. She finds that feminist cities are already emerging, and will be built with care, risk and persistence. Kathryn M. Feltey and Laura Nichols introduce the perspectives, stories and experiences of homeless women into visions of the future. Homeless women in the midwestern United States and in refugee camps in El Salvador talk about the privilege and urgency of thinking into the future: these women resist futurelessness. They provide new pathways that are not readily apparent to those with a measure of protection from homelessness and poverty.

"Borders and New Worlds" includes Sunera Thobani's recent research into the Canadian government's racist and sexist immigration strategies for the 21st century. She argues that contemporary policies rely upon the construction of immigrant women as one of the most significant threats to the nation's well-being. This racist and sexist nation-building is also the subject of Vera Wabegijig's critique of old frontiers and globalization within Canada from an Anishinabwe:kwe perspective. Connecting to Sunera Thobani's work, as well as to Joan Grant-Cummings' article on the New World Order, Vera Wabegijig is asking why Canadians haven't looked more critically at how the government has been implementing this New World Order on Aboriginal Peoples?

In the "Popular Culture" section, Annette Burfoot takes us through plague tales and the *Aliens* movie series, highlighting a range of patriarchal panics about births and invasions and the dominance of masculine citizens in space. Meanwhile, reading our magazines on planet earth, Kate Campbell looks at lesbian chic and asks: where's the revolution? The anti-feminism and heterosexism of the mainstream media glamorizes and recuperates "fun" images of lesbians and portrays lesbian feminist politics as unfashionable and outdated.

This could lead only to "Women in Cyberspace"; and in this section monica schraefel looks at the Web, its claims to be a great, wide, open democratic space. She reminds us that the Net was never constructed to give everyone a voice, and that the protocols of the system screen differences. schraefel discusses *Wired* magazine and media theorist Sherry Turkle and shows that the electronic-frontier mentality goes where it has gone before: harassment and appropriation. schraefel highlights the work of the Nova Scotia feminist web-group, *Women'space*, and the American-based Systers mailing list, and discusses their strategies to facilitate women's communication online.

Virtual reality (VR) immersion and art installations (including Canadian feminist artist Char Davies' site) are the focus of Allison Whitney's speculation about future feminist work in communications media. Patriarchal masteries and fears of female reproductive power link to Annette Burfoot's speculations on the body. Allison Whitney critiques cyberpunk and details some of the activities of cyberfeminist artists and theorists. By explaining what women are "up against," she lays out the types of challenges that will be met in the future.

VR headmounted displays and interface devices such as datagloves exist at one level but the radio remains a powerful tool. The women's radio program, FIRE, in Costa Rica, is a dynamic intervention into everyday local, national and international discussions, connecting women's networks and making alternative perspectives significant. In this section on "Knowledge and Power," Margaret Thompson and María Suárez Toro outline the feminist communication strategies and successes of this women's radio project, which since 1991 has been broadcast in Spanish and English over international shortwave radio to more than 100 countries. FIRE effectively interrupts the global media monopoly that erases the grassroots and stereotypes women.

Mary Beth Krouse's chapter is also concerned with globalization, knowledge and power. She effectively critiques the academic talk show in North America, considers its ideological function in global capitalism and calls on women working there to take back their time and make the connections. She argues that the university is being restructured in a way that increases the exploitation of women, racialized groups, and those who are not economically privileged. This has effects well beyond university campuses.

In the final section, on "The Future of Activism," a feminist gene-alogy of strategies continues. Marina Morrow highlights the experiences of anti-violence activists and the work of Barbara Smith and Angela Miles. Morrow analyses the multi-centred politics and solidarity that feminist activists practise to build coalitions and work responsibly across differences. Many anti-violence workers describe how their contact with women in the global South influenced their strategies and their thinking about violence against women. Interviews with diverse survivors, activists and shelter workers in Toronto, Halifax, Vancouver and Duluth, Minnesota, foreground the issues that women are facing: ethnocentrism, funding cutbacks, state co-optation, and individual, apolitical models that mystify male violence. Joan Grant-Cummings, president of the National Action Committee on the Status of Women, also refers to what women in the North learned from women in the South. If you've been avoiding words like "globalization," "economic restructuring" or "the MAI," read this chapter. Grant-Cummings makes it all clear and compelling. She explains what it is, how it works, and what can be done to counter it. She speaks about the urgency of feminist politics to meet human needs.

Beginning at the end, then, are the calls for action by the World March of Women 2000. "We are counting on the presence of thousands, hopefully millions, of women in the streets in the year 2000!" say the organizers.[7] With participation by first- and third-world groups from North and South, this large-scale mobilization was initiated by the Fédération des femmes du Québec and builds on the Beijing Women's Conference and the 1995 March Against Poverty. The World March brings to light actual strategies against violence and poverty and takes a stand similar to Bernice Johnson Reagon's message: "We are not on the defensive, it's our world and we're here to stay."[8]

Somer Brodribb
July 1999

ENDNOTES

1. Lizzie Borden, *"Born in Flames,"* *Heresies: A Feminist Publication on Art and Politics* 4, 4, 16 (1983), p. 14.

2. Ibid., p. 12.

3. Barbara Smith, "Foreward," in Jayne Meyerding (ed.), *We Are All Part of One Another: A Barbara Deming Reader* (Philadelpia: New Society Publishers, 1984), p. xi. Barbara Smith is the editor of *Home Girls: A Black Feminist Anthology* (New York: Kitchen Table, Women of Color Press, 1983). Her recent book is *The Truth that Never Hurts: Writings on Race, Gender and Freedom* (New Brunswick: Rutgers University Press, 1998) which includes a critique of the Millennium March on Washington and "the elitist and reactionary corporate monster that the mainstream lesbian and gay movement has become" (p. 186).

4. David Ewing Duncan, *Calendar* (New York: Avon Books, 1998), pp. 11-12.

5. Merlin Stone, "9978: Repairing the Time Warp and other related realities," *Heresies: A Feminist Publication on Art and Politics* 2, 1, 5 (1982), pp. 124-126.

6. Duncan (1998), p. xi.

7. Fédération des femmes du Québec, "2000 Good Reasons to March" (see pages 273-283 in this book).

8. Bernice Johnson Reagon, "Coalition Politics: Turning the Century," in Barbara Smith (1983), pp. 365 & 368. See also: Chandra Talpade Mohanty's comparison of Bernice Johnson Reagon's article and Robin Morgan's "Planetary Feminism: The Politics of the 21st Century" in her article, "Feminist Encounters: Locating the Politics of Experience," in Michele Barrett & Anne Phillips (eds.), *Destabilizing Theory, Contemporary Feminist Debates* (Stanford University Press, 1992), pp. 74-92.

PART I

CITIES OF TOMORROW

WOMEN AND THE "CITY OF TOMORROW"

Feminist Transformations of the City in the New Millennium

Mary Ann Beavis

Introduction

At the turn of the millennium, speculation abounds as to what the future will be like. The fascination and fear evoked by the year 2000 are reflected in popular culture by the spate of television shows and movies in the apocalyptic science fiction/fantasy/horror genre;[1] global anxiety over the effects of the Year 2000 date code problem (popularly known as Y2K); and the host of new trade and academic books with the word "millennium" or its equivalent in their titles[2] — including works on women.[3] The new millennium, a notion with biblical overtones, holds out the prospect of both "the end of the world as we know it" and "a new heaven and a new earth."

The source of all this speculation, the Christian Testament Apocalypse, portrays the post-millennial regime as a city (the new Jerusalem) personified by a woman (the grammatically feminine *Yerousal_ma*) decked out like a bride at her wedding (Revelation 21: 2), "coming down out of heaven from Godde, having the glory of Godde, its radiance like a most rare jewel, like a jasper, clear as crystal" (Revelation 21: 10-11).[4] Interpreted from a feminist perspective, this ancient prophecy can be read as a symbol of hope, both for women and for the cities they inhabit and shape in the new millennium.

This article imagines, based on the work of feminist urbanists and on the visions of feminist urban utopian writers, what the future "city of women" will be. However, I shall argue that the city of women of the 21st century will not descend "from above," like the new Jerusalem, but will emerge "from below," as a result of a process that has already begun.

In order to construct a vision of what feminist thought, action and activism might achieve in the 21st century,[5] I resort to three sources of reflection on the future city: (1) "malestream" academic writings on "cities of tomorrow"; (2) the ideas and projects of feminist planners, architects and other feminist urban professionals/academics; and (3) feminist utopian science fiction and fantasy literature in which cities are presented as "good places" for women. I conclude by arguing that the seeds of feminist transformations of cities are already present in contemporary cities.

Founding Fathers of City Planning: "Cities of Tomorrow"

The title of this section is taken from Peter Hall's highly regarded history of urban planning and design in the 20th century. Hall identifies "a few key ideas in twentieth-century planning, which re-echo and recycle and reconnect" throughout the century, all in reaction against the evils of the 19th-century city;[6] he then traces each of these "key ideas" to a few "founding fathers" of city planning. Hall gives the 20th-century approaches to addressing the disease, blight and social decay that plagued large Victorian cities the following highly descriptive titles: "The City in the Garden," "The City in the Region," "The City of Monuments," "The City of Towers" and "The City of Sweat Equity."[7]

The garden city movement, sired by the English gentleman Ebenezer Howard and numerous European and American disciples, sought to remedy urban overcrowding, pollution and lower-class "immorality" by moving large numbers of labourers to idyllic new towns set in the countryside and separated from the slums of the metropolis. Foreshadowing bioregionalism, the Scottish biologist Patrick Geddes took Howard's ideas much further by insisting that cities be planned as part of larger regions, with respect for resource renewal, ecological balance and limitations imposed by natural resources. Concurrently, but in sharp contrast to the humane and environmentally sensitive tendencies of Howard's and Geddes' schemes, the "master planners" Eugène-Georges Haussmann (Paris) and Ildefons Cerdà (Barcelona) revived the ancient monumental tradition of city planning (later reflected in Hitler's Germany, Stalin's Russia, Mussolini's Italy and Franco's Spain), which was "symbolic, expressive of pomp and power and prestige, finally innocent of — even hostile to — all wider social purpose."[8] A strange hybrid of these tendencies was Le Corbusier's Radiant City, a scheme whereby the omnipotent architect/planner would replace existing cities with high-rise towers in park-like settings. At the opposite end of the spectrum is the line of planning thought identified with Frank Lloyd Wright, John Turner and Christopher Alexander, which argues that the built forms of cities should not be imposed "from above" by authoritarian planners, but should come from the citizens who inhabit them. Finally, toward the end of the century, we see the "City of Enterprise," a right-wing style of development determined to simplify planning regimes and processes to make cities — such as London, Baltimore and Hong Kong — "open for business," unimpeded by bureaucratic red tape. In varying degrees and different forms, all of these ideas have found physical expression in contemporary cities, although rarely in the pure form envisioned by the planners, and often with unintended negative results.[9]

Hall's history of city planning ends on a disturbing note. He asserts that after a century or so of utopian schemes for the beautification of cities and the betterment of life for urban citizens, and of real progress in city planning, we have become resigned to the idea of the "city of the permanent underclass," a Dickensian 19th-century metropolis. "The city itself is again seen as a place of decay, poverty, social malaise, civil unrest and possibly even insurrection."[10] Clearly, no matter what their philosophy of planning or political orientation, the "fathers" of the profession wanted, not a return to Victorian social decay, but the betterment of the male-headed nuclear family within a patriarchally defined local, regional and national state. While Hall makes the point that women have had little to do with urban planning and design in the past century, he coyly leaves it to the reader to decide what this means for the shape of cities, today or in the future.[11] Surprisingly, he does not speculate about what the real "cities of tomorrow" — the cities of the 21st century — will be like, but leaves the reader with the question of why, "despite all the massive intervening economic and social improvement, the underclass should appear so steadily to recruit new members to replace those lost to it."[12] Certainly, the implication is that the enduring problem of "the disadvantaged and the underprivileged" is not something that can be effectively addressed by urban planning and the welfare state.[13] In his analysis, there is no foreseeable alternative to the "city of the permanent underclass."

At least part of the reason for the failure of the planning philosophies of the past century to transform cities into healthy and humane environments is hinted at in Hall's admission of women's "absence" from professional planning circles. While feminist women of the 19th and early 20th centuries reflected and wrote with great originality, practicality and creativity on housing and neighbourhood design, "municipal housekeeping" and urban social conditions, all too often their work was dismissed by male authorities as the ramblings of "a bunch of old maid social reformers,"[14] or subordinated to the economic and political agenda of consumerism, suburbanization and gender segregation of postwar North America. This work foreshadows and supplements the work of contemporary feminist planners and designers, whose goal is the "non-sexist sustainable city."[15] In the next section, I sketch the accomplishments of "first wave" feminist urban thinkers, as well as some of the major trends in contemporary urban feminism.

Founding Mothers of Urban and Domestic Reform: "The Grand Domestic Revolution" and Beyond

THE FIRST WAVE

The efforts of 19th- and early-20th-century women to reform housing and community design (referred to as "material feminism") have been documented by the architect and historian Dolores Hayden in the feminist classic *The Grand Domestic Revolution*.[16] Middle-class women's interest in domestic architecture and urban planning was sparked by the beginnings of suburbanization in the 19th century and the resulting "servant problem." Long commutes from city to suburb, as well as the increasing availability of jobs in retail and industry, made working-class women unwilling to work as domestic servants.[17] Suburban women, loath to take on the burdens of housework, child care and food preparation that had previously been relegated to servants, began to devise and advocate alternative housing forms, community designs and services that would free women (or, at least, middle-class women) from domestic work. Some even experimented with communitarian socialism, which entailed socialized domestic work, child care and food service.[18] These communities were founded by both men and women with strong views on women's equality and the need to free women from domestic drudgery.[19] American feminist leaders such as Elizabeth Cady Stanton, Susan B. Anthony and Amanda Bloomer were well aware of these alternatives to the isolated home and housewife, and they advocated for cooperative housing and housekeeping as important steps toward achieving women's equality.[20]

A conservative alternative to communitarian socialism was pioneered by Catharine Beecher, an educator who regarded the home as woman's (as opposed to man's) "commonwealth," and housework as a suitable profession for middle-class Christian women (as opposed to servants).

She proposed all kinds of technical improvements and innovative housing designs to facilitate this new professional role of homemaker for "respectable" women.[21] Her two best-known books, *Treatise on Domestic Economy* (1841) and *The American Woman's Home* (1869, co-authored with her sister, Harriet Beecher Stowe), contained detailed architectural designs for the reorganization of housing space and were immensely popular in the United States (the former was adopted as a school text).[22] Beecher also proposed schemes for housing and services for the urban poor, settlement houses and "model Christian communities," which would include some collective services to lighten women's domestic duties.[23] Beecher's more radical successors included:

* Melusina Fay Peirce (1836-1923), who pioneered the idea of co-operative housing and housekeeping;[24]
* Marie Stevens Howland (1836-1921), a radical and advocate of "free love" who was active in the Owenite movement and co-published plans for a variety of new housing forms, including apartment-hotels, communal courtyard housing and cottages with cooperative housekeeping;[25]
* Mary Livermore (1820-1905), a suffragist and temperance worker who advocated the socialization of housework and child care;
* Ellen Swallow Richards (1842-1911), who, with Mary Hinman Abel, pioneered the idea of public kitchens for the urban immigrants of Boston and brought a scientific approach to the fledgling discipline of home economics at MIT;[26]
* Jane Addams (1860-1935), the Chicago activist who brought the settlement-house movement to the United States in the form of the famous Hull-House; she also established cooperative housing for working women in Chicago;[27]
* Charlotte Perkins Gilman (1860-1935), one of the most prominent feminist activists of her time. She was founder, with Helen Campbell, of the Chicago Household Economics Society, which advocated "both neighborly cooperation and businesslike combination ... cooperative laundries, cooperative bakeries, and public kindergartens."[28] She also recognized the need for "feminist housing for feminist mothers," including both married and divorced women with children, which resulted in a campaign by the New York Feminist Alliance (founded by Henrietta Rodman in 1914) to establish a feminist apartment-hotel

— which would integrate housekeeping, food and child-care services — based on Gilman's ideas;[29]

 ⁺ Ethel Puffer Howes (1872-1950), a psychologist who taught at Harvard University,[30] as well as at women's colleges such as Simmons, Wellesley and Smith. Howes devoted most of her academic career to political organizing on domestic issues, advocating new social arrangements that would accommodate both marriage and career, including part-time work for mothers, and community services to provide cooking, cleaning and child care.[31]

Hayden regards Howes as the last of the domestic reformers of the first wave of feminism. Efforts to alleviate women's domestic burdens by redesigning houses, neighbourhoods and cities were undermined by the so-called Red Scare; by the U.S. policy of promoting dispersed suburban housing for nuclear, male-headed families; and by "selling Mrs. Consumer" on the wonders of household technology.[32]

Another important and overlooked contribution of women to urbanism in this period was the social-scientific research undertaken by women faculty members at the University of Chicago.[33] The geographer David Sibley has documented the work of "the other Chicago School," the so-called mothers of social work — Edith Abbot, Sophonisba Breckinridge, Helen Rankin Jeter, Mary Zahrobsky and Leila Houghteling — who published major research work on social conditions in the inner city of Chicago (the Chicago School of Sociology is well known as the place where urban studies began, around 1910). Jeter analyzed the market mechanisms that consigned low-income tenants to poor-quality housing at relatively high rents; Abbot and Zahrobsky made the connection between racism, high rents and urban spatial segregation for African Americans; and Abbot recognized the social breakdown that occurred when the cultural values of immigrant communities were undermined by poverty and the stresses of adaptation to a new urban American culture. Sibley argues that this group of women urbanists has been relegated to obscurity because of: (1) the blatant sexism of the male sociologists of the Chicago School; (2) the radical political implications of their research; and (3) their use of qualitative, rather than quantitative, research methodology.

Hayden observes that, during the hiatus between the first and second waves of feminism (1920-70), the ideas of the material feminists (as well as those of pioneer feminist social scientists and social reformers) were virtually forgotten.[34] Feminists of the 1970s, while well aware of the "superwoman" syndrome and the double burden of domestic and paid work carried by women working outside the home, had no access to the work of their foremothers and could come up with no better solutions than wages for housework or sharing housework with men.[35]

THE SECOND WAVE

Thanks to the work of feminist architects such as Dolores Hayden and Leslie Kanes Weisman in the 1980s and 1990s, the insights of the 19th-century material feminists have again become available to contemporary women in "urban" professions and disciplines. In particular, the material-feminist insight that gender discrimination has spatial and architectural dimensions that affect women's movements, activities and use of space — that, in other words, urban spaces have been designed by and for men, or by men for women — has affected the practice of women urbanists. Since the 1980s, a substantial body of work has been done by feminists from various urban-related professions and academic disciplines (i.e., planning, architecture, geography, political science, sociology) on what cities designed by women, for women, would be like.[36] This is a kind of utopian exercise, in that it seeks "to make the world a better place, to create supportive, and when possible, beautiful places and things for people."[37]

Initially, the speculations of writers such as Hayden and Weisman on "what a city designed by women would be like" appear rather modest compared with some of the grand schemes devised by 19th-century feminists. In *Redesigning the American Dream*, published in 1984, Hayden recommends incremental measures such as organizing neighbours to re-use existing infrastructure "to transform housework, housing design, and the economics of residential neighborhoods";[38] rezoning to allow accessory apartments;[39] reorganizing tracts for single-family houses into spaces for duplexes and triplexes;[40] relandscaping for a better balance of public and private space;[41] public policy to favour cooperative housing ownership and various forms of public housing;[42] designing for special-needs persons, the elderly and non-traditional family structures;[43] and developing innovative housing forms for "battered wives."[44] One chapter, "Domesticating Urban Space," suggests ways in which women can claim the right to walk city streets without fear of harassment or attack,[45] and also provides a lengthy critique of how public space is used to perpetuate gender stereotypes through advertising and pornography.[46]

Published 10 years after Hayden's book, Leslie Kanes Weisman's *Discrimination by Design* makes very similar proposals[47] — with the addition of a very brief suggestion that suburban shopping malls could be redesigned as public gathering places and resource centres to counteract urban sprawl,[48] and a plea for feminist birth centres as an alternative to the sterility and regimentation of maternity hospitals.[49]

A recent Canadian contribution to this literature edited by Margrit Eichler, *Change of Plans*,[50] contains articles that add a welcome ecofeminist consciousness to the discussion on women and cities. In her introduction to the book, Eichler presents a slightly expanded summary of the political scientist Caroline Andrew's list of the characteristics of the feminist city,[51] a list that draws together many of the insights of a decade of urban feminism, including the work of Hayden and Weisman. The Andrew/Eichler vision of a feminist city includes:

- A well-developed network of services dealing with the issue of violence against women and children;
- A wide variety of services (such services might include alternative forms of transportation, community-based businesses run by and for women, affordable housekeeping and food services, recreational and educational facilities, and feminist resources for psychological and spiritual counselling);
- Elimination of public violence against women through a public agency whose mandate it is to ensure this;
- Friendly neighbourhoods that through a mixed use of space and lively streets are oriented toward pedestrians rather than cars;
- An active social-housing policy, which includes cooperative housing, housing for women leaving transitional homes and special housing for women with disabilities;

- Good daycare in a variety of forms, from drop-in centres to full-day care;
- Active encouragement of community-based economic development, with meaningful jobs for women coordinated with daycare;
- A close physical relationship between services, residences and workplaces, encouraged by mixed land use;
- A feminist planning process, which involves work *with* the population rather than *about* the population;
- Public art that is representative of women and women-centred activities;
- Concern for a healthy environment;

✦   Access to healthy food for all community family members.

While the insights of the second-wave urban feminists have much in common with those of their 19th-century foremothers, contemporary feminist urbanism adds several distinctive emphases, including:

✦   A profound concern for the safety of women and children;
✦   A high level of ecological awareness, including a critique of car-dependency;
✦   Identification with the socially and economically marginalized (racial and ethnic minorities, the disabled, children, abused women, the elderly, etc.);
✦   A high level of class awareness and an ideal of social, as well as gender, equity;
✦   An awareness of the significance of graphic representations of women in public spaces;
✦   Concern with global, as well as local, issues (e.g. food security).

However, perhaps the greatest and most significant difference between the material-feminist activists of the first wave and the urban feminists of the second wave is that the latter are professional academics, architects, planners and policy-makers — women with the power to give their ideas concrete, physical form. Contemporary feminist urbanists also have the benefit of being able to stand on the shoulders of their foremothers, whose work they have access to, thanks to the efforts of historical reclamation undertaken by Dolores Hayden and others.[52] Perhaps as a result, many of the "woman-friendly" features recommended by Caroline Andrew and Margrit Eichler exist in contemporary cities, albeit in partial or piecemeal forms. Services for women, particularly abused women, are far from adequate, but have become an accepted part of the urban landscape since the 1970s. The issues of violence against women and urban safety have by no means been fully addressed, but they are much higher on the public agenda than they were a scant two decades ago.[53] Urban designers are much more aware of the safety implications of their work, and urban safety audits (pioneered in Toronto) are advocated by municipal governments across Canada, as are "safe city" committees and community policing. Architects, planners and policy-makers are also much more sensitive to the special needs of the elderly and the disabled, thanks largely to the efforts of disability-rights activists, both feminist and non-feminist.[54] Women's housing co-ops are scattered in cities throughout the country, although more are needed.[55] Increased urban density and mixed land use have been planning ideals, if not often realities, since the publication of Jane Jacobs' classic work, *The Death and Life of American Cities* in 1961,[56] and problems of urban sprawl are beginning to be seriously addressed in some municipalities.[57] Woman-friendly planning processes have been pioneered in cities throughout the world for more than a decade.[58] Although much remains to be done, these examples demonstrate ways in which feminist professionals, academics and activists have begun to rethink and reshape cities. Arguably, the feminist urban utopia is already present in our cities, in embryonic form.

Visions of the City in Feminist Utopian Literature

First-wave feminist writers of the 19th and early 20th centuries created many utopias, some set in cities, some in idyllic rural settings. In fact, surveys of the literature indicate no strong bias toward either urban or rural settings in this tradition; both city and countryside are envisioned as environments where an ideal society can be realized.[59] Dolores Hayden observes that the utopian novelists of this period, both female and male, "succeeded in encouraging millions of readers to imagine the possibilities of an egalitarian, industrialized, mass society, without all the evils of capitalism."[60] Some of these writers portrayed ideal communities where the kinds of measures advocated by the material feminists had been implemented; Marie Howland and Charlotte Perkins Gilman both wrote about fictional utopias as well as advocating practical social and domestic reform.[61]

In the late 20th century, the genre of feminist utopian writing is highly developed, as the volume of secondary literature on the subject attests.[62] An overlooked topic, however, has been the feminist *urban* utopia, in which the city is depicted as a "good place" (*eutopia*), if not a perfect place (*utopia*, or "no place"), for women to live.[63] Part of the reason for this neglect may be that, within the genre of feminist utopias, feminist urban *eutopias* are relatively rare. Unlike their 19th-century sisters, recent feminist writers have usually constructed the city as a hostile, patriarchal space from which women must escape to build alternative communities in the countryside.[64] The science-fiction writer

Joanna Russ comments on this aspect of feminist utopian writing in the 20th century:

> "If the [feminist] utopias stress a feeling of harmony and connection with the natural world, the authors may be telling us that in reality they feel a lack of such connection. Or perhaps the dislike of urban environments realistically reflects women's experience of such places — women do not own city streets, not even in fantasy. Nor do they have much say in the kind of business that makes, sustains and goes on in cities."[65]

The feminist writers' dislike of urban environments can be connected with a long history of gendered spatial segregation, where women have been conceived of as "out of place" in the public realm.[66] This spatial segregation culminated in the ideal segregation of women and children in "safe" suburban enclaves in the latter half of the 20th century.[67]

I have identified seven contemporary science fiction/fantasy novels in which the city is portrayed as a *eutopia*, or "good place," for women.[68] These seven novels have been selected for their: (1) strong feminist themes; (2) strong utopian/eutopian themes; (3) overall positive portrayal of cities and urban living; (4) clear descriptions of urban environments and lifestyles; (5) popularity and critical acceptance.[69] Six are by American writers: Ursula K. Le Guin, *The Dispossessed* (1974); Sheri S. Tepper, *The Gate to Women's Country* (1988); Pat Murphy, *The City, Not Long After* (1989); Marion Zimmer Bradley, *The Ruins of Isis* (1978); Pamela Sargent, *The Shore of Women* (1986); and Starhawk, *The Fifth Sacred Thing* (1993). One is by a Québécoise Canadian writer: Elisabeth Vonarburg, *The Maerlande Chronicles* (1992).

These works resist the trend of utopian literature in general, and recent feminist utopian literature in particular, to reject the city as a desirable human habitat. They also resist the essentialist impulse to identify woman with nature and man with civilization, an impulse that is so entrenched in Western culture.[70] Perhaps significantly, all of these authors are white;[71] portrayals of the future city by Black feminists tend to be dystopian.[72] Unfortunately, it is outside the scope of this article to speculate at any length about why women writers of colour have avoided the feminist eutopian genre to date, although it undoubtedly reflects important differences between white and non-white women's experiences of urban environments. This may change as the number of women of colour writing in the feminist utopian genre increases.[73]

The feminist urban eutopias under consideration here fall into two broad categories. In the works by Tepper, Bradley, Sargent and Vonarburg, all of which take place in the remote future, cities, civilization and culture are all dominated by women. The women of Bradley's planet Isis have colonized the new world in order to escape a male-dominated interplanetary federation; while a few males are allowed to live on the planet, they are spatially segregated from the women, and are valued mainly for their reproductive role and for their utility as labourers. In the other three novels, the Earth has been devastated by nuclear or other ecological disaster. In Tepper's *Women's Country* and Sargent's *Shore of Women*, women have deliberately adopted the (walled) city as their own place, and have banished men to the hinterland, where they live brutal and futile lives. In Vonarburg's Europe of some 700 years in the future, males are valued for their scarcity (owing to a genetic mutation, only a tiny percentage of the population is born male, and even fewer survive) but live apart from the female majority, and are regarded with some contempt and suspicion. In these novels, men's consignment to dystopia is represented not only as the logical outcome of a violent and patriarchal past, but also as an ultimately undesirable and temporary state that, with great effort and discretion, will eventually be overcome.

In the second group of eutopias — two of which are set in a near-future San Francisco (Murphy and Starhawk), the other on a moon colonized by the followers of a female anarchist philosopher named Odo (Le Guin) — women and men live together in egalitarian urban societies where rigid gender roles have been abolished or are unimportant. These fledgling societies are hedged in by hostile, patriarchal forces that must constantly be resisted. In the novels set in San Francisco, the takeover of the city by egalitarian regimes is the aftermath of ecological disaster (Starhawk) or plague (Murphy). The colonists of *The Dispossessed* inhabit a desert moon (Annarres), to which they have fled to escape what they perceive as the oppression, waste and decadence of their home planet, Urras.

The qualities shared by these urban feminist eutopias correspond to seven "women's ways of knowing," abstracted by Karen Franck from recent feminist psychoanalytic, psychological, philosophical and philosophy-of-science literature.[74] These are:

1. *Connectedness*: The environmental destruction and social devastation wrought by patriarchy prompts the inhabitants of the urban eutopias to be "connected" to the Earth and aware of ecology, the science which recognizes that "everything is connected to everything else." The effects of the past are seen in the present, and it is recognized that remembrance of the past may prevent the repetition of mistakes, as well as provide valuable information that can be used in the present.

2. *Inclusiveness and overcoming dualities*: The distinction between nature and culture, the urban and the rural, is blurred; animals and plants are "at home" in feminist eutopian cities, and agriculture is carried on within and in proximity to urban settlements.

3. *Ethic of care*: An ethic of care and sensitivity to the needs of others (especially other women) is a theme that pervades these novels; supportive households of women (and sometimes men) — mothers, children, lovers, life-partners — live together in comfortable, but rarely opulent, surroundings. Sargent and Vonarburg portray women living in clusters of "towers" filled with interconnected halls and passageways, which link women physically and socially with other women and girls. Vonarburg describes the city of Wardenburg as buzzing like a beehive.

4. *Value of everyday life*: Mixed land use, a vital street life, the presence of children and the visibility of labour are common themes in these novels.

5. *Acceptance of subjectivity and feelings*: The novels' depiction of the city and society is mediated through the experience of characters who are both part of the eutopia and critical of it. The marginalization of males and a tendency toward stagnation are issues that emerge in these near-perfect societies. Experience, emotional growth and empathy, as much as observation and information, provide the impetus for social change.

6/7. *Acceptance and desire for complexity/acceptance of change and desire for flexibility*: Complexity, flexibility and acceptance of differences (especially among women) are features of the physical and, in varying degrees, social landscapes of these feminist eutopias. However, the desire for complexity/flexibility can conflict with the value of inclusiveness and the need to overcome opposing dualities (no. 2, above). The tension between the impulse toward inclusiveness and the desire for complexity and change adds an element of moral depth that is usually absent in utopian literature. Contrary to the static perfection that characterizes traditional utopias, none of the feminist societies portrayed is perfect, nor are the people who inhabit them entirely satisfied with their lot.

The cities of women are good, not perfect, places, and eutopia is conceived as a *process*, not an end state.[75]

The values that underpin these feminist eutopias find physical expression in cities in the following forms:

- *A high level of ecological awareness*: Cities are "designed with nature," using technologies that work in harmony with ecological processes. Recycling and the avoidance of waste and pollution are key principles. City and nature are not regarded as opposites, but as an integrated system.
- *A lively and vital street life*: Whether large or small, the feminist eutopian cities are dense, bustling centres where pedestrians enjoy roaming the streets, work is visible from the pavement, and chance encounters are frequent and welcomed.[76]
- *A lack of disparities between socio-economic classes*: All members of society have satisfying work that meets their economic needs, and that contributes to the well-being of the city.
- *The valuing of children*: Education and child care are high priorities. In Bradley's *Isis*, for example, children's art is featured on the movable screens that serve as indoor walls.
- *Safety and freedom from violence*: These are presupposed in urban life.
- *Communal dwellings*: These make provision for personal privacy.
- *The integration of housing and work*: Work is conducted in, or in close proximity to, residences.
- *An allowance for beauty and pleasure*: This is done in accordance with the aesthetic principles of the respective eutopias (i.e., Annarres' Spartan ethic versus the ease and abundance of Sargent's "cities of women" or the bohemian ethos of Murphy's San Francisco).

As mentioned earlier, although the feminist urban eutopias are good places to live, they are not perfect.[77] In four of the seven imaginary eutopian societies (those of Bradley, Sargent, Vonarburg, Tepper), men and boys are marginalized, both socially and spatially. The women of Sargent's cities are complacent, resistant to change and conformist; the women of Tepper's eutopia are ruled by small councils whose agenda — which involves selective breeding to eliminate aggressiveness in males — is kept secret from most citizens. The radical egalitarianism of Le Guin's Annarres is frustrating to a person of great talent or genius, such as the brilliant physicist Shevek, the protagonist of the tale. Constant vigilance, risk, compromise, effort and *change* are required to keep these fictional cities "good."

Most of these feminist urban eutopias are "millennial" in the sense that they postdate some catastrophic event that marks the end of history as we know it. In three of the seven novels (those of Vonarburg, Tepper, Sargent), all knowledge of the 20th century has been lost; the near-future San Franciscos depicted by Starhawk and Murphy are pockets of resistance to militant, quasi-demonic forces. Urban feminist eutopias are also millennial in a stricter sense; they are societies characterized by "good government, great happiness and prosperity."[78] In most of these stories, eutopia has succeeded dystopia, but reversion to chaos is a dreaded possibility.

Feminist Urban Eutopian Fiction and Urban Feminism

Obviously, there are many similarities between the views of feminist urbanists and the visions of feminist eutopian writers. This begs the question of how aware urban feminist professionals and academics are of the feminist eutopists, and vice versa. There is certainly evidence that feminist urbanists are familiar with at least some of the feminist eutopian literature. Dolores Hayden is well read in the feminist utopias of the 19th century,[79] for example, and Robyn Whittaker and Beth Moore Milroy have wondered aloud whether feminist utopists have something to say to urbanists about their work, asserting that "utopian themes — especially inclusivity and visibility — propose important perspectives from which to analyze how urban practices and plans contribute to consolidating or dispersing power in a given society."[80] Karen Franck refers to Marge Piercy's *Woman on the Edge of Time* in her article on feminist architecture;[81] and Leslie Kanes Weisman has observed that "perhaps the richest source of writing about a future nonsexist scenario is in feminist science fiction."[82] Utopian exercises are sometimes used by academics to encourage students to imagine alternative urban futures.[83] It is more difficult to ascertain whether feminist science-fiction writers read the work of feminist urban scholars and practitioners, although literary critics of this genre often cite Hayden's *Grand Domestic Revolution.*[84]

Whether or not there is direct influence, it is not surprising that two groups of feminists considering the question of what a good city for women would be like have generated similar ideas. Kessler's survey of

American feminist eutopias written before 1950 reveals that the themes of women's eutopian visions have closely paralleled the development and concerns of feminism from the first wave to the second.[85] The first-wave eutopias (1836-1920) are occupied with marriage and domestic reform, suffrage, education, meaningful work and socialism; eutopias of the second wave (1960-83) are more likely to stress communitarian values, ecological awareness and spirituality. In the hiatus between the two waves of feminist awareness (1920-60), Kessler can identify only eight utopias with feminist themes, three of which are preoccupied with improving heterosexual relationships.[86] Of the five remaining examples, one is a late work by Charlotte Perkins Gilman ("Applepieland," 1920) and another is a satire on free love by Clare Myers Spotswood (1935).[87] Kessler explains the dearth of feminist eutopian speculation in this period as being a result of the eclipse of feminism: "This narrowing of focus after the wide-ranging visionary alternatives appearing before 1920 reflects the times: all nonfeminist utopias enclose women in marriages and families that subordinate women's needs to those of the social unit."[88] The decline of women's interest in feminist utopian writing corresponds with the hiatus in urban feminism documented by Hayden.[89]

One way in which the writings of the feminist urbanists and the eutopists differ significantly is that the negativity toward the future of cities, and of humanity generally, characteristic of the feminist eutopian writers is not shared by the professional urbanists. The fictional urban eutopias tend to envision the future city of women as the aftermath of revolution, catastrophic ecological disruption, or both. The feminist urbanists, in contrast, see the city designed by women as a practical, near-future possibility that can be achieved incrementally with planning, effort and commitment. Perhaps the greater optimism shown by the urbanists arises out of their ability, as professionals and teachers, to see their eutopian ideas realized, albeit in partial and provisional forms.

A recent paper by Daphne Spain, "Black Women as City Builders," suggests a helpful way to conceptualize women's historical and future contributions to city-building.[90] Spain has documented the "significant contributions to the urban landscape" made by American Black women in the late 19th and early 20th centuries. Through their involvement with voluntary associations, African-American women created a safety net for Black urban migrants — schools, public baths, boardinghouses, playgrounds, settlement houses.[91] Spain uses a tapestry metaphor to illustrate the relationship between male and female contributions to city-building during this era: "... while men were building the vertical warp of the city — the office buildings, factories, and monuments that formed the skyline — women were constructing the horizontal weft — the ordinary places that held the urban fabric together. Both warp and weft are necessary to complete a successful pattern."[92]

Spain's remarks apply not only to American Black women at the turn of the century, but also to all of the unrecognized and undocumented women whose efforts have contributed to the "weft" of our cities — the hospitals, the schools, the libraries, the colleges, the drop-in centres, the clinics, the daycares, the hospices, the shelters for abused women, the rape crisis centres, the housing cooperatives, the small businesses. In a very real sense, the "city of women," the redemptive space within our cities that women (as well as men) have worked so hard to construct, already exists. To illustrate how feminist planning, design and activism have permeated contemporary cities, I offer a few recent, and very diverse, examples, from large-scale social trends and government-sanctioned programs to small, locally based initiatives:

- The election of increasing numbers of women to positions in local government, an advancement that brings with it changes in role perceptions, governing styles and policy priorities.[93] McManus and Bullock conclude in their review of women in local office in the United States that they are more likely to give priority to women's rights and to women's traditional roles as caregivers; be active on women's-rights legislation, whether or not it is their top priority; be more feminist and more liberal than men in their attitudes toward public-policy issues; have close ties with women's organizations; bring citizens into the governing process; be responsive to groups previously denied full access to the policy-making process.[94]
- The emergence of housing developed by and for women in Canada and internationally.[95]
- The growing presence of feminist women faculty in university planning, architecture and other urban-related disciplines; these women bring an awareness of the gendered aspects of urban design to research and teaching.
- Montreal's "Femmes et ville," a program committed to ensuring the civic participation of women and making municipal government aware of women's specific needs.[96] This is part of an initiative to form an

international network "to link together local authorities, elected women and researchers, as well as nongovernmental organizations," to help create conditions that will "allow women to exercise their citizenship fully; in short, to ensure that women and men fully inhabit the city together."[97]

↝ Initiatives designed to address the issue of violence against women that have sprung up in cities across North America, including "safe city" committees and programs, and the drafting and implementation of urban safety audits.[98]

↝ Small businesses such as Her Hands in Winnipeg, a craft store and cultural centre run by women for women. These businesses provide a place where women can pursue and share their own creative work in an affordable and accessible way.[99]

↝ The Power of Place project in Los Angeles, a non-profit corporation launched by Dolores Hayden in 1984 "to situate women's history and ethnic history in downtown, in public places, through experimental, collaborative projects by historians, designers and artists."[100]

For each of these examples, thousands of others could be adduced. The "city of men" and "city of women," eutopia and dystopia — which, of course, cannot simply be correlated with gender stereotypes — co-exist, in varying degrees and different forms, in all contemporary cities.

Conclusion

We have seen that the feminist writers of urban eutopian literature and the feminist urbanists of the late 20th century have a great deal in common. The two groups share common values, as well as similar concepts of what the city of women should be like (i.e., ecologically healthy and aware; socially and economically egalitarian; safe and free from violence; compact and integrally designed; child-friendly, beautiful and pleasurable, with easy and affordable access to services). In general, the feminist urban professionals are more optimistic than the feminist eutopian writers about how the city of women will come to be. While the eutopists tend to envision the feminist city as springing forth out of the ashes of some patriarchally inflicted catastrophe, or even as a radical alternative to cities of men, the urbanists see it as a practical reality to be realized gradually, partially and incrementally through a continuing and creative process of effort, activism and achievement. But both groups of feminists present a more optimistic view of the future than Peter Hall does with his "City of Tomorrow."

The emergence of feminist urbanism in the late 20th century holds out the promise of cities that will be, if not feminist per se, at least *more* feminist than in the past. In the new millennium, this city of women will expand and contract in different ways, times and places, informing both the weft and warp of the urban tapestry, co-existing with elements of disruption and decay, displacing dystopia and constantly being jeopardized by it. Perhaps the best lesson that can be taken from the fictional urban eutopias is that constant care, risk, persistence and effort will be needed to nurture, restore and maintain the potential that lies dormant in our cities.

ENDNOTES

1. I am thinking particularly of dramas that anticipate the end of the world "as we know it" (i.e., *Independence Day, Dark Skies*, the wonderful *Prey, First Wave, Earth: Final Conflict, Armageddon, Deep Impact, Millennium, The X-Files, Invasion Earth*, to name a few).

2. See, for example: Daniel Wojcik, *The End of the World as We Know It: Faith, Fatalism, and the Apocalypse in America* (New York: New York University Press, 1997); David W. Ehrenfeld, *Beginning Again: People and Nature in the New Millennium* (Oxford: Oxford University Press, 1997); Lon Milo DuQuette, *Angels, Demons and Gods of the New Millennium* (York Beach, ME: Samuel Weiser, 1997); Reginald Stackhouse, *The End of the World? A New Look at an Old Belief* (Mahwah, NJ: Paulist, 1997); and Peter Lalonde & Paul Lalonde, *2000 A.D.: Are You Ready? How New Technologies and Lightning-Fast Changes Are Opening the Door for Satan and His Plan for the End of the World* (Nashville, TN: Thomas Nelson, 1997).

3. See: Catherine Keller, *Apocalypse Now and Then: A Feminist Guide to the End of the World* (Boston: Beacon, 1997); Carol R. Ronai, Barbara A. Zsembik & Joe R. Feagin (eds.), *Sexism: In the Third Millennium* (London: Routledge, 1997); Linda Grant, *Sexing the Millennium: Women and the Sexual Revolution* (New York: Grove/Atlantic, 1995); Fiona Montgomery & Christine Collette (eds.), *Into the Melting Pot: Teaching Women's Studies in the New Millennium* (Brookfield, VT: Ashgate, 1997); Donna J. Haraway, *Modest Witness Second Millennium: Femaleman Meets Oncomouse: Feminism and Technoscience* (London: Routledge, 1996); and Pamela McCorduck & Nancy Ramsey, *The Futures of Women: Scenarios for the 21st Century* (New York: Warner, 1996).

4. The quotation is from the Revised Standard Version of the Bible. I have used the alternative, archaic spelling of God ("Godde") to destabilize the patriarchal associations of the term (see: Edwina Gateley, *A Warm Moist Salty God: Women Journeying towards Wisdom* {Trabuco Canyon, CA: Source, 1993}).

5. Although, arguably, feminist women have been involved in the shaping of cities since the 19th century (see: Dolores Hayden, *The Grand Domestic Revolution: A History of Feminist Designs for American Homes, Neighborhoods, and Cities* {Cambridge, MA: MIT Press, 1981}), explicitly feminist planning and architecture are professions that are still in their infancy (there are few publications in this area that predate the 1970s; most have been published in the 1980s and 1990s). Therefore, any discussion of future feminist transformations of the city can only be preliminary, speculative and suggestive.

6. Hayden (1981), p. 7.

7. Peter Hall, *Cities of Tomorrow* (Oxford/New York: Blackwell, 1988), pp. 8-12.

8. Ibid., p. 9.

9. Jane Jacobs sarcastically calls the cumulative results of the partial implementation of these planning philosophies "the Radiant Garden City Beautiful" (in *The Death and Life of Great American Cities* {New York: Vintage, 1991}, p. 25; this classic of urban literature was originally published in 1961).

10. Hall (1988), p. 11.

11. Hall archly observes that "there were, alas, almost no founding mothers; of the consequences, the reader must judge" (ibid., p. 7), although he does mention the work of Jane Addams (pp. 40, 41, 44, 123, 366) and Jane Jacobs (pp. 230, 234-235, 238, 261).

12. Ibid., p. 400.

13. Ibid.

14. David Sibley, "Women's Research on Chicago in the Early 20th Century," *Women and Environments* 14, 2 (Spring 1995), pp. 6-8.

15. This phrase is taken from the title of: Margrit Eichler (ed.), *Change of Plans: Towards a Non-Sexist Sustainable City* (Toronto: Garamond, 1995).

16. Hayden (1981).

17. Ibid., pp. 22-26.

18. Ibid., pp. 34-53.

19. For example: Robert Owen in England, Charles Fourier in France and John Humphrey Noyes in the United States. To this list should be added Mother Ann Lee, the founder of Shakerism, a movement that established 19 celibate communistic communities, which included innovative communal housekeeping arrangements (ibid., p. 39).

20. Ibid., pp. 50-51. For further information on women's leadership in utopian social experiments, see: Rosemary Radford Ruether, "Gender in Utopian and Communal Societies," in Rosemary Radford Ruether & Rosemary Skinner Keller (eds.), *In Our Own Voices: Four Centuries of American Women's Religious Writing* (San Francisco: HarperSanFrancisco, 1995), pp. 341-382.

21. Hayden (1981), pp. 55-58, 229-265.

22. Ibid., p. 55.

23. Ibid., pp. 59-60.

24. Ibid., pp. 67-89.

25. Ibid., pp. 91-113.

26. Ibid., pp. 115-131.

27. Ibid., pp. 162-179.

28. Ibid., p. 186.

29. Ibid., pp. 188-195. Unfortunately, this promising idea was never realized, owing to ideological disagreements among the project's sponsors.

30. Although Howes had a Ph.D and taught in the Harvard psychology faculty for nine years, her name was never listed in the university catalogue, for fear that acknowledging the presence of a female faculty member might set a "dangerous precedent" (Hayden {1981}, pp. 267-268).

31. Ibid., p. 269. It should be noted that Howes' colleagues at Smith feared that her emphasis on home economics would undermine the academic reputation of the college (ibid., pp. 276-277).

32. Ibid., pp. 281-289. See also: Roger Miller, "Selling Mrs. Consumer: Advertising and the Creation of Suburban Socio-spatial Relations, 1910-1930," *Antipode* 23, 3 (1991), pp. 263-301.

33. The summary of "the Other Chicago School" is based on Sibley (1995).

34. Hayden (1981), pp. 294-296.

35. Ibid.

36. See, for example: Dolores Hayden, *Redesigning the American Dream: The Future of Housing, Work, and Family Life* (New York: W W Norton, 1984); Ellen Perry Berkeley (ed.), *Architecture: A Place for Women* (Washington/London: Smithsonian Institution Press, 1989); Leslie Kanes Weisman, *Discrimination by Design: A Feminist Critique of the Man-made Environment* (Urbana: University of Illinois Press, 1994); Eichler (1995); Ken Norwood & Kathleen Smith, *Rebuilding Community in America: Housing for Ecological Living, Personal Empowerment, and the New Extended Family* (Berkeley, CA: Shared Living Resource Center, 1995); and Clara Greed, *Women and Planning: Creating Gendered Realities* (London/New York: Routledge, 1994).

37. Lynda H. Schneekloth, "Unredeemably Utopian: Architecture and Making/Unmaking the World," *Utopian Studies* 9, 1 (1998), p. 1.

38. Hayden (1984), p. 178.

39. Ibid., p. 179.

40. Ibid., pp. 185-187.

41. Ibid., pp. 189-191.

42. Ibid., pp. 192-196.

43. Ibid., pp. 197-204.

44. Ibid., p. 205.

45. Ibid., pp. 207-217.

46. Ibid., pp. 217-222.

47. Weisman (1994), pp. 124-157.

48. Ibid., p. 49.

49. Ibid., pp. 57-62.

50. Eichler (1995).

51. Ibid., pp. 16-17. This list draws heavily from Caroline Andrew's, "The Feminist City," in Henri Lüstiger-Thaler (ed.), *Public Arrangements: Power and the City* (Montreal: Black Rose, 1992), pp. 109-122. Andrew, a political scientist at the University of Ottawa, has provided a distinctively Canadian voice in urban feminism since the 1980s, as have Beth Moore Milroy, Gerda Wekerle and Fran Klodawsky.

52. Gerda Lerner argues that the ability to dialogue with feminist thinkers of the past is critical to the formation of feminist consciousness and effective social change (*The Creation of Feminist Consciousness* {New York/Oxford: Oxford University Press, 1993}, pp. 274-283).

53. See, for example: Caroline Andrew, "Getting Women's Issues on the Municipal Agenda: Violence Against Women," in Judith A. Garber & Robyne S. Turner (eds.), *Gender in Urban Research* (Thousand Oaks, CA: Sage, 1995), pp. 99-118.

54. For a feminist perspective on disability-rights activism, see: Jenny Morris, *Pride against Prejudice: Transforming Attitudes to Disability* (Philadelphia/Gabriola Island, BC: New Society, 1991).

55. See: Gerda R. Wekerle, "Responding to Diversity: Housing Developed By and For Women," *Canadian Journal of Urban Research* 2, 2 (December 1993), pp. 95-115.

56. Although not explicitly feminist (although she has been called "implicitly feminist" by the environmental activist Sarah Koch-Schulte), Jacobs' critique of "the Radiant Garden City Beautiful" of Le Corbusier and the garden city movement, and her defence of lively, dense, mixed-use urban neighbourhoods, have made her one of the most influential urban thinkers of the 20th century. Jacobs' stature as "urban philosopher" was recently recognized in the international conference held to celebrate her work ("Jane Jacobs: Ideas That Matter," Toronto, October 16-19, 1997).

57. See: Christopher Leo, with Mary Ann Beavis, Andrew Carver & Robyne Turner, "Is Urban Sprawl Back on the Political Agenda? Local Growth Control, Regional Growth Management, and Politics," *Urban Affairs Review* 34, 2 (November 1998), pp. 179-212. See also: Bradshaw Hovey, "Building the City, Structuring Change: Portland's Implicit Utopian Project," *Utopian Studies* 9, 1 (1998), pp. 68-79.

58. Federation of Canadian Municipalities (FCM), *A City Tailored to Women: The Role of Municipal Governments in Achieving Gender Equality* (Ottawa: FCM International Office, 1997); Penelope Gurstein, "Gender Sensitive Community Planning: The Planning Ourselves In Project," *Canadian Journal of Urban Research* 5, 2 (December 1996), pp. 183-98; Penny Gurstein & Vanessa Geary (eds.), *Proceedings of the Workshop: Learning and Connecting: Women as Agents of Change in Their Communities* (Vancouver: Centre for Human Settlements, University of British Columbia, April 1994); Planning Ourselves In Group, *Planning Ourselves In: Women and the Community Planning Process: A Tool Kit for Women and Planners* (Vancouver: Social Planning and Research Council of British Columbia, October 1994); Liisa Horelli, Kirsti Vepsa & Anja Wahlberg, *The New Everyday Life — A Vision and a Way to Plan and Organize Settlement Areas on Women's Terms in Finland* (Strasbourg: Council of Europe, European Committee for Equality between Women and Men, October 1991); Norwegian Association of Local Authorities, *Mobilizing Women in Local Planning and Decision-Making: A Guide to Why and How* (Oslo: Norwegian Ministry of Foreign Affairs, June 1991); Regula Modlich, "Women Plan Toronto," *Women and Environments* 8, 1 (Winter, 1986); and Barbara Taylor, "Women Plan London: The Women's Committee of the Greater London Council," *Women and Environments* 7, 2 (Spring, 1985).

59. Early feminist fantasy writing contains a variety of both urban and non-urban visions of eutopia. For surveys of feminist utopian literature of the 19th and early 20th centuries, see: Hayden (1981), pp. 134-149; Carol Farley Kessler (ed.), *Daring to Dream: Utopian Stories by United States Women, 1836-1919* (Boston: Pandora, 1984); and Carol Farley Kessler (ed.), *Daring to Dream: Utopian Fiction by United States Women before 1950* (Syracuse, NY: Syracuse University Press, 1995). For utopias written about women prior to the 19th century, see the articles in: *Utopian and Science Fiction by Women: Worlds of Difference*, Jane L. Donawerth & Carol A. Kolmerten (eds.) (Syracuse, NY: Syracuse University Press, 1994), pp. 15-92.

60. Hayden (1981), pp. 148-149.

61. Charlotte Perkins Gilman is the author of the well-known *Herland* (New York: Pantheon, 1979); Marie Howland wrote an urban feminist utopia entitled "Papa's Own Girl" (excerpted in Kessler {1984}, pp. 95-103).

62. See, for example: Nan Bowman Albinski, *Women's Utopias in British and American Fiction* (New York: Routledge, 1988); Angelika Bammer, *Partial Visions: Feminism and Utopianism in the 1970s* (New York/London: Routledge, 1991); Marleen Barr & Nicholas D. Smith (eds.), *Women and Utopia: Critical Interpretations* (Lanham/New York/London: University Press of America, 1983); Donawerth & Kolmerten (1994); Margrit Eichler, "Science Fiction as Desirable Feminist Scenarios," *Women's Studies International Quarterly* 4, 1 (1981), pp. 51-64; Libby Falk Jones & Sarah Webster Goodwin (eds.), *Feminism, Utopia, and Narrative* (Knoxville: University of Tennessee Press, 1990); Carol Farley Kessler (ed.), *Daring to Dream: Utopian Fiction by United States Women before 1920* (London: Routledge & Kegan Paul, 1983); Ruby Rohrlich & Elaine Hoffman Baruch (eds.), *Women in Search of Utopia: Mavericks and Mythmakers* (New York: Schocken, 1984); and Lucy Sargisson, *Contemporary Feminist Utopianism* (New York/London: Routledge, 1996).

63. See: Mary Ann Beavis, "Feminist Eutopian Visions of the City," in Mary Ann Beavis (ed.), *Women and Urban Environments Vol. 2: Feminist Eutopian Visions of the City* (Winnipeg: Institute of Urban Studies, 1997), pp. 45-61.

64. The best-known example of a non-urban feminist eutopia is 19th-century feminist Charlotte Perkins Gilman's *Herland*. Some of the best-known feminist eutopias in the anti-urban tradition are: Sally Gearhart, *The Wanderground* (Watertown, MA: Persephone Press,

1978); Suzy McKee Charnas, *Motherlines* (New York: Berkeley, 1978); Marge Piercy, *Woman on the Edge of Time* (New York: Knopf, 1976); and Joanna Russ, *The Female Man* (Boston: Beacon, 1975). Some more recent titles include: Joan Slonczewski's *A Door into Ocean* (New York: Avon, 1986); and Nicola Griffith's *Ammonite* (New York: Del Rey, 1995). By far the majority of feminist eutopias written after 1970 and listed in the appendix to Kessler's *Daring to Dream* (1995, pp. 279-297) are non-urban.

65. Joanna Russ, "Recent Feminist Utopias," in Marleen S. Barr (ed.), *Future Females: A Critical Anthology* (Bowling Green, OH: Bowling Green State University Press, 1981), p. 81. Similarly, see: Marge Piercy, "The City as Battleground: The Novelist as Combatant," *Parti-Colored Blocks for a Quilt: Poets on Poetry* (Ann Arbor: University of Michigan Press, 1982), pp. 161-171; and Marleen S. Barr, "Suzy McKee Charnas, Sally Gearhart, and Marge Piercy Depict Sex and the Single Feminist Utopian Quasi-tribesperson," in Marleen S. Barr (ed.), *Lost in Space: Probing Feminist Science Fiction and Beyond* (Chapel Hill/London: University of North Carolina Press, 1993), pp. 39-49.

66. See: Weisman (1994), pp. 9-34.

67. See: Hayden (1984), pp. 3-38.

68. Marion Zimmer Bradley, *The Ruins of Isis* (New York: Pocket Books, 1978); Ursula K. Le Guin, *The Dispossessed* (New York: HarperCollins, 1974); Pat Murphy, *The City, Not Long After* (New York/Toronto: Doubleday, 1989); Pamela Sargent, *The Shore of Women* (New York: Crown, 1986); Starhawk, *The Fifth Sacred Thing* (New York/Toronto: Bantam, 1993); Sheri S. Tepper, *The Gate to Women's Country* (New York: Foundation, 1988); and Elisabeth Vonarburg, *The Maerlande Chronicles* (Victoria, BC: Beach Holme, 1992).

69. The last criterion ensures that the works selected have enough mass appeal to reach a substantial cross-section of the audience for feminist science fiction/fantasy literature, and that professional urbanists would have access to the novels.

70. See: Gillian Rose, *Feminism and Geography: The Limits of Geographical Knowledge* (Minneapolis: University of Minnesota Press, 1993), pp. 68-88.

71. Three of the feminist urban eutopias recognize the issue of race: the San Franciscos portrayed by both Murphy and Starhawk are clearly multiracial and multicultural; in Vonarburg's Maerlande, most (European) people are brown-skinned, but only one character, the mentor Kelys, is Black.

72. See, for example: Octavia Butler, *Parable of the Sower* (New York/London: Four Walls Eight Windows, 1993) and *Parable of the Talents* (Berkeley, CA: Publishers' Group West, 1998); and Nalo Hopkinson, *Brown Girl in the Ring* (New York: Warner, 1998). Two decades ago, Charles Saunders commented on the lack of interest among Black readers in the science-fiction genre ("Why Blacks Don't Read Science Fiction," in Tom Henigan {ed.}, *Brave New Universe: Testing the Values of Science in Society* {Ottawa: Tecumseh, 1980}, pp. 160-168), hypothesizing that this overwhelmingly "white" genre was largely irrelevant to Black readers' political and sociological concerns. In the past 18 years, the number of non-white science-fiction/fantasy authors has burgeoned and includes: William Sanders (Cherokee), Brenda Clough (Chinese American), Michelle Sangara West (Japanese Canadian), Somtow Sucharitkul (Thai), Eric Kotani (Japanese American), Virginia Hamilton (African American), Steven Barnes (African American), William Wu (Chinese American), Tannarive Due (African American), Jewel Gomez (Afro-Hispanic American), Craig Kee Strets (Native American), Jamal Nasser (Palestinian), Walter Dean Meyers (African American), Misha (Native American); R. Garcia y. Robertson (Hispanic American), Ernest Hogan (Hispanic American) and Mary Soon Lee (Irish-Chinese-Malaysian American), as well as the pre-1980 non-white science-fiction authors Samuel R. Delaney, Charles Saunders and Lester Del Rey. Also noteworthy is the DeColores Project, which "attempts to locate, recognize, and publicize the works of people of color in the field of speculative fiction (science fiction, fantasy, horror, magical realism, and fantastical literature of any type)." The project can be visited at http://www.netgsi.com/~obelesk/DeColores.html. Thanks to members of the Feminist Science Fiction, Fantasy and Utopia ListServe for these suggestions.

73. For a more ambivalent, non-fictional view of the city from a Black feminist writer, see: Rebecca Johnson, "New Moon Over Roxbury: Reflections on Urban Life and the Land," in Carol Adams (ed.), *Ecofeminism and the Sacred* (New York: Continuum, 1993), pp. 251-260.

74. Beavis (1997). See also: Karen Franck, "A Feminist Approach to Architecture: Acknowledging Women's Ways of Knowing," in Berkeley (1989), pp. 201-216.

75. See: Lenard Hart, *Utopia as Process* (Toronto: Faculty of Environmental Studies, York University, 1996).

76. An exception is Murphy's San Francisco, which is populated only by scattered plague survivors. However, the spirit of the city is so strong that the streets are haunted by shadows of its former ambience.

77. This "imperfection" is a common feature of feminist eutopias (Kessler {1983}, p. 7).

78. *The Concise Oxford Dictionary, 7th Edition* (Oxford: Clarendon Press, 1982), p. 642.

79. Hayden (1981), pp. 134-149.

80. Robyn Whittaker & Beth Moore Milroy, "Do Feminist Utopists Have Something to Say to Urbanists about Work?" *Canadian Journal of Urban Research* 6, 1 (June 1997), p. 37. The authors referred to in this article are Marge Piercy, Elisabeth Vonarburg, Margaret Atwood, Louky Bersianik, Ursula Le Guin and Sheri S. Tepper.

81. Franck (1989).

82. Weisman (1994), p. 167 refers to Ursula Le Guin, Joanna Russ and Marge Piercy as authors of such fiction, although she notes that these authors portray built space "vaguely, if at all," perhaps because (female?) children's spatial imagination is often stifled by our "rational" Western culture (p. 168).

83. See, for example: Beavis (1997); Karen A. Franck, "Imagining as a Way of Knowing: Some Reasons for Teaching 'Architecture of Utopia,'" *Utopian Studies* 9, 1 (1998), pp. 120-141; and Weisman (1994), pp. 168-179.

84. See Donawerth & Kolmerten (1994), p. 223, n. 14; Kessler (1995), p. 324; and Jones & Goodwin (1990), p. 80, n. 1.

85. Kessler (1995), pp. xxv-xxvii.

86. Ibid.

87. Ibid., p. xxvi.

88. Ibid., p. xxv.

89. Hayden (1981).

90. Daphne Spain, "Black Women as City Builders," Urban Affairs Association Annual Meeting, Toronto, April 16-19, 1997.

91. In referring to the examples adduced by Spain, I do not mean to discount the contributions of other women to the shaping of cities; much work needs to be done in documenting the city-building activities of women of diverse ethnicities and nationalities. In Canada, for example, two notable women founders of Montreal are Jeanne Mance and Marguerite Bourgeoys (see Patricia Simpson, *Marguerite Bourgeoys and Montreal, 1640-1665* {Montreal and Kingston: McGill-Queen's University Press, 1997}); women's contributions to the settlement-house movement in Toronto are documented by Allan Irving, Harriet Parsons & Donald Bellamy in *Neighbours: Three Social Settlements in Downtown Toronto* (Toronto: Canadian Scholars Press, 1995); Becki L. Ross has traced the development of lesbian community in Toronto (*The House That Jill Built: A Lesbian Nation in Formation* {Toronto/Buffalo/London: University of Toronto Press, 1995}); the current work of Eleanor J. Stebner on Sister MacNamara, the founder of Winnipeg's Rossbrook House, is also relevant.

92. Spain (1997), p. 2.

93. Susan A. McManus & Charles A. Bullock III, "Electing Women to Local Office," in Garber & Turner (1995), pp. 155-180.

94. Ibid., pp. 173-174.

95. Gerda R. Wekerle, "Responding to Diversity: Housing Developed By and For Women," *Canadian Journal of Urban Research* 2, 2 (December, 1993), pp. 95-114; and UNCHS (Habitat), *Women Constructing Their Lives: Women Construction Workers: Four Evaluative Case Studies* (Nairobi: UNCHS, 1997).

96. Federation of Canadian Municipalities (1997).

97. Ibid., p. 4.

98. See Caroline Andrew, "Getting Women's Issues on the Municipal Agenda: Violence against Women," in Garber & Turner (1995), pp. 99-118.

99. "Women Artisans Create Unique Cultural Space," *Winnipeg Sun*, September 29, 1997.

100. Dolores Hayden, *The Power of Place: Urban Landscapes and Public History* (Cambridge, MA/London: MIT Press, 1995), p. xi.

"THE ONLY THING YOU REALLY GOT ... IS THIS MINUTE"

Homeless Women Re-visioning the Future

Kathryn M. Feltey & Laura Nichols

Introduction

As we enter the millennium, growing numbers of women and children join the ranks of the homeless around the globe.[1] Common factors contributing to homelessness include the feminization of poverty, a shortage of affordable low-income housing and welfare policies focused on short-term relief. Unique factors include wars and political upheaval that produce a mobile population of refugees who are homeless.

In thinking about the coming millennium, feminists are challenged to envision a future where the economics and politics of gender do not inevitably produce poverty and homelessness. Homelessness in women's lives is both a symptom and an outcome of their economic dependence within the private household and the wage-labour market. Women become homeless when relationships end and economic support is withdrawn, labour does not generate a "living wage," illness drains the family resources, or other factors intersect to make them vulnerable. In addition, homelessness often occurs in the aftermath of natural disasters, such as floods, earthquakes and hurricanes, and man-made disasters such as wars. Women and children are the most visible among the displaced; in Central America 90 percent of the families living in refugee camps are headed by women.[2]

While collective homelessness (i.e., when an entire village is displaced) is a vastly different social phenomenon than individual or family homelessness, where particular groups (i.e., single poor women heading families) are overrepresented, the experience of displacement or homelessness for women is tied to the disruption of caregiving roles within the family. Therefore, regardless of the contributing factors, the core experience of homelessness for women is the loss of a physical context in which social relationships are sustained and nurtured, bodies and souls are fed.

Women's relationship to housing and human settlements, as Caroline Moser demonstrates, is an outgrowth of both economics and gender.[3] Women are, for the most part, outside of the planning process that produces housing options for low-income families. Moser explains that the reality of women's lives does not inform or guide the planning process:

> "Policy-makers, planners, architects, and designers both within government and international agencies, all perceive themselves as planning for people. But regardless of the reality of the particular planning context there is an almost universal tendency to make two assumptions: first, that the household consists of a nuclear family of husband, wife, and two or three children and, second, that within the family there is a clear sexual division of labour in which the man of the family as the 'breadwinner' is primarily involved in productive work outside the home, while the woman, as housewife and 'homemaker,' takes overall responsibility for the reproductive and domestic work involved in the organization of the household."[4]

While women may be excluded from formal policy/planning arenas, they certainly are not absent from political and social activism addressing issues of housing and homelessness. For example, Montserrat Sagot, in her research on Costa Rica's women-led housing movement, found that women "in their role as main providers for their families and as developers and sustainers of the networks of human relations inside the community are potentially the primary builders of social movements that struggle for issues of daily subsistence and collective consumption."[5] Further, these social movements serve to politicize the private domain of women, transforming them into "conscious political actors." In Costa Rica this resulted in planned new communities where housing was the primary focus. At the same time, the organization of communal life addressed so-called women's issues such as child care and domestic violence, which were defined, not as private matters, but as community concerns.

Our goal is to introduce the perspectives of homeless women into our visions of the future. We are interested in how homeless women view their circumstances and in what they feel needs to happen for change to occur. By pivoting the centre so that homeless women are integrally engaged in the analysis and critique, we hope to discover pathways to the future that might not be readily apparent to those who have been protected from immediate experience with homelessness and poverty. As the feminist political scientist Rhadha Jhappan points out in her problem that includes rehabilitating communities and neighbourhoods.[9] The power of homeless women's stories to explain the causes and consequences of their situation is illustrated in Elliot Liebow's work *Tell Them Who I Am*.[10] Meredith Ralston uses the stories of drug- and/or alcohol-addicted homeless women to move beyond an individual-level explanation for homelessness to a critique of non-feminist theories of the welfare state.[11] And Marjorie Bard relates how storytelling and narrative serve as the springboard for women's organizations that are designed to redefine individual problems as collective concerns (i.e., Women Organized Against Homelessness).[12] Our goal is to construct a set of collective stories about homelessness that will allow us to see beyond and through to a future for women who are homeless in the present.

Stories are the starting point for what the peace activist and sociologist Elise Boulding calls "imaging the future." She uses this term in her workshops, which are designed "to encourage people to dare to imagine best-case scenarios for the future and invent creative strategies to realize them, rather than becoming trapped in fashionable worst-case scenarios with their military focus."[13] Boulding observed that she was empowered as an activist by her ability to imagine the way things could be. Therefore, imaging is the first step to empowered activism, which is where significant social change can occur.

In this article, we are guided by Boulding's ideas about how to responsibly "image" the future.[14] First, we present, in response to Boulding's call for indepth knowledge of the past, the reflections of homeless women on the causes and consequences of homelessness in the United States. The women's critique of the system and advice to decision-makers provide insight that is often overlooked and devalued: "The bag lady ... is not viewed by well-dressed and working community members as capable of articulating legitimate personal, social, and political concerns — and positing solutions."[15] We challenge this view by giving precedence to the concerns of homeless women about social, political and economic inequality, and to the very direct effects of this inequality on their lives. We end this section with a description of three different community projects organized by women to create alternative opportunities for poor and homeless women in the United States.

Second, we present stories of women who are homeless in Central America in response to Boulding's concern that imaging the future has excluded non-Northern populations. She calls for the North to "develop more inclusive imagery, more inclusive identities, and to learn from the countries of the South about history, cultures, lifeways and traditions of community and problem solving not based on high-tech lifestyles."[16] Our hope is that such cross-cultural visioning will help to create the structures and spaces from which alternative futures can be imagined and constructed.

The feminist theorist Chandra Talpade Mohanty's notion of the politics of location provides further support for acknowledging and including individual experience, especially the experiences of the "colonized," or in our case, the homeless. Their location, according to Mohanty, "forces and enables specific modes of reading and knowing the dominant."[17] Therefore, by drawing on the perspectives and understandings of homeless women — who are deeply embedded in, yet located outside of, the dominant systems (where a future is being constructed for them in the form of social and economic policies) — we propose to shift the discourse to the level of personal experience and knowledge.

Gathering Women's Stories

The perspectives presented are derived from two sources: (1) a decade-long study of homeless women and children in the Midwestern United States (1988–98); and (2) observations, interviews and published stories gathered in El Salvador during the rebuilding of communities in 1993 at the end of a civil war. These two sources provide a method of imaging the future that is based on Boulding's work. While we are not claiming a systematic comparative analysis, we do believe that weaving our observations from different cultures broadens the future of possibilities for women across time and space.

HOMELESS WOMEN IN THE NORTH AMERICAN MIDWEST

Today, women's homelessness in this particular region of the United States is based on the dependency of women on men, poor countries on rich countries, and hierarchical systems of oppression linking race, class, nationality, sexuality, ability and so on. Like the communities they call home, homeless women in the Midwest have seen their lives shaped by deindustrialization, declining levels of public-welfare support and an increasing stigmatization of the poor.

Our research involved indepth interviews with several hundred women living in homeless shelters, battered women's shelters and transitional housing during the study period. The interviews included accounts of the women's lives, the events leading up to and producing their homelessness, their survival strategies, their dreams and hopes for the future, and the advice they had for people making the economic and political decisions in the country and their communities. In short, we asked them to tell us their stories using a before-during-afterwards framework, with their current homeless experience as the pivotal point.

True to feminist methods, the research was designed for women, to "serve the interests of the poor, exploited and oppressed."[18] The sheltered women (the "subjects" of the research) were approached in the spirit of a teaching relationship — they had something to teach the researchers about the experience of living through homelessness. In establishing the relationship, it became clear that the issue was often one of power and resources: sheltered women would agree to be interviewed because they saw the interviewer as someone who could get them something they could not get on their own. For example, shelters often have a "time out" policy, which requires all residents to be out of the shelter for several hours during the day. During the coldest months, it was never difficult to find women to interview, since shelter staff allowed them to stay inside. On several projects we were able to get funding to pay a stipend for the interview. We often had sheltered women calling us to set up interviews once word got around that there was payment for their stories. Ultimately, we did not have what they most needed, however. One sheltered woman, approached about an interview, asked, "Do you have a home for me?" When she was told no, she said, "Then I got nothing for you."

The issue of power and privilege was one the research team has addressed continually in this decade-long project. While that issue has never been resolved, the process has helped us identify expectations and biases that we take into the field with us. This is one way feminist methods have been used to test and retest what the researcher knows versus what the researcher comes to learn from the interviews and the stories told.

In addition to the homeless women, we interviewed social-service providers and community organizers about their experiences with home-lessness, the response to homelessness in their communities, and their visions for a future without homelessness (and what it would take to get there). Focus-group discussions were conducted with representatives from community organizations and industries, including churches and synagogues, social-action and community groups, planning agencies, women's entrepreneurial and business support organizations, and financial institutions. These discussions focused on perceptions, attitudes and beliefs about homelessness, and the community's response to it.

HOMELESS WOMEN IN EL SALVADOR
We also present the voices of women from El Salvador as they reflect on their experiences during a civil war that lasted from 1980 to 1992 and left more than 70,000 people dead. The United States helped to finance El Salvador's military and government action against the rebellion of the poor, who were demanding a just distribution of land for farming, and basic civil rights. The war destroyed whole villages and forced thousands into homelessness and "countrylessness" as they became refugees in neighbouring nations.

In order to more fully understand the past, we read women's accounts of the war and then, in July 1993, visited repatriated villages and talked with women who had been refugees. We were identified as members of a delegation from the United States, and continually had to acknowledge the role U.S. military support had played in destroying the villages and the lives of the people we met. We heard countless women tell us how the war had taken the lives of their children, as well as describing the torture they endured and the hardship they experienced living as refugees. Then we were told of the role we were now asked to take: to know their experiences and to monitor what went on in their country. They wanted us to understand their past and move with them in imaging a different future. The tension between our understanding of the part the United States had played in fuelling the war and the power we had as U.S. citizens to make demands for the people of El Salvador allowed us to see our stories as interrelated. Further, it became painfully clear that U.S. citizens play a role in reproducing the inequalities that exist throughout the world.

To gain knowledge of the past, we must hear about, and learn from, the lived experience of homeless women. Engaging in cross-cultural imaging involves shifting the perspective from a culturally situated homelessness to an understanding of how the local and global context shapes women's choices, as well as the way they respond to their individual and shared circumstances. From there, we can envision and move toward futures that encompass the perspectives and actions of women around the globe.

Knowledge of the Past: The United States

PATHWAYS INTO HOMELESSNESS

Women residing in shelters and transitional housing share common paths to homelessness. The events leading them to the shelter system include individual-level factors — such as relationship disruption, the breakdown of social networks, domestic violence, drug or alcohol addiction and mental-health problems — and structural-level factors, such as the loss of employment or underemployment, lack of subsidized or low-income housing options, disruption or cuts in welfare benefits, and dependence on short-term emergency social services. These factors are interrelated, making it difficult to identify a single root cause of homelessness in a particular woman's life. For most of the women, homelessness resulted from a combination of economic and personal crises, as these stories illustrate:

> "I ended up here because [public housing] put me on a list. They couldn't find a place for me, so I waited and waited and I stayed with friends. They my friends and family couldn't afford to have me anymore."

> "To make a long story short, I hurt my knee and I was unable to work. [My husband] deserted me and the kids, and I was unable to pay the rent and I got evicted. All of my clothes and belongings were set out."

> "When I was in the hospital having my baby, my apartment was robbed and they took everything. They broke the windows and I was afraid to stay there, so I moved in with my sister. She didn't really have enough room for me, so I moved in with my other sister. Section 8 [the Public Housing Authority] called her [threatening to evict her for having more occupants than her lease allowed], so I had to leave and I ended up here."

The homeless women, almost without exception, turned first to family and friends, members of their social support network, when they found themselves in need of shelter. For most, the formal shelter system was a last resort, in large part because of the stigma attached to being a shelter resident ("People look at you in the category of being a bagwoman, or you are a runaway, or you are a drug addict"). Rebecca Koch, Mary T. Lewis and Wendy Quinones describe the strategies used by homeless mothers to avoid shelters as "resistance for survival ... resistance to the demeaning label of 'homeless.'"[19]

The women enter the shelter as "resistance for equality," making a claim, in other words, that they and their children "are deserving of available community resources."[20] Once in the shelter, the women expressed both relief and frustration. One woman, describing the positive side of the shelter, said, "They provided me with clothing and with food. We have group sessions where they make you feel like you are somebody, like what has happened to you doesn't make you any less of a person." On the other hand, the shelter was a temporary, short-term, limited option for people who have complicated and complex factors operating in their lives. Another woman explained:

"You are in a situation [where] you have a place to stay today, but everyone here knows there is an end date. What if you are not together by then? You don't have a permanent place. You know you could do something wrong and, hey, you are gone. You have no security and it is always on your mind. The more it is on your mind the more it wears you down. The time you need to be together is the time you are the weakest. It is like a vicious circle. Because the only thing you really got when you don't have a home is this minute. You can work towards it and you can try. But after you go to all of the agencies, after you do so much, and after you do everything you can do, you still haven't got an answer."

INSIDE THE SHELTER SYSTEM

As the woman quoted above observed, the social-service system, which is made up of various agencies, including shelters, does not provide an answer to homelessness. Barbara Arrighi points out in her work on homeless families that the shelter system is set up as temporary because of the assumptions that family crisis is short-lived and derived from individual circumstances (i.e., job loss or divorce).[21] She argues that systemic factors, "such as a shortage of full-time jobs, increased part-time and temporary service work, declining wages, a decrease in affordable housing, and cuts in federal and state assistance for families, have contributed to a crisis-based way of life for increasing numbers."[22]

The crisis-based nature of the response to homelessness means that the symptoms are treated (i.e., homeless women have a place to sleep), while the root causes are unchallenged and unchanged. When we asked homeless women to reflect on their circumstances and to share their perspectives, they focused, not on their unique problems, but on their shared position and what they needed *collectively* to move out of homelessness: "We're all homeless and need a home, attention, jobs, low-income housing, because we can't afford to pay the skyrocketing rent landlords are demanding. Even though we are from different races, we all in the same boat," said one woman. In addition to sharing a need for housing, they also share a desire to belong: "We have nowhere to go, but we all want to have a place to raise our children. We want to belong, you know, not just to the homeless, but to society and to ourselves."

The social-service response to homelessness transfers private family life to the public realm. In the United States this is not about taking public responsibility for changing the conditions producing home-lessness. Rather, it is about processing and monitoring homeless individuals and families in the agencies and organizations that have developed in the wake of the situation. One shelter provider explained her job this way:

> "I think that what happens is that we are so concerned with the quantity of our work. You know, Do we have x amount of clients on our case load? Are all of our forms correctly done? Do we need any more forms? It is like quality assurance through professionalism rather than quality assurance through care of the client. So, sometimes the system takes its eye off the real goal, the individual, and places it on the organization or statistics."

As this provider indicates, the "clients" in the system are treated as "cases" and success is measured solely by how many shelter residents are moved into "permanent" housing (public or private market) and how many find employment. Funding is tied to performance criteria that include decreased dependence on public assistance (i.e., moving "clients" off the welfare rolls).

The homeless women report that the way the system operates is a detriment to their efforts to succeed. As one woman, a recovering drug addict, said, "I would really like to see if I couldn't make something of myself. Do something before I die. But the system just beats you into the ground." Another, referring to the intensive demands for resident participation of the transitional housing program, said:

> "Sometimes I struggle with ... having other people suggest and tell me what to do. I don't need to be told I have low self-esteem every week. It knocks me down as a person, makes me feel less of a person. Somebody from the program comes to my house once a week and you really do get bombarded, like what else do I have to tell you that I haven't told you already?"

The structure of the programs brings together women from two classes: the homeless and the providers. Some of the providers clearly saw their shared circumstances of gender and sometimes class and race. "I never realized how true it was until I came to work here, [but] you know the only thing between us and being homeless is one paycheque," said one woman. Another, expressing a spiritual connection to the women she serves, explained: "You know this woman that walks in the door could be any of us and really a part of us is linked to her. There is a little of me in her and a little of each one of these homeless people reflected in ourselves too."

For their part, the homeless women often perceived the providers "not as helpers but as agents of an oppressive system that distrusts and maligns those who are living in poverty."[23] They expressed ambivalent feelings about providers as gatekeepers of the resources and as agents of control, even over very basic day-to-day decisions like bedtime and child discipline. As one mother complained: "It is like [the staff] is the mom and I am the child." In fact, many of the women talked about the parent role adopted by staff, and about the "tough love" strategies used to make women comply with shelter and housing rules and regulations. The perception that the providers did not see the commonalities between themselves and the homeless women was expressed by a resident in the following way:

"The one common denominator we all have in this program, whether we work for it or live in it, is that we are all women. We are capable of having babies or adopting them. We are all capable of working. The difference is that people who are working in the program do not see it that way. It is kind of like that question of how hard do women have to work to prove everything that they can — that is an age-old question. That has been going on for hundreds of years. [The staff] has got to stop looking at women in this program from an outside view."

THE VIEW FROM INSIDE

Asked to give advice and direction to decision-makers and leaders in government, the homeless women wanted to communicate several main points. First, they want those making the decisions to use humanity and empathy as guiding principles. They want decision-makers to subjectively understand their circumstances as they allocate resources:

"It is not that we are not as good as everybody else as far as being on welfare and all of that. We love and care for our kids as much as they do theirs. We want a home for them just the same as they want a home for their kids. A lot of these decisions I don't under-stand. They read the paper and they know how much it costs to rent a two-bedroom apartment. I would tell them to live what I have lived and then tell me that you would make the same decisions. Everybody was not born with a silver spoon in their mouth. I don't expect you to give me anything. I expect you to give me a chance. That is what I expect you to give me — a chance."

The women also stressed that being given a chance should include more than being offered a temporary housing program. The issues confronting women, especially single mothers, need to be addressed in a permanent, comprehensive way, as this mother from the transitional housing program explains:

"There are so many issues that women as a whole need to be addressed, and they are just not being addressed. You just cannot take women and kids and throw them into a program and say this is it. And then when our time is up, a lot of us will be going right back to [project] housing. Then all of a sudden we will be hit with

[handwritten margin note: common sense, that women, no matter what class, want what's best for their kids]

the changes in [welfare]. All of a sudden [welfare] is going to be cut off. The system is just not geared or organized to help single women [who] have kids."

The women not only asked for understanding, they also expressed anger at a political system where militarism and capitalism set national priorities:

"If they can spend millions of dollars on the defence budget when the country's not at war, then they could do something for the homeless. It's just a situation where they are not [apportioning] money in the right places. Economics have affected a lot of people — like when the plants closed. They don't want to look at the blue-collar workers [who] have worked to keep this country alive. Then when their jobs fold up, they have nowhere to go. This is supposed to be the land of plenty and people are [living] in the streets. They wonder why women are turning to prostitution and stuff, where are we going to get the extra money from?"

"They spend billions of dollars ... on the weapons that just sit there. They're never gonna use them, unless they plan on blowing up the world. Can you imagine how many women and children that [money] could help? You know in Canada their medical expenses are paid by their government. Why can't America look at that and say we can do that too? We got enough weapons sitting around to blow the world up. How about putting some of that money into human beings, the people that are out here starving, instead of [for] those rich people that sit there with their millions of dollars and the Republicans [who] look down [on us]?"

Ultimately, the enormity of the obstacles to moving women out of poverty in our current economic system and political climate contributes to feelings of hopelessness and a sense that change is not possible:

"The more you look around every day somebody becomes homeless. It really happens and with the children. I think with all of the money that is in our government and these empty buildings that they have around here in almost every city that you go to ... in the projects it is so bad. I mean, there are rats running on babies while they are sleeping. There are drug addicts everywhere. People just don't care. You know what? I believe times are going to get worse. I cannot see really any improvement. Maybe I am just pessimistic. I just don't really see any change in the future, because the rich just want to keep getting [richer]."

These views, critical as they are of structures that do not support communities of people, represent a "vision of transformation" that is defined by Koch and colleagues as "the ability to think and act in ways that change reality for oneself and for one's society."[24] While some of the homeless women we talked with expressed this type of vision, most were engaged in the daily struggle for survival and were not in a position to work for change beyond their own circumstances. To explore transformation in practice, we turn to three community organizations in the United States where women have come together to create alternative futures. These organizations reflect the possibility of transcending current systems to create opportunities for women and their children. These examples are presented as models to spark our imaging as we move into the millennium.

WOMEN TRANSFORMING THE FUTURE

The Community Housing Coalition of Cincinnati is one example of an alternative program that bridges differences to improve the lives of women. The coalition was formed to address the issue of housing in women's lives. The group separated its mission from the public response to homelessness, which founder Maureen Wood described as "having the potential for creating permanent dependency by focusing on temporary shelter over permanent housing."

The first effort of the group was an international conference held in the late 1980s. Women who were architects, builders, developers, social-service providers and low-income earners came together to reconceptualize housing to fit the needs of women. Together, they designed and developed blueprints of model homes. After the conference, 25 participants from Cincinnati formed a development enterprise to build housing for women. Housing was envisioned as community-based and included 24-hour childcare, cafeteria services and shared meeting space, in addition to apartments for women of all ages, with and without dependent children.

In addition to planning, fundraising, and imaging the future of housing, the coalition conducted home-repair training for women who had their own homes, bringing those who attended the sessions into the coalition. As a result, the coalition came to include women who were city planners, council women, professional women, low-income women, women of colour and lesbian/bisexual women. While the diversity of the group often proved to be a challenge, members were committed to staying with the process and saw themselves as benefitting from their differences. As Wood said, "We don't miss the details."

Rowan Homes in Philadelphia is a second example of an alternative program that brings the resources of women with class privilege together with the needs of disadvantaged women. Rena Rowan, a one-time homeless refugee in Siberia and a single immigrant mother, established Rowan Homes as a foundation for the homeless. The group's projects include a transitional shelter for homeless women and children and a 75-unit complex that will provide long-term housing for women and children (with nearby or on-site support services such as health and daycare and after-school programs). Rowan explains, "We want every Rowan Homes family to know ... they will have a community behind them who will support their efforts."[25]

The Women's Economic Agenda Project (WEAP) in Oakland, California, is a third example of women coming together to share their stories — in this instance, their perspective on the ways that the needs of women of colour and poor women had been neglected by the women's movement in the United States. "WEAP's primary agenda is to fight for economic justice for poor women and their families and for basic human rights, such as decent and safe housing, food, education, and health care."[26] The goal is to empower women to organize themselves against economic injustice, with projects that include national summits for low-income women, a speakers' bureau, and the Women and Family Center, which offers education, business development and skills training for women. The group has been active against welfare-reform legislation in the United States and has worked with organizations responsible for funnelling federal money into communities. Accordingly, WEAP addresses how structural changes in the economy and in policy making "affect low-income women and women of color, and, at the turn of the millennium, [the organization is] committed to empowering these women to fight for their rights."[27]

Broadening the base of the movement to centre the experiences and perspectives of women of colour and low-income women also requires moving beyond the borders of the United States. We turn now to the South to cross-culturally vision the future for homeless women.

Cross-Cultural Visioning: El Salvador

Boulding encourages us to engage in dialogue across cultures to better understand the history, traditions and problem-solving techniques of people living in areas different from our home countries. She calls specifically for peoples in Northern countries to try to understand the experiences of people who live in Southern countries and to use such knowledge to imagine a future different from the one that is limited by the Northern dominant ideology. This process, which Boulding refers to as "cross-cultural imaging," encourages us to learn from the stories of women in other countries and combine them with a deeper understanding of our own cultures of homelessness and poverty as we work toward a different future.

WAR AND HOMELESSNESS IN EL SALVADOR

The openness and willingness of women in El Salvador to share their experiences with people in North America provides an opportunity to engage in cross-cultural imaging. Their stories take place in a very different context than do the stories of women in the United States. Their most recent memories are of war, a 12-year civil war between the Farabundo Marti National Liberation Front (FMLN), who called for basic human rights for the country's poor citizens, and the U.S.-supported Salvadoran military. Yet war and extreme inequality between the poor and the rich are not new realities in this small country. El Salvador has been a site of unrest since the 1880s, when the ruling elite bought up land and created large plantations for export crops such as sugar and coffee. This created widespread poverty, as *campesinos* (peasants/farm workers) were displaced from their communally owned land and left without a place to grow their own food. They were subsequently forced to work for substandard wages on large plantations, farming sugar and coffee for export, living only where the landowner allowed.

In 1932 Farabundo Marti led a rebellion of rural peasants against the government. This resulted in what is referred to as *la mantanza* (the massacre), wherein 30,000 civilians were killed by members of the country's military. Those who did not own land were pushed farther into the isolated hillsides, forming small villages on land that was not claimed by landowners because it was unfarmable. There, people attempted to grow corn and other staples on the steep hillsides. There was no electricity and their only source of water was from nearby streams or rivers. The poor also crowded around the capital city of San Salvador, living in shanties on land owned by the government or private landholders.

In the 1970s people again began to protest economic inequality and unsafe living conditions. This led to the creation of the FMLN, and from 1980 until 1992 a bloody civil war ensued between the nation's military and the FMLN. Although a number of women participated in the FMLN, the force was made up primarily of men, drawing more men out of cities and small villages, and away from their families. The war was heavily financed by the United States, which provided training, equipment and even some personnel to help the government fight individuals they labelled communists. Countless human-rights violations committed by members of the military were documented by various groups both within and outside the country. One of their most common activities was to "disappear"[28] people and to kidnap young boys to conscript them into the army. Women, besides joining the FMLN and various political groups, also created some of the most visible protests against the actions of the Salvadoran military and government, defying the subordinate status of "woman" and claiming a power that grew out of the truth of their suffering.

WOMEN AS ACTIVISTS AND COMMUNITY-BUILDERS

The materially poor women in El Salvador were realizing the depth of the injustices they faced, "because on top of suffering at the hands of the rich oligarchy, we also suffer as women. That's why we call it double oppression, and that is why we struggle."[29] Carmen Virginia Martinez said, in a speech she delivered at the International Women's Day Forum about the legal structure of El Salvador:

"[It is] a structure rendered by tradition into civil code that conceives of women as dependent, submissive, and passive beings, and thus reveals the basic sexist design of this society ... The majority of women are employed in service or secondary, marginal activities that do not produce capital, so that consequently they have little clout as a labor force. We have also dealt with women's role in domestic labor — labor which provides for the reproduction and sustenance of the workforce but which is given no economic value."[30]

During the war, women played an active role in protesting the injustice they saw in their country and helping to rebuild their communities. In the larger cities, women who lived primarily in shanties on the outskirts became political activists, protesting in the streets and making demands on government and church officials. In 1977 they formed the group COMADRES, which captured public attention by staging demonstrations and vigils, calling for the release of political prisoners, for knowledge about those who had been disappeared and for the prosecution of death squads who had murdered thousands of Salvadorans. A member of COMADRES, who lost 14 members of her family to the war, said of her role in the struggle for justice, "I'm fighting for my suffering people, and this is the struggle of all the mothers in my country. And so we go out into the streets without fear ... We won't be silenced. And we know that one day we will win and the situation will change."[31]

While the women of San Salvador were visible in political protests in the capital city, women living in the countryside became key players in the refugee camps. The camps became necessary when the Salvadoran military moved into the remote villages, massacring those they claimed were members of the FMLN. As a result, more than a million people, mostly women and children, fled their villages, and were forced to live in refugee camps in Honduras and Guatemala. Some stayed for more than 10 years, isolated on barren land and reliant on international relief agencies for food, water and other goods. Although dependent on others, the refugees began to develop a sense of community and to plan for their return to El Salvador. Community councils were formed, and training, literacy and other learning opportunities were provided.

Beth Cagan, a professor of social work, and Steve Cagan, a photographer, are two Northerners who spent a significant amount of time with a refugee community in Honduras. On their return to El Salvador, the community members built a new city — Segundo Montes. The Northerners wrote about their experiences learning from the people of this community in their book, *This Promised Land, El Salvador*.[32] The city of Segundo Montes, with a population of more than 8,000, has been touted as one of the most successful of the repatriated communities. When they arrived at the camp in Honduras in the early 1980s, 85 percent of the refugees were illiterate; when they left nine years later, fewer than 20 percent were. During their time in the camps, the refugees established community-based systems of government, created architectural plans, provided educational opportunities, and rationed resources so as to meet the needs of each individual in the camp. Women became active leaders, empowered by the unjustness of their oppression. They became skilled in technical crafts such as construction and weaving, as well as in health care, education, dentistry, nutrition and sanitation, and they formed democratic governments and teaching cooperatives. Finally, in 1989, a woman led the first group of refugees back to their homeland, in defiance of the Salvadoran and Honduran governments (which had not given permission for the move).

When a group of us from the United States visited Segundo Montes and other repatriated communities in 1993, many of them were just beginning. Most of the repatriated Salvadorans had chosen to return to the site of their former villages, which were usually in complete ruin as a result of the war. Despite the harsh conditions and lack of resources, people worked collectively to rebuild their communities. Women were major leaders, not only serving on leadership boards and councils, but also working in jobs that previously had been considered appropriate only for men. And the structure of daily life changed significantly. Women no longer worked alone, spending most of their time preparing their family's food and caring for their own children. Under their leadership, activities such as tortilla production and child care became cooperative ventures. A collective kitchen and several daycare centres were constructed, effectively moving family life to the heart of community life.[33]

Similar activities were occurring in other parts of El Salvador. In the small village of Santa Marta, the four women and three men of the community council told us of the priorities of the community: first, they hoped to build a church, then a bakery, a health clinic and 42 one-room houses for single women with children. Meanwhile, the children were collecting pieces of the bombs they had found lying throughout their community to build the Bells of Life, which would signal the people of the village to come together. They held school sessions, in open-air classrooms, taught by the most educated members of the village:

typically 12- and 13-year-old children. No community member, no matter what age or physical ability, would be left behind.

They dreamed of obtaining electricity for the whole village, and were developing radio contact with other villages to minimize their isolation. They asked us to go back to the United States and tell others of their plans, their hopes, their dreams. The women asked us to take their stories back to the people of North America because "so many North Americans don't realize what is happening in our country, they don't see us as human beings with the same aspirations that they have. They want peace, justice, well-being, schools, education, work, health, and religious freedom. Well, these are the same things our people want."[34] And to achieve all this, they needed resources: medical equipment, building supplies, more training in health care, books and pencils for the schools. The community would gratefully accept contributions, according to the members of the community council, but would not allow their development planning to be influenced by external sources of aid and support. The vision was theirs.

The repatriated people of El Salvador took the skills they had learned in the refugee camps and the empowerment they felt as a community to create for themselves what their government refused to provide. Although they had seen death and experienced the fear and destruction that come with war, they had hope for a better future and vowed to work together to make that happen. They struggled to maintain the democratic structures they had established in the refugee camps and to make sure that the needs of all were provided for — regardless of their abilities. All contributed, in some way, to the vision of the community, and all felt responsible for its success.

The greatest lessons we learned in engaging in cross-cultural imaging with the people of El Salvador were of the power of hope and community. We witnessed a people who had nothing, but who, by coming together, were able to develop a community — a community where access to food, shelter and health care was not dependent on family or marital status, educational achievement or class position. In this place, if one was homeless, all were homeless, and if one was housed, all would be housed. Each villager we spoke with talked about his or her role in relation to other members of the community. It was evident that, while resources continued to be limited, no individual would be denied the assistance of the community. And although the journey has been difficult, and women still struggle to maintain their independence and face continued obstacles from their government, the stories of the past are fresh and the vision for the future is strong.

Women in Community Creating the Future

Despite very different histories and circumstances, homeless women in both Central America and the United States experience extraordinary barriers to moving forward in hope. The women of El Salvador lived with political unrest and the constant threat of danger. They experienced homelessness as a community displaced by the horrors of war. They had little support from their government and relied on international groups for resources and protection. They struggled every day to maintain the sense of solidarity, community and vision that was born in the refugee camps.

The women from the United States, meanwhile, faced the daily struggle of living in poverty in a land of many resources. They were blamed as individuals for their poverty and were not seen as part of a larger community, nor were they encouraged to form alliances with others. Instead, they were dependent on a social-service system that does not guarantee assistance and encourages individual success at the expense of the community, as well as on a low-wage labour market that does not allow them to move their families out of poverty.

Despite these seemingly insurmountable obstacles, women have been able to move forward in hope by critiquing the political and economic structures that keep them poor. By understanding the shared experiences of women through story, and not allowing ourselves to be limited by the ideas of others, we can form policies and programs that are different from those prescribed by the dominant system — policies and programs that recognize women's multiple roles as caretakers, community-builders and underpaid workers.

Poverty and homelessness are inevitable when women are dependent within the family and underpaid in the wage market. The dependency inherent in the roles of wife and mother places women at risk. As Esther Ngan-ling Chow and Catherine White Berheide demonstrate in their feminist analysis of policy, gender inequality that is embedded in family structures and political economies produces disadvantage for women around the globe.[35] Basically, women's labour, waged and unwaged, is controlled under patriarchal family and political systems. Women around the globe are burdened with, and disadvantaged by, their "triple role" as mothers and caretakers within the household, workers in the wage-labour market, and participants in their communities and neighbourhoods.[36]

The exclusion of women from policy-making and planning means that their experiences are peripheral in the state-level response to the housing side of the homeless problem. However, there is much to be learned from women's ways of organizing and taking action. Feminists are challenged to envision a future where "women-centred" policies are developed out of women's experiences and perspectives.[37] The goal is to move into a future, not where the homeless are sheltered, but where homelessness for women and children is a rare event.

A dominant theme expressed by both the people in El Salvador and the women's groups in the United States is the importance of community over the individual in responding to the problems of homelessness and poverty. These women have rejected the dominant ideology that encourages individual achievement and family success above the good of the community, and they have become political actors and visionaries working for their communities. Said a 19-year-old woman who grew up in a camp of Salvadoran refugees, "Most of us were very little when we went into the refuge, and we hadn't yet accepted the values of capitalism, individualism, selfishness; they hadn't yet entered our consciousness ... We've come back into a capitalist system, the same one our parents lived in, but we've had the experience of being in an autonomous community, of deciding for ourselves what our values are."[38] The challenge for women becomes how to maintain this vision for the future while fighting for its realization in the moment. Women's own stories of homelessness should be guiding the vision; however, it is up to those of us who are privileged in the dominant system to help clear a protective place so that change can occur.

so diff from Young! (handwritten marginal note)

ENDNOTES

1. The authors would like to thank Diane Moran and the anonymous reviewers who gave a thoughtful and thorough review of earlier drafts of this article. We are grateful to Somer Brodribb for creating the space for this type of visioning work for the future. And we are indebted to the women in the United States and El Salvador who chose to share their stories, with the hope that their experiences could be used to create change. The research on homelessness in the United States has been supported by the Ohio Urban University Research Program through various grants awarded from 1989 to 1999.

2. Caroline Moser, "Women, Human Settlements, and Housing: A Conceptual Framework for

Analysis and Policy-Making," in C. Moser & L. Peake (eds.), *Women, Human Settlements, and Housing* (London: Tavistock, 1987).

3. Ibid.

4. Ibid., p. 13.

5. Montserrat Sagot, "Women, Political Activism, and the Struggle for Housing: The Case of Costa Rica," in Esther Ngan-ling Chow & Catherine White Berheide (eds.), *Women, the Family, and Policy* (Albany, NY: SUNY Press, 1994), p. 191.

6. Rhadha Jhappan, "Post-Modern Race and Gender Essentialism or a Post-Mortem of Scholarship," *Studies in Political Economy* 51 (1996), p. 30.

7. Marie Kennedy, "A Hole in My Soul: Experiences of Homeless Women," in D. Dujon & A. Withorn (eds.), *For Crying Out Loud: Women's Poverty in the United States* (Boston: South End Press, 1996), p. 54.

8. Alice Walker, *By the Light of My Father's Smile* (New York: Random House, 1998), p. 149.

9. Kathleen Hirsch, *Songs from the Alley* (New York: Ticknor & Fields, 1989).

10. Elliot Liebow, *Tell Them Who I Am: The Lives of Homeless Women* (New York: Free Press, 1993).

11. Meredith Ralston, *"Nobody Wants to Hear Our Truth": Homeless Women and Theories of the Welfare State* (Westport, CT: Greenwood, 1996).

12. Marjorie Bard, *Organizational and Community Responses to Domestic Abuse and Homelessness* (New York: Garland, 1994).

13. Elise Boulding, "The Cultures and Futures of Peace," *Futures* 28 (1996), p. 537.

14. Elise Boulding, "The Challenge of Imaging Peace at Wartime," *Futures* 23 (1991), pp. 528–533.

15. Bard (1994), p. 39.

16. Boulding (1991), p. 529.

17. Chandra Talpade Mohanty, "Feminist Encounters: Locating the Politics of Experience," in M. Barrett & A. Philips (eds.), *Destabilizing Theory: Contemporary Feminist Debates* (Stanford, CA: Stanford University Press, 1992), p. 88.

18. Ralston (1996).

19. Rebecca Koch, Mary T. Lewis & Wendy Quinone, "Homeless: Mothering at Rock Bottom," in Cynthia Garcia Coll, Janet L. Surrey & Kathy Weingarten (eds.), *Mothering against the Odds: Diverse Voices of Contemporary Mothers* (New York: Guildford, 1998), p. 72.

20. Ibid., p. 73.

21. Barbara Arrighi, *America's Shame: Women and Children in Shelter and the Degradation of Family Roles* (Westport, CT: Praeger, 1997).

22. Ibid., p. 65.

23. Ibid., p. 48.

24. Koch et al. (1998), p. 77.

25. Earnie Young, "She's Giving by Design: Rena Rowan's $1.5M Helping Home Project," *Philadelphia Daily News* (September 25, 1998), p. 119.

26. Taken from the WEAP Web site at www.iww.org/whip/weap.html.

27. Ibid.

28. "Disappeared" refers to a common practice of El Salvador's military, where people were kidnapped either because more men were needed to serve in the army or because they were considered dangerous because of their assumed political connections to the FMLN or human-rights organizations. The bodies of the disappeared were often found in mass graves or dumped throughout the country; many have never been found at all. Women were at the forefront in demanding that the government reveal the whereabouts of the disappeared. Many were subsequently jailed and tortured because of their activism. For more information on this practice and on the work of women in El Salvador, see: Lynn Stephens (ed. & trans.), *Hear My Testimony: Maria Teresa Tula, Human Rights Activist of El Salvador* (Boston: South End, 1994).

29. Reina Isabel, "Returning Home," in New American Press (ed.), *A Dream Compels Us: Voices of Salvadoran Women* (Boston: South End, 1989), p. 238.

30. Carmen Virginia Martinez, "Women and the Family in El Salvador," in ibid., p. 117.

31. COMADRES Testimony, in ibid., p. 59.

32. Beth Cagan & Steve Cagan, *This Promised Land, El Salvador* (New Brunswick, NJ: Rutgers University Press, 1991).

33. Ibid.

34. Martinez (1989), p. 160.

35. Chow & Berheide (1994).

36. See, for example: Moser (1987); and Rae Lesser Blumberg, *Gender, Family, and Economy: The Triple Overlap* (Newbury Park, CA: Sage, 1991).

37. Chow & Berheide (1994), p. 26.

38. Quoted in: Cagan & Cagan (1991), p. 181.

PART TWO

BORDERS & NEW WORLDS

CLOSING THE NATION'S RANKS

Canadian Immigration Policy in the 21st Century

Sunera Thobani

The Founding of the Canadian Nation

Immigration policies have historically been central to the production and reproduction of the Canadian nation. The nation's very founding was predicated on the colonization of Aboriginal peoples and the appropriation of their lands.[1] During this first phase of capitalist globalization, Canada's national territory was acquired by Europeans through colonization/racialization, central to which were the state's racialized land policies.

Simultaneously, racialized immigration policies enabled the settlement of Aboriginal lands by Europeans who were subsequently integrated into the "national" population. Indeed, Canadian immigration policies overtly distinguished between immigrants of "preferred races" (initially British and French immigrants, and later various other European immigrants) and "non-preferred races" (immigrants from Asia, the Caribbean and Africa) until the 1960s and 1970s. While policies such as the Head Tax, the Exclusion Act and the Continuous Passage requirement[2] all sought to severely restrict the immigration of third-world peoples for permanent settlement, European immigrants were actively and aggressively recruited. These racialized immigration policies resulted in the definition of the British and French as the two "founding" nations of Canada.

In the post-World War II period, national liberation movements in colonized countries forced the dismantling of the British Empire, as well as of other empires organized by other European colonizing powers. Growing anti-racist and anti-fascist movements in advanced capitalist countries also forced the abandonment of the "scientific" racist theories of the previous era. With immigration from Europe also declining in the changed global economy after 1945, the Canadian state pragmatically removed overt references to race in its immigration policy.[3]

During the later 1960s and 1970s, the state finally entrenched the point system in the Immigration Act of 1976-7, which largely based selection criteria for immigrants on skills, occupation and family relations.[4] The introduction of the point system has enabled a shift in source countries, so European countries are no longer the top sources. By 1993, 51.08 percent of all immigrants came from Asia and the Pacific, 18.19 percent from Europe, 14.31 percent from Africa and the Middle East, 13.28 percent from South and Central America and 3.14 percent from the United States.[5] While immigration from Europe continues to remain significant, the domination of European immigration in absolute numbers, as had been the case in the pre-1960 period, had ended by the 1990s.

The Immigration Act has also enabled third-world women to gain increased access to Canada, and subsequently to make claims to citizenship. In fact, under the "family" category, third-world women have entered Canada in greater numbers since the 1970s. It is in the context of this increased access that the Canadian state organized the 1994 Immigration Policy Review (IPR) as part of the process of restructuring immigration.

Restructuring the Immigration Program

The 1994 IPR was mandated to develop, through extensive public consultations, an immigration strategy for the 21st century.[6] The state argued that policy changes were made necessary by new global conditions which posed challenges to the "effective management" of the program.[7] While the Immigration minister repeatedly stated his commitment to "include" Canadians in "making choices" for the future, the review began with a private meeting of 30 individuals.[8] Ten key issues for discussion in the public consultations were identified in this meeting, as were the "elements of an approach" for "the most productive discussion of these issues."[9] Extensive public consultations were then organized across the country.

While the public consultations gave the appearance of a democratic process that would allow Canadians to raise their concerns about immigration, the prior identification of the issues for discussion meant that the specific "problems" Canadians were to be concerned with were predefined by the state. The framing of these particular issues, and the specific questions raised for discussion, would, of course, shape the responses and policy recommendations which participants could be anticipated to make. In this way, the public consultations enabled the "problems" defined by the state to be made into the major concerns of

Canadians.[10] The consultations therefore became an exercise to draw *Canadians* into a preset agenda, and to popularize it by giving participants a stake in solving the problems. The state constructed immigration as a problem shared by the state and *Canadians*, and in this way, invited *Canadians* to own the subsequent policy changes as being in the nation's, and therefore in their own, interest.

Framing the Consultations

The first issue identified for discussion was the developing of a "vision" of Canada. The texts raised specific questions about the impact of immigration on the population, on cultural diversity and on the economy.[11] The background information provided states: "In 1991, the Economic Council of Canada found that immigration has a small but positive impact on our economy."[12] This is an extraordinary starting point for a discussion of immigration policy in a settler colony that was established and populated by European immigrants. The statement makes sense only if the reader focuses on recent immigration (which is predominantly of third-world peoples) as the "problem" and forgets the pre-1970s immigration (which was predominantly of European immigrants). This particular reading of Canadian history is racialized, as it defines *Canadians* as not having themselves been immigrants. The starting point for the consultations naturalizes the nation, presupposing that it has naturally existed, and that its existence is not deeply connected to the colonizing migrations of Europeans at an earlier stage of globalization. This effectively separates *Canadians*-as-members-of-the-nation from *immigrants*-as-outsiders-to-the-nation.

Having thus appealed to *Canadians*, the text informs them that *immigrants* make a contribution to "our" economy. Here "our" economy is defined as belonging to all of us equally, and although *immigrants* make a contribution by working and living in this same economy, it is not "theirs." Of the three questions that frame this part of the discussion — (1) "What role should immigration play in fostering the development of Canada's economy?"; (2) "How does immigration affect the social and cultural life of Canada?"; and (3) "What are the benefits of cultural diversity?" — two (nos. 2 and 3) draw attention specifically to cultural diversity.[13] The text thus separates economic development from social and cultural life, setting the stage for the weighing of economic benefits against social and cultural benefits.

In linking questions of social and cultural diversity to immigration, the text defines *Canadians* as those who are socially and culturally homogeneous. And by questioning the benefits of cultural diversity, the text makes it clear that the *immigrants* whose benefits are to be evaluated are those who are culturally and socially diverse. As a number of theorists have demonstrated, the phrase "cultural diversity" has come to stand in for "racial" diversity in the "new" racism of the post–World War II period.[14] The texts invite *Canadians*, as a culturally and socially homogeneous group, to work in partnership with the state in assessing the impact of diverse *immigrants* on the nation. In this very first issue, the text places Canadians who are culturally and socially diverse outside the partnership being developed with the state, giving people of colour who are legally Canadian citizens no authority to speak. Their diversity silences them. In defining *immigrants* as different culturally and socially, the text prohibits all people of colour who are citizens from taking part in the defining of the national interest. This racialized use of the category "immigrant" identifies all people of colour as part of the same "problem" that the *immigrants* under discussion are said to represent.

The background information framing the second issue directs attention to two categories of immigration: the "independent" category — also referred to as the "economic" category — and the "family" category. I have argued elsewhere that the organization of immigration under these two categories accomplishes the gendering of immigration: the "independent" category becomes masculinized by its definition as a category of independent, economic agents who make contributions to the economy, while the "family" category simultaneously becomes feminized in its definition as a category of dependants who have to be sponsored as family members.[15] The "family" category therefore becomes ideologically constructed as a feminine one, with the economic contributions made by its members rendered invisible. In the consultation text, the reader is informed that the criteria for admission in the "independent" category are based on the education, skills and occupation of the applicants. It also points out that this category is easily managed through the adjustment of the allocation of points. In this way, this category is defined as allowing the immigration of future members of the nation who will make contributions to "our" economy. This category is not linked by the texts with questions of social or cultural diversity, nor is it associated with any costs to the nation.

The text's presentation of the "family" category stands in stark contrast. No references are made to the economic contributions of people in this category; rather, they are constructed as making no contributions whatsoever to the nation. The text presents this category of immigrants as having easy access to Canada as long as they have family members in the country and meet "standards for good health and character."[16] It does not reveal that immigrants under this category need sponsors who are specified family members, and who have to meet specific financial requirements under the sponsorship regulations. Annual plans tabled by the Immigration minister set numerical targets for the "family" category, as they do for the "independent" category. The text therefore hides the reality that the "family" category is also subject to control and management, presenting it instead as potentially allowing limitless and uncontrollable immigration.[17]

Because the "family" and "independent" categories have been defined in this particular way, when the discussion question "Should immigration be managed according to business cycles or long-term social goals?"[18] is asked, the response involves making a choice between opposing economic and social goals. When the text asks, "How much importance should the principle of family reunification be given?"[19] it specifically calls into question the principle underlying this category. Through these strategies, it is the "family" category that becomes defined as the source of diversity, as not making economic contributions and as allowing potentially limitless entry into the country. In this way, the texts come to set up the "family" category as the problematic one, the one in need of increased control and management.

Six of the 10 issues raise specific questions about the costs of immigration and link increased demands on social programs with *immigrants*.[20] They are: "Have recent immigration and economic trends created needs which current programming and resources cannot meet?"; "Should newcomers receive materials explaining the rights and responsibilities of consuming public services?"; "How far are Canadians prepared to go to ensure their generosity and openness are not abused?"; "What are the groups, institutions and programs which need to be protected?"; "What factors should we consider in shaping our immigration programs to increase economic benefits at low cost?"; and "How do we build partnerships among all levels of government [to] improve the detection of abuse?"[21] These questions direct attention to the range of fiscal, social and political "problems" with immigration, and to the need to "protect" *Canadians* from *immigrants*.[22] Three of the 10 issues directly construct *immigrants* as threatening national institutions by abusing social services. The text's linking of *immigrants* with criminality and the abuse of social services sets up every *Canadian* as vulnerable to being taken advantage of by *immigrants*.

The text hides the reality that regulations require sponsors to undertake financial responsibility for sponsored family members and expressly forbid those in the "family" category from accessing social-welfare programs such as those related to housing and social assistance. Further, the text's linking of *immigrants* with increased demands on social services provides the motive for the involvement of all *Canadians* in the subsequent restructuring of the immigration program: it gives every *Canadian* a direct investment in protecting him/herself individually, as well as his/her fellow citizens collectively, against being taken advantage of by *immigrants*.

Even as the text links *immigrants* in general — and the "family" category in particular — with economic costs and the abusing of the "generosity of Canadians," it constructs all *Canadians* as citizen-taxpayers who are equally in danger of being taken advantage of by the potentially abusive *immigrant* women who enter under this category and, legitimately or otherwise, overburden social programs. The text constructs for *Canadians*, as taxpayers, a common interest in restricting the access of *immigrant* women to social programs, and gives then a direct stake in further restricting immigration under the "family" category.

None of the issues identified for discussion address the inequalities *immigrant* women are subjected to in Canada, or the deeply entrenched racism in Canadian society. The only exception is one question that raises the problem of the non-recognition of "foreign" educational and professional credentials of *immigrants* in Canada.[23] The text does not mention the reality that sponsored *immigrants* are made into second-class citizens by regulations that give them unequal access to social entitlements (although sponsored immigrants can become citizens after living in the country for three to five years, their financial dependency on their sponsor lasts for 10 years). Nor does it mention that sponsors, who are citizens and landed immigrants, have to forfeit their own claims to social assistance in order to sponsor family members. Throughout the document, it is *immigrants* who are presented as the problem, not the various agencies of the state that reproduce racialized inequalities. Nor are *Canadians* and the racism they help to perpetuate raised as a problem.

None of the 10 issues refers to the unequal treatment of workers who enter the country under the Live-in Care Giver Program, which allows domestic workers to apply for landed status after doing domestic work for two years (during which period they are dependent upon their employers for their continued stay in the country). Nor is any mention made of the Non-Immigrant Employment Authorization Program, which has allowed increasing numbers of workers to enter the country on temporary work permits. The existence of both these programs is made invisible in the immigration review.

The consultation texts produced the conceptual framework for the restructuring of the immigration program, and specifically identified "problems" that needed to be solved. In this way, the state imposed an ideological knowledge of the problems onto the lived experiences of the consultation participants, shaping their relationship to reality through the lens of these "common-sense" problems.[24] Where the framework being produced by the state would conflict with the lived experiences of individual participants, the consultations compelled these individuals to articulate their experiences as a subjective, individual reality, while the texts were made to represent an objective, collective reality shared by the nation. If the individual experiences of participants contradicted the texts' definition of the problems, their individualized experiences became juxtaposed in the consultations with the collective problems facing the nation. Therefore, once the conceptual framework for the textual reality was produced and entered, as was necessary to engage in the consultations, individual participants could challenge this framework only within its own terms of reference. Their lived knowledge of problems would be awed by the state's knowledge of the problems confronting the nation. In short, the consultation texts constructed a textual reality through which participants were to view actual reality, and the conceptual framework became the lens through which participants, as *Canadians*, were asked to relate to *immigrants*.

What the State Heard

The contributions made, in response to the discussion questions during the public consultations, fall under the following four major themes: defining a national vision for the 21st century, defining the desired quality of *immigrants*, finding an appropriate balance between the "independent" and "family" categories and protecting the security of *Canadians* and national institutions.[25]

DEFINING A NATIONAL VISION

The first theme in the reports of the consultations defines both a national vision and a national character, and calls for their preservation to be a key goal of future immigration. Here the texts define *immigrants* as threatening national values by their cultural and social diversity. *Immigrants* are defined not only as not sharing *Canadian* values, but also as threatening these values and the cohesiveness of the nation. The texts use cultural and social diversity to reconstruct racialized definitions of *immigrants* and *Canadians*, and in the process to define all people of colour as outsiders to the nation (regardless of their actual legal status).

The views of the majority of *Canadians* are summarized as being in cautious agreement with continuing immigration, although some participants called for an end to immigration altogether, and others for a reduction in the numbers. The texts immediately counter this cautious support by repeatedly raising the so-called problems with immigration. Therefore the support for continuing immigration is made conditional on recognizing the potential dangers of racial diversity, as the following comments demonstrate: "... the importance of the whole must be emphasized. We must be a choir, not a cacophony"[26] and "ethnic diversity has no benefits, it only creates tension."[27]

The text's construction of diversity as a characteristic of *immigrants*, not of *Canadians* — and a divisive and fractious one at that — is achieved through its repeated warnings about the dangers diversity presents to the national vision and to national values shared by *Canadians*. These values are defined as including freedom; democracy; the rule of law; the principles of justice, fairness, tolerance and respect for our fellow citizens; and equality.[28] One submission is singled out for special mention as capturing the *Canadian* character: "Canadians value honesty and fairness. They respect hard work and people with integrity. And they are willing to give people a second or even third chance. But Canadians also expect their fellow Canadians to respect the system that is in place, and to not take advantage of their generosity."[29]

The texts' repeated definitions of a *Canadian* identity and core *Canadian* values construct a national self-image, a national character, that *Canadians* are said to have defined. However, the texts themselves shape this national character while simultaneously inviting *Canadians* to claim it as their own. The ideological construction of this national character as being committed to tolerance, as accepting of differences and as being humane stands in sharp contrast to the actual recommendations of many of these *Canadians*, who want to end immigration altogether; allow immigration only from European source countries; and contain, and even eliminate, cultural diversity. Frequent recommendations to close the doors to all *immigrants* are not allowed to interfere with the text's construction of the *Canadian* character as fair and just.

The texts hide the actuality that people in Canada are divided by the social relations of race, class and gender. The significance of the text's production of a unitary national character lies in its countering, at the ideological level, the increasing material polarization that is a result of economic restructuring in the 1990s. Race, class and gender inequalities are increasingly significantly in the 1990s, as a number of studies have demonstrated.[30] This polarization, which intensifies economic inequalities, and hence further entrenches differing interests among *Canadians*, is not allowed to enter the textual reality. The texts construct the national character as a unified one with a shared national interest, and work to counter and transcend the increasing internal polarization within the nation.

Significantly, the national character is given substance and concrete meaning, in direct opposition to *immigrants*, who are defined as threatening its continued existence:

> "Throughout the consultation process, Canadians have expressed concern that their Canada is disappearing; that '... *its values and lifestyle are being eroded and degraded* [emphasis added].'"[31]

> "Yet, a number of thoughts were expressed with respect to Canada's character. A list of the elements of the country's basic belief system should look something like this: non-violence, justice, democracy, equality, honesty, acceptance, and fairness. There is no doubt that Departmental personnel want these core values to be retained and strengthened by immigration, not threatened."[32]

The problem constructed by the texts is not so much that *immigrants* do not share national values; rather, it is that they erode and degrade these values. As the values of *immigrants* become constructed as being the opposite of *Canadian* values, the texts actually delineate the ideological borders of the nation in direct relation to *immigrants*. Where *Canadians* are defined as respecting the rule of law, honest, hard-working and fair, *immigrants* are defined as abusers or as representing criminality, disease, laziness and ignorance of democratic values and the rule of law (when not openly flaunting them). The texts continue to present the state as being committed only to protecting the nation and national values in partnership with *Canadians*.

IMPROVING THE "QUALITY" OF IMMIGRANTS

While the first theme racializes the quality of *immigrants*, the second theme specifically genders this problem by constructing *immigrant women* as threatening to erode the nation with their boundless fecundity. *Immigrants* are defined in the texts as threatening the national way of life, and this problem is associated with the dangers of *immigrants* overwhelming the nation's resources through overpopulation. The following statement is offered as one that "reflects the views of many": "Growth as an ever increasing and self-sustaining way of life, leading to increased consumption, has been our North American way of life. All of these treasured ideas and much of what we call `our way of life' is now ending."[33]

The IPR enabled the association of immigration with the ending of "our" way of life. The text's defining of "our" treasured North American way of life as leading to increased consumption negates the reality of First Nations, whose experience of "our" way of life has been one of ongoing colonization. The actuality that "our" North American way of life increased consumption for only some sectors of the population, at the expense of the exploitation of the resources of Aboriginal peoples, is made invisible, as is the reality that the overconsumption of the planet's resources by the majority populations in the West threatens the very future of the planet.

In particular, the texts present the dangers of overpopulation as a widespread concern of *Canadians*. Canada has a "fragile ecology,"[34] and climatic conditions and geography are cited as unable to sustain more than the "ideal population," which has already been surpassed.[35] The use of geographical and climatic conditions to justify curtailing immigration from third-world countries is a familiar theme in Canadian history: arguments that Asian and African immigrants were incapable of adapting to the climate were used to restrict their immigration in the late 19th and early 20th centuries. As the IPR gives new currency to these older rationales, the dangers of population growth through immigration are summed up by the texts as follows:

> "The effect that population growth will have on our environment and quality of life seems to be of primary concern. Environmental deterioration, air and water pollution, traffic congestion, increased crime rates, over-burdened social services, garbage disposal problems and shortages in housing, food and energy are some of the problems that people identify with over-population. They are concerned as Canada's population grows, these problems will increase in severity."[36]

In the quote above, the text begins by associating immigration with population growth, which it then immediately equates with over-population. *Immigrants* become responsible for environmental deterioration, pollution, increased crime, overburdened social services, food and housing shortages, and so on. The complexities of these wide-ranging problems become reduced simply to the presence of *immigrants*, and attention becomes directed away from the consumption patterns of *Canadians* and the impact of capitalist development on the environment. As *immigrants* are made the cause of these various, and extremely serious, problems, the text also directs attention away from the responsibility of the state for these problems. The texts actually accomplish a reversal of existing social relations: *immigrants* become attributed with the power to devastate and overwhelm both the nation and the environment. Although population levels in Canada actually face decline and will fall below replacement levels in the year 2010 without continued immigration, the texts incorporate, and thereby legitimize, this unfounded concern.

The texts also clearly signal that the problem of population growth is a selective one, created only by immigration and not by the reproduction of *Canadians*; in fact, it puts forward a specific proposal for increasing population levels by giving *Canadians* incentives to reproduce.[37] The population growth of *Canadians* is therefore not the problem; it is not anticipated to devastate the environment as the population growth of *immigrants* will. In blaming *immigrants* for overpopulating and graphically listing the specific problems associated with overpopulation, the texts link *immigrants* with the problems third-world peoples have historically been associated with in the Western imagination, problems such as increased crime, disease, pollution, excessive breeding and excessive demands on resources. Indeed, one would be hard-pressed to find a more racially charged representation of *immigrants* than the one constructed in the texts' discussion of overpopulation. In contrast, the texts point out that *Canadian* society is "dedicated to the preservation of a healthy environment."[38]

The gendered consequences of the texts' linking of *immigrants* with overpopulation are also unmistakable. It is women, after all, who populate, and it is third-world women, in particular, who have been associated in the Western imagination with overpopulating the planet. Contemporary population debates draw on Malthusian theories[39] and define population growth in third-world countries as an explosion endangering the very survival of the human species. High population levels are blamed for causing economic stagnation, environmental devastation and poverty. Overpopulation has created excessive demands on scarce resources, the popular argument goes, and population control is the only solution. Third-world women have been the specific targets of population-control programs in India, Bangladesh and Brazil, as well as in the United States and Britain. Indeed, the "excessive" fertility of third-world women has long served in the *Canadian* imagination as presenting a danger of "polluting" the whiteness of the nation. So, for example, in the early part of the 20th century, South Asian and Chinese women were specifically identified as a threat to the "purity" of the nation, and were defined as undesirable for Canada because they had the power to reproduce and thereby undermine the whiteness of the nation. The IPR texts' discussion of overpopulation draws upon these racialized/gendered historical undertones of previous immigration policies that specifically sought to prevent the entry of "non-preferred race" women into the country. The text uses these concerns in the 1990s to rally *Canadians* against the "menace" of the "abundant" fecundity of *immigrant* women. *Immigrant* women become attributed with the power to literally reproduce "garbage" in quantities enough to overwhelm the nation. *Immigrant* women themselves, and their fertility, come to be equated with "garbage" and "pollution" by the writers of the texts.

That the problem of overpopulation also selectively applies to different categories of immigrants also becomes clear in subsequent sections of the texts, which make repeated recommendations for aggressively increasing the recruitment of the "independent" category, as well as for recruiting more immigrants who speak English and

French.[40] Very explicitly, the text repeatedly states that the problem is one of the quality of *immigrants*, not their quantity,[41] and records numerous recommendations to return to the original European source countries to attract *immigrants* who are compatible with the nation.[42] Fluency in English and French is repeatedly recommended as the criterion by which the "quality" of potential *immigrants* should be evaluated. Using the criterion of social and cultural compatibility with the nation, in tandem with strengthened language criteria for selection processes, can, of course, be anticipated to privilege Europeans because they would be most likely to meet those requirements.

The defining of the problem of overpopulation thus operates at two levels: the presence of both *immigrant* women themselves and their fertility becomes the problem. In this way, the problems of the quantity and "quality" of *immigrants* become very specifically, and literally, inscribed onto the bodies of *immigrant* women.

BALANCING IMMIGRATION CATEGORIES

The third theme relates to finding the appropriate balance between the "independent" and "family" categories. The framing of these two categories by the questions for discussion shaped the responses from participants in such a way that, with very few exceptions, most reproduced the state's own ideological constructions. The texts continue to define the "independent" category as making economic contributions and, by simultaneously defining the "family" category as one of dependants, make it responsible for the costs of immigration and for overburdening social programs. The "independent" category is not associated with social, cultural and linguistic diversity, nor is it associated with any costs to the nation. The economic contributions of this category are repeatedly reinforced, and its compatibility with the nation is not questioned. Therefore, it is the "family" category, and *immigrant* women in particular, who are made responsible for lowering the "quality" of *immigrants*.

In response to the question "What criteria should we set for selecting *immigrants* in order to achieve our social and economic objectives?"[43] the responses call for increasing restrictions and reducing the family category because it is unaffordable. "Weight must be given to official language ability, education levels and potential to contribute to Canada ... Potential to contribute to Canada must be viewed in terms of (a) ability to demonstrate willingness to integrate socially and culturally; and (b) proven ability and demonstrated willingness to be productive economically."[44]

Given that the starting point for the public consultation was the construction of the "family" category as not economically productive, recommendations for increasing the economic benefits of immigration inevitably translate into recommendations for reducing immigration under the "family" category, as well as for increasing internal controls to limit the access of sponsored *immigrants* to social programs. Further recommendations call for requiring *immigrants* to pay the costs of settlement services themselves,[45] and requiring "immigrant communities" to fund settlement services for new *immigrants*:

> "Immigrant communities can play an important role in the integration of new arrivals. They should be encouraged in this respect to provide language and settlement services to other immigrants, particularly where existing delivery mechanisms are underfunded or overburdened, and if possible to provide Canadian job experience as a transition into the broader labour market (perhaps through a form of sponsorship). These measures will help raise the economic contribution of immigrants while reducing the costs of traditional settlement delivery mechanisms."[46]

This extraordinary recommendation constructs all people of colour as "immigrant communities," regardless of their citizenship status, and makes them responsible for "their" own kind. The reality that "immigrant communities" — as taxpayers — fund "our" national social programs is made invisible by this recommendation. Other measures recommended by the text to reduce the costs of immigration by strengthening the sponsorship agreement include the introduction of a sponsorship bond (one specific recommendation calls for this bond to be set at $20,000).[47] One recommendation calls for raising the income levels of prospective sponsors before they can qualify for sponsorship;[48] others recommend the outright ending of family sponsorship for low-income *immigrants*, arguing that "being separated from one's family is a choice that every immigrant must make."[49]

While the texts recommend restrictions on the numbers of *immigrants* in the "family" category and their access to social programs, they simultaneously call for increasing and supporting the immigration of the "independent" category. The texts recommend aggressive recruitment and "promotion" of this category, specifically calling for increasing the numbers of economic immigrants by correspondingly decreasing the "family" category to keep overall immigration levels low. In this way, the feminized "family" category, and *immigrant* women in particular, come to be defined as one of the biggest burdens the immigration program places on the nation.

"PROTECTING" NATIONAL INSTITUTIONS

The fourth theme focuses on alleged threats to national institutions by *immigrants* who are portrayed as engaged in widespread criminal activities and abuse of social services. Every *Canadian*, as taxpayer, is said to be in danger: "There is increasing concern that immigrants are not respecting these responsibilities [of sponsorship], thus placing demands on already over-burdened social support programs, funded by Canadian taxpayers."[50]

Participants are said to want "a government which takes effective action against abuse of our systems instead of allowing chronic abusers of our immigration and welfare systems to go unchecked."[51]

State officials are reported to be frustrated with a system that stops them from dealing quickly and efficiently with fraud and abuse. They are disturbed by the fact that some people arrive at "our" borders with "*instructions* on how to use the system to their advantage [emphasis added]," the text records.[52] Here, the effective use by *immigrants* of the system becomes equated with fraud and abuse. The texts present *immigrants* who know how to use the system as a problem because they abuse it, and they present those *immigrants* who don't know "our" system also as a problem because they don't understand democracy and the rule of law!

Contributions that challenged the state's racialized construction of *immigrants* can be found in the reports of a number of study groups, but these reports were simply left out of the final reports of the IPR. Contributions that challenged the racist stereotypes that immigrants "live off the fat of the taxpayer"[53] were ignored, as were contributions that challenged the view that *Canadians* and *immigrants* have opposing values.

The practices of the state during the IPR did not allow these oppositional views to enter the framework being constructed for the restructuring of the immigration program. These contributions would have disrupted the framework's reality by challenging its fundamental assumptions about the nation, as well as about the threats *immigrants* present to it. These contributions were silenced by being denied entry into the final report, which ends by reiterating the numerous threats *immigrants* present to the health and safety of *Canadians* and their national institutions.

The framework being produced through the IPR brings both right-wing anti-immigrant views and more liberal views to the same conclusion. If it is accepted that *immigrants* are engaged in the massive abuse of social services, as the right wing claims, then the solution to cutting costs becomes one of restricting immigration. A more liberal view might reject this wholesale stereotyping and instead define *immigrants* who claim assistance as victims of economic conditions beyond their control and, as such, unwittingly precipitating a crisis in social services. The solution to reducing costs in this liberal view would also be to reduce immigration levels, even if only as a temporary measure. The problem constructed in the IPR framework is such that there is only one solution. The state's ideological construction of *immigrants* as outsiders to the nation makes their unequal treatment by the Canadian state politically acceptable.

The important point here is not whether *immigrants* use social services. After all, the very basis for the creation of social programs, especially social assistance, was the recognition that individuals are not responsible for the conditions which create unemployment and poverty, and that they need protection from economic cycles through access to social programs. Rather, the point is that defining *immigrants* as outsiders to the nation legitimizes their unequal access to these programs. This is the state's way of legitimizing and normalizing unequal rights and entitlements for *immigrants* through its ideological practices: "they" should not have the same rights as "us."

What the Consultations Accomplished

By appealing to *Canadians* in overtly racialized ways, the state sought to nationalize them into supporting its practices for the 21st century. The review enabled the state to present itself as the defender of the national interest against *immigrant* women. It enabled the state to claim a partnership between nation and state on the basis of "shared goals" and "shared responsibilities" between "government and its citizens."[54] In the textual reality produced by the state, the family category is placed in a no-win situation, whether economic, social or cultural criteria are used for immigrant selection. It would come up short on economic criteria because it has been ideologically constructed as making no economic contribution to the nation. It would likewise come up short on the social and cultural criteria because it has been ideologically constructed as culturally and socially diverse, and, as such, potentially undermines national cohesion by increasing racial tensions. Once the textual reality produced by the IPR is entered, the only way to maximize the economic contributions of the immigration program and to reduce racial tensions is to reduce immigration under the "family" category. The texts' construction of this particular problem leaves no other option, unless of course the textual reality, its entire conceptual framework and its underlying assumptions, are rejected.

Throughout the review texts, the construction of *immigrant* women as presenting various threats to the nation remains constant, as does the construction of the state as the defender of the interests of *Canadians* against *immigrants* in general, and *immigrant* women in particular. The reality being constructed through the IPR texts presents the state as committed only to protecting the nation, and the public consultations were used as demonstration of the state's commitment to creating a democratic process, to building a partnership with an active citizenry to resolve its problems. The IPR enabled the state to present itself as the protector of the nation by constructing *immigrants*, and *immigrant* women in particular, as a problem-in-common; thus creating the political climate for a closing of the nation's ranks against them. In the process, it also built the necessary political support to reduce the ability of third-world women to come to Canada as permanent residents, and therefore to subsequently make claims to citizenship. Further policing the access of all *immigrant* women in Canada to social-security programs was made not only feasible, but also absolutely necessary, in the name of protecting *Canadians* and "our" economy and national institutions.

The IPR ended with the tabling of the annual report *A Broader Vision: Immigration and Citizenship* (which outlined immigration levels as set by the government for the years 1995-2000), and of a long-term strategy plan, *Into the 21st Century: A Strategy for Immigration and Citizenship*. This plan outlines the future direction for immigration policy, and as such is an extremely significant document. A number of its recommendations have been implemented since 1995.

The annual plan for the years 1995-2000 recommended an outright reduction in overall immigration levels and also a significant reduction under the "family" category. Restrictions on eligibility criteria for sponsorship were increased; sponsors have to sign a contract, and sponsors can be prosecuted by provincial governments for defaulting. An increase in the surveillance of sponsored *immigrants'* access to social-assistance programs will be organized by the federal Immigration Department and provincial social-service agencies. A $975 Head Tax was introduced, which will disproportionately limit poorer third-world women's immigration. The state subsequently commissioned a report, *Not Just Numbers*, that echoed many of the recommendations made in the IPR, including that fluency in English or French be made a selection criterion. This report also called for a new Immigration Act, for restricting the grounds on which claims to Canadian citizenship can be made, and for privatizing the costs of all settlement and language training programs.

Notes toward Strategies for Resistance

People-of-colour communities, along with immigrant- and refugee-rights groups, have responded to the changes discussed above by organizing campaigns against the Head Tax and against making fluency in English and French a selection criterion. While these are certainly very important initiatives, challenging state-organized racism against women of colour, as *immigrant* women, is much more fundamental. Rather than feminist and anti-racist organizations focusing only on the discriminatory treatment of third-world *immigrants* — and these policy changes are specifically aimed at them — what is urgently required is a challenge to the racialization of the *Canadian* nation itself.

A fundamental principle underpinning the Canadian nation is the ongoing colonization of Aboriginal peoples. Ending this colonial/racial domination through Aboriginal self-determination and title to land is key to realizing any progressive social change in Canada. As long as Canada remains a white settler colony, the nation will continue to be racialized.

The second principle underlying the Canadian nation is the racialization of all *immigrants*: white immigrants have historically been, and continue to be today, integrated into the ranks of the nation, while people of colour are bordered as *immigrants*, as outsiders to the nation. Therefore, challenging and transforming the fundamental racialization of the nation as bilingual and bicultural is necessary if Canadian society is to become more just. As long as this racialized definition of the nation is accepted, membership in it will remain exclusionary, and the racialized bordering of *immigrants* as outsiders, inevitable. An examination of how nation-building is currently being organized demonstrates that, although the specific content of the national interest has changed over time, the state's construction of the nation as "white" (and the definition of women of colour as representing a threat to it) has not. As long as the nation is defined by racialized cultural, linguistic and social characteristics, women of colour will continue to be defined as outsiders who undermine the "unity" of the nation.

My discussion of immigration also recognizes that there is an urgent need for building coalitions between Aboriginal women and women of colour. A dialogue on immigration between Aboriginal communities and people-of-colour communities is urgently needed if we are to stop the state from pitting these communities against each other. Aboriginal voices were given no space in the Immigration Policy Review, and the struggles of Aboriginal peoples today receive little support from people-of-colour communities. Coalitions of Aboriginal women and women of colour committed to working across our historical divisions have to be a priority for the anti-racist organizing of women of colour.

While women of colour are organizing against racist immigration policies, it is up to *Canadians* to challenge their own racialization (which is the basis of their membership in "their" nation), and to rupture their partnership with "their" state. The question women of colour need to ask *Canadians* is this: If the state is not acting in your interest in closing the nation's doors to *immigrant* women, then where are your voices?

Conclusion

Immigration policy regulates access to citizenship in Canada, as well as organizing membership in the nation. As long as this policy continues to distinguish between those whom the state defines as compatible with a racialized nation and those whom it constructs as outsiders and dependants (and hence a burden on the nation), the unequal treatment of *Canadians* and *immigrants* will be inevitable.

As long as immigration policy controls borders to organize the unequal treatment of citizens, immigrants and non-citizens, it cannot help organizing and regulating inequalities between them. Once we accept that there should be unequal treatment of citizens, immigrants and non-citizens, the question which remains is only that of how unequal that treatment should be.

The current phase of globalization has made increased international migration inevitable. The growing global polarization between the North and South, and the environmental devastation that is the fruit of the neo-conservative "free trade" agenda promoted both within Canada and at the international level, are forcing people to migrate in increased numbers. And it is the very people who are forced to migrate as a result of the policies that the Canadian state is pursuing internationally that the Canadian state seeks to keep from entering Canada as permanent residents who can subsequently claim citizenship.

ENDNOTES

1. For a more indepth discussion of these issues, see: Dara Culhane, *The Pleasure of the Crown: Anthropology, Law and First Nations* (Burnaby, BC: Talonbooks, 1998); Noel Dyck, *What Is the Indian "Problem": Tutelage and Resistance in Canadian Indian Administration* (St. John's, NF: Institute of Social and Economic Research, 1991); James S. Frideres, "Policies on Indian People in Canada," in Peter Li (ed.), *Race and Ethnic Relations in Canada* (Toronto: Oxford University Press, 1990), pp. 47-68; Joyce A. Green, "Towards a Détente with History: Confronting Canada's Colonial Legacy," *International Journal of Canadian Studies* 12 (Fall, 1995), pp. 85-105; and Lee Maracle, "Racism, Sexism and Patriarchy," in Himani Bannerji (ed.), *Returning the Gaze: Essays on Racism, Feminism and Politics* (Toronto: Sister Vision, 1993), pp. 148-158.

2. A Head Tax of $10 was imposed on Chinese immigrants in 1885. The tax was increased to $50 between 1886 and 1900, to $100 for the next three years, and to $500 from 1904 to 1923. The 1923 Exclusion Act sought to prevent all immigration from China; and only 50 Chinese immigrants were allowed to enter the country between 1923 and 1947. The Continuous Passage requirement was introduced in 1908 to restrict immigration from India and Japan. It required immigrants to travel from their country of origin to Canada in a continuous, unbroken journey at a time when such passage was not available to people from those countries.

3. With immigrants from Europe declining in numbers, third-world countries became correspondingly important as sources for labour. In *Critical Years in Immigration: Canada and Australia Compared* (Montreal/Kingston: McGill-Queens' University Press, 1989), Freda Hawkins also makes the argument that Canadian bureaucrats recognized "that Canada could not operate effectively within the United Nations, or in a multiracial Commonwealth, with the millstone of a racially discriminatory policy round her neck."

4. The point system organized immigration largely under the two categories of "independent" and "family" classes. Additionally, it has organized temporary workers under the "business" and "domestic workers" categories. The refugee program is, of course, organized under different selection criteria.

5. Citizenship and Immigration Canada (hereinafter CIC), *Facts and Figures: Overview of Immigration* (Ottawa: Ministry of Supply and Services, 1994), p. 5.

6. My analysis of this review is based on an examination of the consultation documents, the reports of working committees, the report of the national conference, the interim and final reports, and the reports tabled in Parliament.

7. CIC, *Canada 1005: A Strategy for Citizenship and Immigration, Conference Proceedings* (Ottawa: Ministry of Supply and Services, 1994), p. 1.

8. This meeting was organized by the Public Policy Forum, and drew participants from the three levels of government, from "international and social organizations, business, labour, academic institutions, and media representatives," and "public safety and service agencies" (CIC, *Canada 2005: A Strategy for Citizenship and Immigration, Background Document* {Ottawa: Ministry of Supply and Services, 1994}, p. 2). Organizations representing *immigrants* and *immigrant* women are not recorded as having participated.

9. CIC, *Immigration Consultations Report* (Ottawa: Ministry of Supply and Services, 1994), p. 2.

10. While in a technical sense the terms "Canadians" and "immigrants" would be expected to refer to legal status within the country, these terms have been historically racialized and express everyday racism in common-sense terms. When I refer to the racialized meanings of these categories, the words are italicized.

11. I would like to remind the reader that the principles and criteria underlying the acceptance of immigrants and refugees are different. In this article, I am not addressing the refugee program, although this program, too, was included in the Immigration Policy Review. For various reasons, the refugee program is beyond the scope of my present inquiry.

12. CIC, *Canada and Immigration: Facts and Issues* (Ottawa: Ministry of Supply and Services, 1994), p. 3.

13. Ibid.

14. See, for example: Martin Barker, *The New Racism* (London: Junction, 1981); Paul Gilroy, *There Ain't No Black in the Union Jack* (Chicago: The University of Chicago Press, 1991); and Etienne Balibar, "Racism and Nationalism," in Etienne Balibar & Immanuel Wallerstein (eds.), *Race, Nation, Class: Ambiguous Identities* (London: Verso, 1991), pp. 37-68.

15. Sunera Thobani, "Nationalizing Citizens, Bordering Immigrant Women: Globalization and the Racialization of Citizenship in Late 20th Century Canada," Ph.D thesis, Simon Fraser University, 1998.

16. CIC, *Facts and Issues* (1994), p. 3.

17. For example, in June 1989, immigration policy allowed sponsorship of single, adult children of sponsors. Adult children were previously not defined as eligible for family sponsorship. When this attracted more applicants than the department had anticipated, changes were introduced in April 1992 to reduce the eligibility of adult offspring. See: CIC, *A Broader Vision: Immigration and Citizenship Plan 1995-2000* (Ottawa: Ministry of Supply and Services, 1994), p. 8.

18. CIC, *Facts and Issues* (1994), p. 3.

19. Ibid.

20. Questions 5, 6, 7, 8, 9 & 10 (ibid.). In the background to the first issue, there is a reference to *immigrants* being less likely to claim welfare and other benefits than *Canadians*, and an acknowledgement that *immigrants* contribute more in taxes than they consume in social services. But this information is not used in the framing of the questions for discussion, and the rest of the document reiterates the view that *immigrants* represent a burden on social services.

21. Ibid., pp. 3-6.

22. The range of institutions across which the "problems" of immigration have to be managed are specified for Working Groups 6A and 6B as including housing, health, education, social assistance and policing.

23. CIC, *Facts and Issues* (1994), p. 5.

24. See: Dorothy Smith, *The Conceptual Practices of Power* (Toronto: University of Toronto Press, 1990) for a full discussion of how central the social construction of knowledge and the framing of reality through textual practices are to the reproduction of relations of ruling in advanced capitalism.

25. These themes are summarized at the end of the reports. A fifth theme dealing with the refugee program also runs throughout the texts, but as this program lies outside the scope of my present inquiry, I do not address it in this article.

26. CIC, *Immigration Consultations Report* (Ottawa: Ministry of Supply and Services, 1994), p. 19.

27. Ibid.

28. Ibid., p. 21.

29. Ibid., p. 20.

30. See, for example: Punam Khosla, *Review of the Situation of Women in Canada, 1993* (Toronto: National Action Committee on the Status of Women, 1993); D. Ralph, "How to Beat the Corporate Agenda: Strategies for Social Justice," in J. Pulkingham & G. Ternowetsky (eds.), *Remaking Canadian Social Policy* (Halifax: Fernwood, 1996), pp. 288-302; and J. Brodie (ed.), *Women and Canadian Public Policy* (Toronto: Harcourt Brace, 1996).

31. CIC, *Immigration Consultations Report* (1994), p. 22.

32. CIC, *Employee Consultation Report* (Ottawa: Ministry of Supply and Services, 1994), p. 1.

33. CIC, *Immigration Consultations Report* (1994), p. 17.

34. Ibid., p. 18.

35. Ibid.

36. Ibid.

37. Ibid.

38. Ibid.

39. Thomas Malthus, a British economist, argued in the 1700s and early 1800s that human population increases in geometric terms (i.e., 1, 2, 4, 8), while the capacity to increase food production is possible only in arithmetic terms (i.e., 1, 2, 3, 4). Increases in agricultural production would never be able to meet the needs of population growth, he argued, and called for population growth to be curtailed.

40. CIC, *Immigration Consultations Report* (1994), pp. 26, 65.

41. CIC, *Canada 2005: Background Document* (1994), p. 61.

42. CIC, *Immigration Consultations Report* (1994), p. 26.

43. CIC, *Facts and Issues* (1994), p. 3.

44. CIC, *Immigration Consultations Report* (1994), p. 26.

45. CIC, *Employee Consultation Report* (1994), p. 7.

46. CIC, *The Report of Working Group #8* (Ottawa: Ministry of Supply and Services, 1994), p. 11.

47. Don J. De Voretz, "New Issues, New Evidence, and New Immigration Policies for the Twenty-First Century," in Don J. De Voretz (ed.), *Diminishing Returns: The Economics of Canada's Recent Immigration Policy* (Ottawa: C.D. Howe Institute, 1995), p. 8.

48. CIC, *Working Group #8* (1994), p. 11.

49. CIC, *Immigration Consultations Report* (1994), p. 28.

50. CIC, *Working Group #8* (1994), pp. 10-11.

51. CIC, *Canada 2005: Background Document* (1994), p. 42.

52. CIC, *Employee Consultation Report* (1994), p. 6.

53. CIC, *Canada 2005: Conference Proceedings* (1994), p. 6.

54. CIC, *Immigration Consultations Report* (1994), p. 1.

AN ANISHNAWBE:KWE PERSPECTIVE ON NEW WORLD ORDER

Vera M. Wabegijig

The New World Order is nothing new. It has been happening throughout the world since land was first privatized and people, communities and nations were conquered. But we've been made more aware of the New World Order through consciousness-raising and resistance against government control and its corporate inclination to dominate the global economy. We understand that the New World Order threatens us all. Now what I wonder is: Why haven't Canadians looked more critically at how the government has been implementing this New World Order here in Canada, on the Aboriginal peoples?

We don't have to look far to find the effects of the New World Order. It thrived here before Canada was even incorporated as a country. Canadians should be outraged by and disgusted with the treatment of Aboriginal people. Through colonialism, segregation, the reservation system, the residential-school system, the Indian Act and assimilation, the government engaged in the genocide of Aboriginal peoples. The effects are evident within every Aboriginal community and nation, whether it be on- or off-reserve.

This is what the New World Order has wrought: high unemployment, poverty, abuse of alcohol and drugs, family violence, sexual abuse, suicide, low self-esteem, loss of language and traditions, poor health care, poor education, increase of HIV and AIDS cases and the initial breakdown of ancient societies within Aboriginal social structures.[1] This has all been regularly maintained and regulated by the federal government and its enforcer, the Department of Indian and Northern Affairs. Now, however, the government is switching its control to our own people through the Aboriginal band chief and the band councils. The chief and council members are becoming the new oppressors, and they demonstrate and exercise a foreign policy: the Indian Act.[2]

Some Aboriginal History

The Indian Act is a tool used to further the assimilation of Aboriginal peoples into the Canadian colony. Adopted in 1951, this tool was used by the federal government to absolve it of responsibility toward the First Nations. The Indian Act is a piece of paper that says who is and who is not Indian, what an Indian can and cannot do, where an Indian can and cannot live, where an Indian can and cannot go, and who an Indian can and cannot marry.

This last provision was a highly effective way of reducing the government's responsibility. An Indian woman kept her status if she married an Indian man, but lost it if she married a non-Native or a non-status Indian. At the same time, however, if an Indian man married a non-Native woman, she would become an Indian with full status. A woman who lost her status would no longer have a house on the reserve and her children would automatically be considered Canadian. The government held no responsibility for the education, health-care and housing needs of non-status Indians; they were also stripped of other rights that status Indians had.[3]

These injustices and indecent acts were supposed to annihilate Aboriginal people. Through the (ab)use of media and the misinformation of history books, the Canadian population has been conditioned to believe that Indians are a burden to the economic state. Most Canadians think that all Indians get a free education; get all their health, eye and dental care paid for; and are given a free ride paid for by Canadian tax dollars. The sad truth is that our Aboriginal ancestors honestly believed in the treaty process. In fact, the federal government constantly lied, tricked, deceived and fooled Aboriginal people into signing treaties that placed them on desolate, barren lands and turned them from independent to dependent nations.

These in-faith negotiations have left many First Nations communities two steps behind the rest of Canadian society. The Canadian government continues to condition the general public to believe in and depend on what the media and history books teach. This conditioning in fact instils the notion that students cannot question teachers' twisted pronouncements. Who has the dominant voice/opinion in the educational system? The same group that controls and dominates the government and the economy: the white-male-dominated, privileged elitists and neo-liberalists who govern the corporate-minded club. Will we ever learn the whole truth behind all of the lies that have been created through the conditioning and programming of economic colonialism?[4]

The Power of Resistance

The New World Order is rooted in racism, white supremacy, sexism and other oppressions. Why do we continue to support a system that is biased toward, and exploitive of, at least 80 percent of the world's population?[5]

What we need is resistance. When people unite together as a collective, such as indigenous militant groups and women's groups, they can inform the general public of the need to question the policies and the laws of governments. People have the power to elect their representatives and government leaders because their taxes pay the salaries of every government employee, including the prime minister; it is these taxes that are misused, however, and in the end it is the social programs that get the drastic cuts. Take a look at how far the government has cut health care, child care, education, social assistance and employment insurance, for example. These cuts are happening in every province. And it is the general public who feels the effects of losing these social institutions — especially the poor, who are mostly women and children. Resistance must be the cord that connects all people together.

People have the right to join together and fight the oppressor, demand change, demand restructuring of an existing government or a new government all together. But the government employs various institutions to convey misleading information and eliminate any opposition. Remember the Oka crisis?[6] This is an important example of how the media is used to manipulate the general public. On all Canadian television stations we were faced with the image of masked Kahnesatake Mohawk warriors. These warriors were portrayed as a threat not only to the Canadian government, but also to all Canadians. What was not said or reported was that innocent women and children made up the majority of people behind the barricades, and that they were actively involved in this crisis. The Mohawks of Kahnesatake simply wanted to honour and respect their ancestors, to protect their burial grounds when the town of Oka wanted to add another nine holes to a golf course. Absurd, isn't it? Yet this truth was quickly obscured by the images of that familiar confrontation between a soldier and a masked warrior. This type of media manipulation resulted in mass confusion and mass misinterpretation, and eventually led to the weakening of the strong Kahnesatake and Kahnawake-Mohawk collective.

There are other resistance movements that are constantly being attacked, such as the women's movement. The government came to the conclusion that the women's movement was a man-hating lesbian regime, a conclusion that only adds to the existing negative connotations attached to feminism. The government, aided by the media, broadcasted this conclusion to the general public. It is this type of portrayal that perpetuates the idea that women who are involved in the movement are spinsters, lesbians and troublemakers.

Of course, the women's movement represents a threat because it questions the ideology behind the patriarchy and demands that women's voices be heard and taken seriously. This questioning by women was unheard of — after all, a woman's place is in the home, not in the political arena. But this resistance created a raising of consciousness in all women, and the once all-male government was finally being challenged and threatened. It was these new challenges, of course, that made the government construct feminism as bad and advance the notion that a good woman would not question a man's opinion.

Another tactic the government employs to disengage a collective is the use of the armed forces. Look at the Oka crisis, the Lubicon Cree, Restigouche, Gustafson Lake, Ipperwash — the list goes on and on. The difference between the government's approach to Aboriginal and non-Aboriginal resistance is that it routinely uses the armed forces to occupy Aboriginal territory. This threatens all people who create Aboriginal communities.

These are major human-rights violations, but who sees it this way? Only the Aboriginal people and a few others are aware of these inhuman acts of violence. The general public is informed by the corporate media, but the media is there to serve the purposes of the government and the governments within governments. Their twisted lies feed the misinformed, and thus create dissension and division within Aboriginal communities and among the Canadian population. It is this divide-and-conquer mechanism that the government favours the most. It is used all the time against every collective that screams for change.

It is easier to pass bills and treaties such as the North American Free Trade Agreement (NAFTA)[7] when the general public is blindsided. It is easier to be tricked and deceived when people and collectives are tangled up with internal politics and in disarray. The Canadian government and the neo-liberalists who dominate and control the economic neo-colonialist agenda thrive on manipulating and weakening people. But the Canadian government is not the only guilty party. Equal responsibility must be borne by all governments and corporations in all countries that have conquered the human race, the environment, the land and its resources, the economy, the social structure — all to the point of destruction. The power lies in resistance through political collectives, spiritual awakening, community strengthening, consciousness-raising and the power of knowledge. If people do not wake up and stand up, the New (Economic) World Order will bring about global genocide, global slavery, destruction of global environment and the end of the world as we know it.

ENDNOTES

1. Anne McGillivray & Brenda Comaskey, "'everybody had black eyes ... nobody don't say nothing': Intimate Violence, Aboriginal Women, and Justice System Response," in Kevin Bonnycastle & George Rigakos (eds.), *Unsettling Truths: Battered Women, Policy, Politics and Contemporary Research in Canada* (Vancouver: Collective Press, 1998); Sharon McIvor & Teressa Nahanee, "Aboriginal Women: Invisible Victims of Violence," in ibid.; "Eco-Justice and Health: Indigenous Communities at Risk," Special Issue, *Abya Yala News: Journal of the South and Meso American Indian Rights Center* 11, 1 (Spring 1998); and "Honor the Earth 1997," Special Issue, *Indigenous Women's Network* 2, 5 (1998).

2. Renae Morriseau (dir.), *Indigeni: Native Women: Politics* (The Coyote Collective, 1996).

3. Shirley Bear, "You Can't Change the Indian Act?" in Jeri Wine & Janice Ristock (eds.), *Women and Social Change: Feminist Activism in Canada* (Halifax: James Lorimer, 1991); and Teressa Anne Nahanee, "Indian Women, Sex Equality and the Charter," in Caroline Andrew & Sandra Rodgers (eds.), *Women and the Canadian State* (Montreal/Kingston: McGill-Queens University Press, 1997), pp. 89-103.

4. Sharon Venne, "Whose Law? Whose Land?" *Overview* (May 1998), pp. 8-9.

5. Joan Grant-Cummings, "Feminism: The Antidote to the Global Capitalist Economic Agenda" (see pages 259-271 in this book).

6. Christine Welsh (dir.), *Keepers of the Fire* (National Film Board, 1994); Alanis Obomsawin (dir.), *Kanehsatake: 270 Years of Resistance* (National Film Board, 1993); Alanis Obomsawin (dir.), *My Name Is Kahentiiosta* (National Film Board, 1995); Donna Kahenrakwas Goodleaf, "'Under Military Occupation': Indigenous Women, State Violence and Community Resistance," in Linda Carty (ed.), *And Still We Rise: Feminist Political Mobilizing in Contemporary Canada* (Toronto: Women's Press, 1993), pp. 225-242; and Frances Abele, "Beyond Oka: Dimensions of Mohawk Sovereignty, Interview with Kahn-Tineta Horn," *Studies in Political Economy: A Socialist Review* 35 (Summer 1991), pp. 29-41.

7. Donna Goodleaf, "Self-Government and NAFTA: Tools of Genocide," *Entering the War Zone: A Mohawk Perspective on Resisting Invasions* (Penticton, BC: Theytus, 1995), pp. 173-83; and Sharon Venne, "Aboriginal Peoples and NAFTA: Colonization Continues to Run Amok," *Constitutional Forum Constitutionnel* 5 (1994), pp. 78-80.

PART THREE

POPULAR CULTURE

HOW CHIC ARE WE?

Lesbian Chic in Mainstream Print Media

Kate Campbell

After decades of relative invisibility, lesbians and lesbianism have become very popular media topics in the 1990s. In 1993, which was the peak of the so-called lesbian-chic trend, the television show *Roseanne* introduced a regularly appearing lesbian character, and many of the biggest-selling American magazines, including *Newsweek*, *Cosmopolitan*, *Vogue*, *Mademoiselle*, *Harper's*, *New York*, *Vanity Fair* and *Us*, ran lengthy feature articles in which lesbianism was presented as fun, fashionable and trendy.

Although the increase in visibility attained through this trend can be seen as a positive step toward social change, the representation of lesbianism in the mainstream press can also be viewed as part of the current backlash against feminism, particularly against the radical feminism and lesbian feminism of the 1970s and early 1980s.[1] As I will argue, lesbians who are viewed by the press as "overly political" or "strident," usually those who are over age 35, are derided, while younger, "fun" lesbians are applauded. In this way, the important social criticisms made by second-wave feminists, including critiques of capitalism, North American beauty imperatives, and mainstream media, are undermined and even ridiculed.

I became interested in media representations of lesbians in 1993, when my friends and I began noticing a sudden increase in the number of lesbians appearing in mainstream magazines, in movies and on television shows. We began having discussions about the impact of this "lesbian chic" trend, and about our reactions to it. At that time, I was glad to see lesbians in media and, along with my friends, followed the coverage avidly. However, I was somewhat disturbed by what I saw. There were thin, white women with make-up and designer clothes, but nowhere did I see lesbians who looked like me, or who looked like the majority of lesbians I knew. It is important not to disregard the importance of media visibility for any social movement, and this is particularly the case with lesbians, who have been largely invisible in society for so long. For many people, especially youths in non-urban areas, the popular media is their primary source of information about lesbians, and may in fact be the only place they ever hear the issue discussed. Thus, as I will argue, it is essential to examine the kind of information being produced by the mass media, to lobby to change homophobic and heterosexist representations and to create positive alternatives.

The term "lesbian chic" refers not only to the increased volume of media coverage about lesbians in the 1990s, but also to the nature of that coverage. If the portrayal of lesbians had been overtly negative and derogatory, it would not be described as "chic." The word "chic" suggests a current fashion or a trend, as well as sophistication or exoticism. Thus, in the lesbian-chic trend, lesbians are presented as fashionable, sophisticated and often exotic. In addition, the images associated with lesbian chic frequently fail to reflect any racial, age, class or political diversity among lesbians, and for the most part fail to challenge traditional stereotypes of femininity, female sexuality and attractiveness. The lesbians who are represented most frequently, and most sympathetically, tend to be those who are stereotypically attractive and not overtly radical in their politics.

This sudden increase in media attention in the early to mid-1990s can be demonstrated by looking at the number of citations in the *Canadian Business and Current Affairs Index* under the categories "lesbian," "lesbians" and "lesbianism." In 1983 there were 3 articles indexed, in 1989 there were 30 and in 1992 there were 96. One year later, in 1993, there were 317 articles. Thus, there was a slow increase in media interest throughout the 1980s, but a sudden jump between 1992 and 1993, the year the lesbian-chic trend hit the newsstands. This mainstream-press attention seems to have peaked in 1994, but it has remained relatively high since then. Of the 317 lesbian-chic articles appearing in 1993, I obtained 65 from some of the best-known Canadian and American newspapers and magazines; these 65 articles give a broad sense of the variety and frequency of coverage of lesbianism as a journalistic subject during that period. Although there were also some very interesting lesbian-chic articles published in Britain, Australia and elsewhere, I restricted my search to Canadian and American sources, owing to the breadth of the topic.

"The Problem That Is Never Mentioned"

In order to understand how and why lesbian chic has developed as a trend in the 1990s, it is important first to examine some of the history of how lesbians, and to some extent gay men, have been represented in the press. Prior to 1950, homosexuality was never overtly discussed in the North American media. There were some very vague references to "perversion" and "inversion," but in general the subject of homosexuality was considered too obscene to write about. In the late 1940s and early 1950s, however, this very gradually began to change. The Kinsey reports prompted a certain amount of public interest in and media discussion about sexuality in general, and some sexologists began to publish books and articles on the subject, such as *Female Homosexuality* by Frank Caprio, published in 1954. Also in this period, visible gay and lesbian communities and bar cultures began to develop in urban centres.

Because gays and lesbians were more visible than ever before, they began to be perceived as a social threat by both the media and government agencies. These fears about the perceived spread of homosexuality led to an increase in violence against lesbians and gays, usually in the form of street bashings, increased harassment and persecution by the police and the government, and an increase in media articles denouncing homosexuality.[2] McCarthyism also had a significant impact on the media representation of lesbians, in both the United States and Canada. A woman interviewed by the Lesbians Making History Collective recalled that many lesbians, especially those employed in areas considered sensitive, such as teaching and the military, feared losing their jobs and falling victim to increased violence.[3]

Largely in response to McCarthyist persecution and the rise in gay bashings, homophile organizations (made possible by the growth of lesbian and gay communities) began to be formed in the United States in the early 1950s. Some the earliest and most well-known American homophile organizations were the Mattachine Society, which was founded in 1951, and the Daughters of Bilitis, an all-lesbian group formed in 1955.[4] The first Canadian homophile group, the Association for Social Knowledge (ASK), was formed in 1964.[5] These organizations did increase the overall visibility of lesbians and gay men in North American media, and for the first time announced homosexual rights as a political issue.

In the 1950s and 1960s, the majority of articles and stories about lesbians were to be found, not in the mainstream press, but in the so-called yellow press, or tabloid newspapers, and in the dime novels that proliferated in the period. Many gay and lesbian historians have argued that, despite the largely negative and homophobic messages contained in these articles and novels, they were avidly read by many gays and lesbians, and were the primary source of information on homosexuality for many people.[6] The articles and stories of this period were profoundly influenced by the psychological and sexological literature of the era. One example, published in the Toronto tabloid *Flash* in 1951, under the pseudonym Sapho, includes the following passage:

> "[L]esbians fall into three groups: those who are homosexual because of a glandular deficiency; those who, while normal at birth, become homosexual as a result of a psychic shock, and those who, in maturity, turn voluntarily to Lesbianism as a release from the vulgarity and bestiality of men ... This latter group is largely made up of prostitutes ... [b]ut these girls are not true Lesbians."[7]

Although this description is lurid, it is a fairly good summary of the theories of lesbianism informing articles published in more reputable newspapers and magazines during this period. It is important to note that this view of lesbianism as a psychological illness persisted in both the media and medical institutions well into the 1970s, as evidenced by the fact that the American Psychological Association considered homosexuality an illness until 1973.[8]

During the 1950s, there were a few articles published about lesbians in women's magazines such as *Canadian Home Journal*[9] and *Chatelaine*.[10] But these early articles took a very negative view of lesbianism, or inversion, as it was frequently called, and focused on the "social problem" it presented. Here is a passage from an article published in *Canadian Home Journal* in 1951, called "The Problem That Is Never Mentioned," which captures the general tone of these early writings very clearly: "Although lesbianism is a very different matter from venereal disease, there is the same need to have more than a vague and horrified notion of what it is if we are to understand and help to solve the social problem it presents."[11]

This article begins with a lurid description of a lesbian who murders her lover out of jealousy, and then goes on to discuss how dominating mothers and effeminate fathers will make a young girl into a lesbian (because, as the author notes, "lesbianism begins at home").[12] The article concludes: "There you have the chief reason why lesbianism is a social problem that directly or indirectly affects every one of us ... It must and should be condemned, but as the preventable disease it essentially is rather than as a hideous, shameful degradation to which only a kind of moral monster would succumb."[13]

By the late 1960s, the impact of the newly emerging gay liberation and women's movements becomes visible in media representations of lesbians and gay men. On June 27, 1969, lesbians and gay men fought back against police harassment at the Stonewall Inn in New York's Greenwich Village. As the Australian queer theorist Annamarie Jagose has suggested, the Stonewall Riots symbolize the beginning of the gay and lesbian movement, and the rejection of the assimilationist politics of earlier homophile activists. Jagose argues that the notions of gay identity and gay pride that cemented in this era led to a politic which was less intent on proving that lesbians and gays were just like heterosexuals, and more embracing of sexual difference.[14] Many newspaper and magazine articles throughout the 1970s were critical of the gay and lesbian liberation movement, and other articles hinted derisively at the connection between lesbianism and the women's liberation movement. However, as the feminist writer Sue O'Sullivan has argued, these representations, despite their underlying hostility and homophobia, did constitute a reaction by the mainstream media, and as such challenged common assumptions about sexuality and gender roles.[15]

The 1970s also saw an explosion in the number of feminist and lesbian-run alternative publishing houses, journals and newspapers in North America and Europe.[16] These publications not only served to replace pulp novels and tabloid papers as the primary source of information about lesbian lives, but also led to led to changes in the representations of lesbians in mainstream culture. For example, in 1977 *Chatelaine*, a Canadian women's magazine, under the editorship of the feminist Doris Anderson, published a very sympathetic article entitled "Gay Women: A Minority Report."[17] This piece was more positive than any article previously published in a mainstream magazine and was clearly influenced by the women's movement.

Acceptance or Backlash?

The American journalist Susan Faludi argues compellingly that, throughout the 1980s, "backlash" was a trend, played out particularly in the media and popular culture, that blamed feminism and women's struggles for equality for many social problems, as well as for widespread stress and unhappiness among women. Faludi argues that the purpose of this trend was to "thwart women's progress"[18] and to contain the serious threat to the status quo that feminism represented. Although Faludi does not refer to lesbianism or homophobia in her discussion of anti-feminist backlash, lesbian chic can be seen to fit into this trend.

In *Backlash*, Faludi identifies "trend stories" as a new type of journalistic writing that arose in the 1980s.[19] She argues that these trend stories, articles that describe shifts in social behaviour, are a part of the anti-feminist backlash because they almost always focus on female behaviour, they are based on conjecture rather than fact and they frequently prescribe behaviour rather than describe the lives of real people.[20] These articles rarely cite hard evidence of the trends they identify, and they maintain authority by repeating the same points over and over, and by quoting other trend stories on the same subject.[21] Many of the lesbian-chic articles can be identified as trend stories, as they contain frequent repetition of ideas and sweeping generalizations about social behaviour. These articles also are part of a chain reaction; almost every large-circulation publication published an article on lesbianism within the space of a few months in 1993. Thus, lesbian chic can be seen as one of the many media trends of the 1980s and 1990s; others include the biological clock, the new monogamy, the new femininity, the celibacy trend and the new morality.

In addition to the anti-feminist backlash identified by Faludi, I would argue that a similar and closely related backlash against the gay and lesbian movement also appeared in the 1980s. This right wing, anti-feminist, anti-homosexual backlash has been linked to the Reagan and Bush administrations in the United States, and to Thatcherism in Britain. In a number of articles published in this period, gay and lesbian activists are presented as having gone too far, or as being "too militant,"[22] and are repeatedly referred to as "aggressive."[23] Many articles on the AIDS epidemic vilified gay men, and sometimes even lesbians, and portrayed homosexuals as diseased, malevolent and a threat to "innocent" members of society."[24]

The appearance of openly gay men in mainstream politics, along with the newly perceived political power of lesbians and gays, attracted considerable media attention and was portrayed as a threat by conservatives in Canada and the United States.[25] By the early 1980s, most major newspapers and newsmagazines in Canada had run features on the emerging political power of gays, and throughout the 1980s right-wing magazines such as *Alberta Report* ran dozens of articles on the threats to society posed by homosexual men. The emergence of radical queer-rights and anti-AIDS groups such as ACT-UP[26] and Queer Nation in the mid to late 1980s also attracted a great deal of media attention, much of which was very judgmental and warned against political tactics that would cause "divisiveness" and "alienation."[27] But some Canadian journalists did begin to take lesbian and gay politics more seriously. The nature of the coverage varied, depending on the management of the paper, however, and gay and lesbian politics were often framed as "lifestyle" stories, rather than as political or social issues.[28]

Why Lesbian Chic?

Various journalists and theorists have speculated on the media's recent "discovery" of lesbians, but there is no single reason why this virtual silence was broken relatively suddenly. It is important to note, however, that while the number of articles published on lesbianism increased dramatically in the early 1990s, the lesbian-chic trend was ultimately the result of slower, more gradual political and social shifts, including the growth of gay and lesbian political organizing, AIDS activism, shifts in feminist politics, and the identification of lesbians and gays as a potentially lucrative consumer market. Thus, while the trend arrived suddenly, the factors that led to it had been developing since the earliest gay and lesbian organizing in the 1950s.

The first, and possibly the most significant, factor contributing to the development of lesbian chic is the AIDS epidemic. As Sue O'Sullivan has stated, "It was the unexpected, the wild card of AIDS, which … served to prise open the magazines' covers slightly and allowed a sexual diversity to seize some space within their pages. AIDS forced a recognition that sexual diversity existed and it did it relatively quickly."[29] AIDS has made frank discussions of sexuality and sexual practices much more common, and has spurred many lesbian and gay celebrities to come out publicly.

Most significantly, the organizing of lesbians, gay men and allies in the wake of the AIDS epidemic has attracted media attention and, as I noted earlier, triggered anti-gay backlash. In an era of enormous public fear of AIDS and other sexually transmitted diseases, lesbians have been characterized as safe and appealing.[30] A *Harper's* magazine editor stated in 1993, "Lesbianism is the big thing at the moment ... It's the ultimate form of safe-sex, completely risk-free."[31] Thus, lesbians became chic partly because they were (somewhat inaccurately) perceived as being "safe" from AIDS, and in this way were presented as a foil to gay men, who were viewed in the media as unsafe, unhealthy and dangerous to the population.

Politics has also played an important role in the development of lesbian chic. U.S. president Bill Clinton received a great deal of media attention during his 1992 election campaign for being the first U.S. presidential candidate to actively seek the support of the gay community, and for having an openly gay man (whom he subsequently fired) as a senior official in his election campaign.[32] The widespread debate over the status of gays and lesbians in the military sparked an enormous amount of media interest, and the controversial 1993 appointment of the openly lesbian Roberta Achtenberg as under-secretary of the Department of Housing and Urban Development (HUD) was also a significant media event.[33] Events in Canadian politics, such as the debate over Bill 167, a bill defeated in the Ontario provincial legislature which would have granted same-sex benefits and family recognition to gays and lesbians in Ontario, also sparked media attention in the early 1990s.[34]

In looking at media representations of lesbianism, it is important to consider the dramatic increase in the coverage of heterosexual sex by the mainstream media over the past 20 years. The enormous success of *Cosmopolitan* magazine, which began publishing in the late 1960s, demonstrates the increasing popularity of sex as a subject of public discussion. The mainstream media is constantly seeking stories that are considered "new." Because lesbianism is an aspect of sexuality that has rarely been dealt with in the media, it can be presented to heterosexual readers as new and unusual.

Economics can also be identified as a key factor in the development of lesbian chic. As the feminist economists Amy Gluckman and Betsy Reed have stated, "Liberation is not the bottom line for many of the interests that have molded ... depictions of lesbians and gay men — money is."[35] Lesbianism, as a subject for media articles, attracts a great deal of attention, creates controversy and sells magazines. The notorious issue of *Vanity Fair* with k.d. lang and Cindy Crawford on the cover had the third-largest sales in the magazine's history.[36] This may be due in part to the popularity of the two stars, but much of its consumer appeal came from the shock value of the titillating cover photo. Similarly, both *Essence* and *Cosmopolitan* received record amounts of reader response when they ran articles on lesbianism.[37]

The "Gay Market"

Throughout the 1990s, dozens of articles on the growing popularity of the "gay market" were published in advertising-industry journals and business sections of Canadian and American newspapers.[38] Gays and lesbians were, and are, touted as a very lucrative market for advertisers, because they are supposedly upwardly mobile, fashion-conscious, brand-loyal and relatively wealthy. Different articles cite varying statistics, but overall it is suggested that lesbians and gays have more disposable income than do heterosexuals. These data are in fact highly questionable, particularly in relation to lesbians, and are based on some rather broad stereotypes and class assumptions.[39]

The feminist theorist Nicola Field is highly critical of this type of lifestyle marketing, arguing that targeting gays and lesbians as upper-class consumers serves to erase race and class differences, and disguises the fact that this media-constructed lifestyle is "largely unattainable and meaningless to many."[40] This construction of lesbians and gays as an upper-class consumer market hides the widespread discrimination that many lesbians face in the job market, because of both their sexuality and their gender, not to mention the widespread racism faced by many women. With gay and lesbian communities constructed as rich, urban and white, those who do not fit this artificial mould are further marginalized, and the systemic barriers they encounter go unnoticed. In addition, the historian Steven Maynard has pointed to the tendency of marketing firms that target gays and lesbians to depoliticize sexuality, stating that they "define being lesbian and gay in terms of what we buy. Such a view of our sexualities may define us as consumers, but not necessarily as people with political rights."[41] Regardless of the accuracy of these marketing surveys, lesbians, and especially gay men, are definitely perceived by advertisers and publishers as a lucrative consumer group.

There is a long history in the advertising industry of appropriating the language and images of counter-cultural social movements in order to sell products. Susan Faludi refers to the commercialization of feminism in the 1970s, when advertisers equated products such as menstrual pads and pantyhose with freedom and liberation for women.[42] In the 1980s, targetting environmental consumerism through "green products" was a popular marketing strategy. In the 1990s, lesbianism is used to sell a range of products. Many clothing manufacturers, including Calvin Klein, Guess!, J. Crew, Victoria's Secret, Club Monaco and Benetton, have used pictures of women models embracing, or images of androgynous or "butch-looking" women, in advertising campaigns. This type of marketing is often referred to as "gay window advertising," as the ads are carefully constructed to be interpretable from more than one perspective. For example, a recent full-page ad for a clothing store, run in many mainstream fashion magazines, portrayed two young women in formal clothing. One woman had her hand on the zipper of other's dress, and it was deliberately unclear whether the women were lovers or merely friends getting ready to go out. This "gay window ad" is deliberately ambiguous, and is just one of many double-entendre ads currently in circulation. This type of advertising is designed to appeal to queers without alienating more conservative consumers. While many advertisers want to reach the so-called gay market, they often don't want their products to be too clearly associated with gay people. Other less subtle ads include a recent tequila promotion that featured an attractive man and woman on a motorcycle with the caption "She's using you to get to your sister." This advertisement relies on shock value and, more interestingly, alludes to the chic factor of lesbian sexuality without visually representing it, which, as I will discuss, is a common theme in recent depictions of lesbianism.

Lesbians and Popular Culture

The final, and perhaps most complex, factor in the development of lesbian chic comes, in part, from lesbians and bisexual women themselves. The feminist activist and writer Sarah Shulman has argued that lesbians of different generations have varying responses to popular culture. She states that lesbians who came of age before the mid-1980s tended to be more suspicious of popular culture and feared assimilation and co-optation; however, the younger generations of lesbians are more attracted to popular culture, and demand to see themselves represented in it.[43] Others, such as Danae Clark, argue that with the development of identity politics and the lesbian "style wars" of the late 1980s, lesbians have been able to consider style and cultural representations in a way that is more open to the images of popular culture.[44] Rather than rejecting popular culture and mainstream fashion as entirely patriarchal and exploitive to women, many lesbians and feminists, influenced by postmodern theory, have accepted that representations can be ambiguous. The view that audiences are not passive viewers, but can interact with and influence the ways that images are interpreted, has much more currency today than in the 1970s. Some feminists now see mainstream fashion as a potential site of pleasure, political choice and self-representation, rather than as purely oppressive to women. Clark attributes this in part to a rebellion against lesbian feminism and "political correctness," but notes that this shift may also have been triggered by consumerist marketing strategies.[45] As the feminist anthropologist Joyce Hammond has noted, sexuality, as a cultural construction, is often represented in ways that are fluid, interactive and contested.[46] This means that, when looking at popular portrayals of lesbians, there are frequently numerous, often contradictory, interpretations possible. Many lesbians have commented on the contradictory nature of the lesbian-chic trend. While they applaud the increase in visibility, they are critical of the nature of these representations and suspicious of some of the consumer-driven motives. Feminist authors Diane Hamer and Belinda Budge have stated that popular culture is an important arena for feminist political intervention: "Popular culture is a site where meanings can be contested, and where dominant ideologies can be disturbed. It is here, in television, magazines, films, books, music, that we are offered culture's dominant definition of ourselves."[47]

It is for this reason that many lesbians have engaged with mainstream media, and have in this way contributed to the rise of the lesbian-chic trend, by demanding their place in popular culture.

"Do Lesbians Have More Fun?"

One of the primary criticisms that can be made of the lesbian-chic trend is that it lacks almost totally representations of lesbian sexuality.[48] Although this may seem ironic, given the "sexy" image the trend connotes, very few actual references to lesbian sexual practices are included in lesbian-chic articles, images or films. For example, an article that discusses the lack of safer-sex information for lesbians and the dearth of research on female-to-female HIV transmission fails to specify what kinds of sexual practices are high risk for lesbians, or how these risks might be decreased.[49] A number of the lesbian-themed films released in the early 1990s also demonstrate this erasure of lesbian sexuality. The controversial television show *Ellen*, and mainstream films such as *Fried Green Tomatoes*, *Three of Hearts* and *Boys on the Side* include lesbian characters, but lesbian sexuality remains curiously absent.

As the feminist philosopher Marilyn Frye has pointed out, because lesbian sex does not fit into the heterosexual notion of what sex is, it is invisible and is often not considered to be sex at all.[50] In media articles, lesbianism is more often defined in terms of love rather than lust or desire.[51] In many of the articles that describe the coming-out process, falling in love is emphasized, while first sexual experiences are almost never mentioned. At times, lesbian attraction seems to be almost deliberately separated from sexuality. One article included the following description: "It was like I had been hit by lightning. I didn't have a name for what I was feeling. All of my attention was suddenly sucked in her direction ... It was a really strong attraction, *but not sexual*."[52] Although this passage seems to describe sexual attraction, readers are given the contradictory message that this is not, in fact, sexual. And despite the many articles that feature the subject of lesbian marriages and commitment ceremonies, I could find very few that described or interviewed lesbians who chose to be single or non-monogamous. Even an article that described a lesbian strip club focused on the attire of the dancers and the club patrons, and did not discuss sex explicitly.[53] The journalist Katherine Monk has argued that "this whole idea of `lesbian chic' really has nothing to do with sex. All the images we've seen over the last year or so have been completely de-sexed."[54]

A 1995 *Chatelaine* article entitled "Do Lesbians Have More Fun?" is an interesting example of the de-sexualized depiction of lesbians in the mainstream press. The author, Judith Timson, portrays lesbian relationships, not as sexually passionate, but as intimate and emotional. The subheading to the article reads: "Many straight women believe a relationship with another woman would offer a fusion of mind and body, emotional support and mutual friendship."[55] Thus, lesbianism is represented as appealing for its emotional and spiritual benefits, but not necessarily for the sex.

According to Timson, many of her heterosexual friends see lesbian relationships as utopian, but she assures readers that this has nothing to do with sex. She states that, although she and a female friend have joked that they should be married to each other, "we both know there is not a scintilla of sexual attraction involved. It would be ... more relaxing. There'd be more laughs ... We could trade clothes ..."[56] Timson's piece is typical of 1990s articles on lesbianism in its denial of sexuality. Lesbianism is presented as appealing because of shared housework, borrowed clothes and female camaraderie; sex is not mentioned as a part of the appeal.

Another article, published in the *Globe and Mail* and entitled, "Happily Hetero, But Hankering after a Lesbian Fling,"[57] describes three married heterosexual women who fantasize about (and in one case pursue) lesbian relationships in order to fulfill their needs for friendship, emotional intimacy and sexual variety, which they do not receive from their husbands. The author, Beverly Kemp, emphasizes that the women she interviewed were not lesbians, latent or overt, "nor have they ever felt a vital ingredient was missing in their relationships with men."[58] The article is in fact very contradictory, because, in spite of Kemp's assurances that the three women are all happily and irrevocably heterosexual, one woman has been having a lesbian relationship for 18 months, and another states, "I have absolutely no desire for sex with my husband now; any we do have is purely penetration. It feels like a violation of my body, almost like a quiet form of rape."[59] I think that the contradictory nature of this article points to the fact that the mainstream media is beginning to grapple, however unsuccessfully, with the notion of fluid sexual identities. Although these articles tend to overlook lesbian sexuality, they do break new ground insofar as they reveal something that has rarely been acknowledged in mainstream media: heterosexual women think about lesbianism, and sometimes even find it appealing.

Generally, sexual orientation has been presented in mainstream media as rigid and unchanging, particularly for heterosexuals, and bisexuality is rarely referred to at all. The journalist Lisa O'Kelly has argued that magazines such as *Vanity Fair* have found that "featuring straight-looking lesbians is a way of tapping into non-lesbian women's fantasies about each other."[60] To acknowledge in a major newspaper that heterosexual women fantasize about each other may contribute to breaking down these rigid categories of sexual orientation, and may eventually move toward an acceptance of sexual diversity. But this trend is ambiguous because lesbians themselves, particularly those who do not look traditionally feminine, are still excluded. O'Kelly includes a quote from the novelist Joanna Briscoe, who states, "This sort of thing [chic, straight-looking lesbians] is much nearer to where most women are than any previous imagery of lesbianism."[61] Thus, lesbian sexual imagery in popular culture is still being defined by what is thought to be appealing to the heterosexual majority.

Lesbian Politics: Highlighting Divisions

Susan Faludi has argued that the press, as part of its anti-feminist backlash, frequently focuses attention on conflicts between women to further the notion that they cannot get along with each other, and to make the women's movement seem less threatening.[62] Recent media articles indicate that a similar process of divide and conquer is taking place regarding the lesbian and gay rights movement. Many articles that discuss lesbian and gay political issues emphasize divisiveness among activists, including conflicts between gay men and lesbians, between lesbians and heterosexual feminists, between homosexuals and bisexuals, and between different generations of lesbians. These divisions do exist, and have been the subject of debates within gay, lesbian and feminist communities for the past two decades. However, by stressing the weaknesses rather than the strengths of lesbian and gay political groups, the mass media often portrays them as disorganized and politically immature. While it is the case that lesbian and gay male activists do not always have the same priorities or interests, they have nonetheless been organizing together to fight homophobia for at least 40 years. Thus, the characterization of the bond between gay and lesbian activists in the 1990s as "fragile," as in a 1993 *Globe and Mail* article,[63] is somewhat misleading.

In addition to focusing on the divisions between lesbians and gay men, the mainstream press often highlights divisions between different generations of lesbians. Although these divisions do exist, this press coverage serves to construct an image of feminists, especially lesbian feminists, as excessive, humourless and out of date. A 1993 *Newsweek* article covertly criticizes lesbian feminism by stating that "in the '70s, the prevailing outlook was separatist and even prudish," and contrasts this with the current "vital, 'sex-positive' scene."[64] In the glossary included with this article, "sex-positive" is defined as "Flaunts female-to-female eroticism, no-guilt, feel-good sex."[65] Although the connection is not made overtly, one assumes that lesbian feminism is therefore sex-negative, guilty and secretive. Another article, published in the March 1993 issue of the American fashion magazine *Mademoiselle*,[66] had a subheading that read: "Young lesbians: . . . having staked out their own issues, they're now defining a new style."[67] The words "youth" and "young" are repeated throughout the article, and young lesbians are described as "fresh," which suggests older lesbians compare unfavourably, as presumably, stale. Although there is no overt discussion of feminism, the "older" lesbians referred to in the article are clearly feminists of the 1970s and early 1980s. Readers are told that: ". . . so different is the baby dyke from the previous generation of lesbians that every aspect of her experience — from dating to politics — is different. Her issues are her own, not her older sister's."[68]

This statement very clearly separates the "young lesbian" from all older lesbians. This categorization of "young lesbians" into a monolithic group erases the enormous cultural and political diversity that exists among them. As well, according to this statement, young lesbians share nothing at all with lesbians who came out earlier, and apparently the gay and lesbian movement is not relevant to their lives. This clearly demonstrates a critique made by the journalist Rachel Giese, who argues that lesbian chic presents lesbianism without any kind of historical context. She states, "It was as though the Stonewall Riots, the feminist and civil rights movements and the creation of a rich feminist/lesbian culture of writing, film and music never existed."[69]

Many of these lesbian-chic articles criticize lesbian-feminists by portraying them as intolerant, judgmental and prudish, and make no references to the important work they've done, such as speaking out against homophobia, fighting against violence against women, fighting for women's rights to abortion and birth control, and naming the tyranny of the fashion and beauty industries. It is certainly true that the climate and focus of feminist political organizing have shifted since the 1970s, and there has been internal criticism, and even conflict, between feminists of different generations. However, the media's representation of these political struggles has been largely shallow and misleading, especially in its failure to contextualize the substance of the ongoing debates among feminists, and in its reliance on the misogynist stereotype of quarrelsome women.

Conclusion

As Joyce Hammond has argued, visibility can often be a double-edged sword for minority groups.[70] Media visibility is important in increasing social awareness, and the lack thereof can have a significant psychological impact on members of the group in question. However, as demonstrated by the popular representations of lesbians in the 1990s, visibility also often serves to reinforce negative stereotypes. A number of feminist writers, including Hammond, Rachel Giese and Sue O'Sullivan, have commented that lesbians are currently chic, to the extent that they are thin, white, able-bodied and appropriately feminine. Other lesbians are conspicuously absent, and lesbian feminists are figures of ridicule and derision.[71]

In the 1970s and 1980s, many lesbians and feminists attempted to deconstruct notions of female beauty and reject, or at least rethink, mainstream fashion. Conversely, lesbian chic is more a creation and a tool of consumer culture than a challenge to it. Lesbians (at least the chic ones) are no longer seen as "ugly" and "man-hating"; instead, they are attractive and somewhat titillating. The public can now enjoy the bad-girl image of the attractive, sexy, "lipstick lesbian," without having to deal with feminism or radical politics. Fashion and women's magazines in the 1990s have in almost every instance portrayed lesbians as young, white, middle class, thin and fashion-conscious. Thus, these magazine articles do little to challenge stereotypes, and give readers the false notion that lesbians are a homogeneous group. There are still almost no lesbians of colour represented in the mainstream media, leaving the impression that all or most lesbians are white, and that lesbianism is a predominantly North American phenomenon.

One of the most disturbing aspects of lesbian-chic media coverage in the 1990s is the assumption, or even insistence, that discrimination is no longer an issue for lesbians. Almost none of the articles uses words such as "homophobia" or "oppression." This denial of homophobia allows heterosexual readers to avoid confronting their own biases, and promotes the misleading view that lesbians have achieved full equality. The feminist media theorist Janice Winship has argued that women's-magazine articles on lesbianism present homophobia as a personal prejudice rather than a cultural problem, and the magazine audience is assumed to be liberal, tolerant and not in need of education. Thus, everyday homophobia and heterosexism become further normalized; homophobes are seen only as terrible bigots who physically attack gays and lesbians, rather than as teachers, bosses and family members who simply fail to question their heterosexism. Although lesbianism has attained some degree of acceptability and trendiness in the 1990s, it is still a very marginal identity, and the normality and centrality of heterosexuality are not fundamentally challenged. In the media of the 1990s, the blatant homophobia of earlier eras has been replaced by heterosexism. Although lesbians are more visible, and the images of lesbians in the mainstream media are not as blatantly hateful as they were in previous decades, the cultural dominance of heterosexuality is rarely questioned, and the systemic barriers that lesbians face are largely invisible.

In February 1999 the *Globe and Mail* published an article entitled "Girls Just Wanna Have Fun," in which the journalist Stephanie Nolen asserts that lesbianism "is not about feminist response to patriarchal society, it's about girls on a Saturday night," and interviews a number of young women who support her view that identity politics are passé.[72] This article argues that for young "queer kids," labels such as "lesbian" and "bisexual" are no longer necessary and lesbian activism is irrelevant, because they are able to have sex with whomever they want without consequence. Although in many ways this article can be seen as a sign that heterosexism is becoming less dominant, it is in fact very contradictory. Readers are told that "sex is overpoliticized. Sex is just a pleasurable experience."[73] Clearly, this article represents a rejection of the central feminist tenet: the personal is political.

In looking at the future of lesbian political organizing, it is important not to underestimate the widespread acceptance and power of these anti-feminist arguments. Many theorists, having examined the lesbian-chic trend, conclude that, although these representations are "contradictory and ambivalent," they can be at least partially reclaimed, and potentially hold positive value.[74] However, given the corporate interests driving the mainstream media, I would argue that this reclamation is perhaps too hasty. Although media messages are indeed mutable and complex, the mainstream media is still largely controlled by a small group of wealthy individuals, and the anti-feminism and heterosexism observable in much mainstream media should not be underestimated. I would argue that the backlash against lesbian-feminism is not an accident, nor is it a passing trend. As we move into the 21st century, we must not forget the history of activism that has brought forth the current media "acceptance" of lesbianism, and we should not dismiss the critiques of consumer capitalism put forward by feminists of the 1970s. It is clear that the mainstream media will continue to be a central site of struggle for feminists in the next millennium, and it is equally clear that we need to understand and learn from the lessons of lesbian-feminism, rather than rejecting it as dated and unfashionable.

ENDNOTES

1. For a more indepth discussion of radical feminism and lesbian feminism, see: Becki L. Ross, *The House That Jill Built: A Lesbian Nation in Formation* (Toronto/Buffalo/London: University of Toronto Press, 1995); and Lillian Faderman, *Surpassing the Love of Men* (New York: Morrow, 1981).

2. See, for example: Albert Warson, "Degenerates Parade, Inspector Says: Blames Lack of Public Disgust for Growth of Homosexuality," *Globe and Mail* (November 14, 1963), p. A13.

3. Lesbians Making History Collective, "People Think This Didn't Happen in Canada," *Fireweed* 26 (Spring 1989), p. 84.

4. Elizabeth L. Kennedy & Madeline Davis, *Boots of Leather, Slippers of Gold: The History of a Lesbian Community* (New York: Routledge, 1993), p. 67.

5. Gary Kinsman, *The Regulation of Desire: Homo and Hetero Sexualities*, 2nd ed. (Montreal: Black Rose, 1996), p. 203.

6. Lillian Faderman, *Odd Girls and Twilight Lovers: A History of Lesbian Life in Twentieth-Century America* (New York: Penguin, 1991).

7. Sapho, "`Women Shun Us! — Men Scoff at Us!' Toronto Lesbian Tells All," reprinted in *Jim Egan: Canada's Pioneer Gay Activist*, Jim Egan (Toronto: Canadian Lesbian and Gay History Network, 1987), p. 24.

8. Faderman (1991), p. 132.

9. C.K. Cameron, "The Problem That Is Never Mentioned," *Canadian Home Journal* (November 1951), pp. 12, 103-106.

10. Renate Wilson, "What Turns Women to Lesbianism," *Chatelaine* (October 1966), pp. 32, 130-132, 134.

11. Cameron (1951), p. 12.

12. Ibid, p. 106.

13. Ibid.

14. Annamarie Jagose, *Queer Theory: An Introduction* (New York: New York University Press, 1996), pp. 30-32.

15. Sue O'Sullivan, "Girls Who Kiss Girls and Who Cares," in Belinda Budge & Diane Hamer (eds.), *The Good, the Bad and the Gorgeous: Popular Culture's Romance with Lesbianism* (London: Pandora, 1994), p. 79.

16. Rodger Streitmatter, *Unspeakable: The Rise of the Gay and Lesbian Press in America* (Boston: Faber & Faber, 1995).

17. Dorothy Sangster, "Gay Women: A Minority Report," *Chatelaine* (July 1977), pp. 24, 79-84.

18. Susan Faludi, *Backlash: The Undeclared War against American Women* (New York: Crown, 1991), p. 454.

19. Ibid., p. 79.

20. Ibid.

21. Ibid.

22. David Lewis Stein & Erna Paris, "Homosexual Rights: Is Militancy Necessary?" *Chatelaine* (July 1979), p. 24.

23. See: ibid.; and Herbert Gold, "Frisco's Homosexuals Show Way Out of the Closet," *Toronto Star* (November 5, 1977), p. C5.

24. Barry D. Adam, *The Rise of a Gay and Lesbian Movement* (Boston: Twayne, 1987), p. 157.

25. Kinsman (1996), p. 203.

26. AIDS Coalition To Unleash Power.

27. See: Eloise Salholz, "The Future of Gay America," *Newsweek* (March 12, 1990), pp. 20-25; Howard Fineman, "Marching to the Mainstream," *Newsweek* (May 3, 1993), pp. 42-45; and Bruce DeMara, "New-Style Activists in Gay Rights Fight," *Toronto Star* (January 3, 1994), p. A14.

28. Fred Fejes & Kevin Petrich, "Invisibility, Homophobia and Heterosexism: Lesbians, Gays and the Media," *Critical Studies in Mass Communication* (December 1993), pp. 403-404.

29. O'Sullivan (1994), p. 82.

30. Rachel Giese, "Lesbian Chic: I Feel Pretty and Witty and Gay," *Border/Lines* 32 (1994), p. 27.

31. Lisa O'Kelly, "Lesbian Chic: Sapphic Sisterhood Goes Mainstream," *Vancouver Sun* (June 18, 1994), p. B5.

32. Jeffrey Schmalz, "Gay Politics Goes Mainstream," *New York Times Magazine* (October 11, 1992), p. 18.

33. Kate Brandt, "From 'Lesbian Chic' to 'Damn Lesbians': The Mainstream Media Discover (Some) Dykes," *Deneuve* (July/August 1993), p. 56.

34. Susan Ursel, "Bill 167 and Full Human Rights," in Katherine Arnup (ed.), *Lesbian Parenting: Living with Pride and Prejudice* (Charlottetown, PEI: gynergy books, 1995).

35. Amy Gluckman & Betsy Reed, "The Gay Marketing Moment: Leaving Diversity in the Dust," *Dollars and Sense* (November/December 1993), p. 16.

36. Brian D. Johnson, "A Lighter Side of Lang," *Maclean's* (November 6, 1995), p. 69.

37. Peter Freiberg, "Women's Magazines Take on the `L' Word," *Washington Blade* (January 14, 1994), p. 35.

38. See, for example: David Isrealson, "Tapping the Gay Market," *Toronto Star* (September 18, 1994), pp. D1, D8; and Nancy C. Webster, "Playing to Gay Segments Opens Doors to Marketers," *Advertising Age* (May 30, 1994), p. S6.

39. Gluckman & Reed (1993), pp. 16-17.

40. Nicola Field, "Identity and the Lifestyle Market," in Rosemary Hennessy & Chrys Ingraham (eds.), *Materialist Feminism* (London: Routledge, 1997).

41. Steven Maynard, "What Colour Are Your Underwear? Class, Whiteness, and Homoerotic Advertising," *Border/Lines* 32 (1994), p. 9.

42. Faludi (1991), p. 76.

43. Sarah Shulman, interviewed in the film *Thank God I'm a Lesbian* by Laurie Colbert & Dominique Cardona, 1992.

44. Danae Clark, "Commodity Lesbianism," in Henry Abelove, Michele Aina Barale & David M. Halperin (eds.), *The Lesbian and Gay Studies Reader* (New York: Routledge, 1993), p. 199.

45. Ibid., p. 189.

46. Joyce D. Hammond, "Making a Spectacle of Herself: Lesbian Visibility and k.d. lang on *Vanity Fair*'s Cover," *Journal of Lesbian Studies* 1, 3 & 4 (1997), p. 3.

47. Hamer & Budge (1994), p. 2.

48. See: Giese (1994), p. 29. Giese states that "the `chic media lesbian' is sexy but never has sex."

49. "Lesbians Upset Over Exclusion from AIDS Debate," *Toronto Star* (February 10, 1994), p. E10.

50. Marilyn Frye, "Lesbian 'Sex'," in *Willful Virgin: Essays on Feminism* (Freedom, CA: Crossing Press, 1992), pp. 109-119.

51. See, for example: "From Dyke to Transgender: A Glossary of Gay and Lesbian Terms," *Vancouver Sun* (July 29, 1994), p. B4.

52. Mia Stainsby, "Coming Out: An Odyssey Through Hell to Happiness," *Vancouver Sun* (September 21, 1991), p. D8 [emphasis added].

53. Laura Blumenfeld, "Dancers, Feminists at Odds Over Lesbian Strip Club," *Toronto Star* (September 13, 1991), p. F1.

54. Katherine Monk, "All-Women Sexpertease Attracts Both Buzz-Cut Butches and White-Haired Grannies," *Vancouver Sun* (February 17, 1994), p. C6.

55. Judith Timson, "Do Lesbians Have More Fun?" *Chatelaine* (April 1995), p. 46.

56. Ibid.

57. Beverly Kemp, "Happily Hetero, But Hankering after a Lesbian Fling," *Globe and Mail* (November 13, 1993), p. D5.

58. Ibid.

59. Ibid.

60. Lisa O'Kelly, "Lesbian Chic: Sapphic Sisterhood Goes Mainstream," *Vancouver Sun* (June 18, 1994), p. B5.

61. Ibid.

62. Faludi (1991), p. 82.

63. Naomi Klein, "Coming Out Isn't Everything," *Globe and Mail* (July 15, 1993), pp. A1, A4.

64. Eloise Salholz, "The Power and the Pride," *Newsweek* (June 21, 1993), pp. 54-60.

65. Ibid, p. 58.

66. Elise Harris, "Women in Love," *Mademoiselle* (March 1993), pp. 180-183, 208.

67. Ibid, p. 180.

68. Ibid.

69. Giese (1994), p. 28.

70. Hammond (1997), p. 30.

71. O'Sullivan (1994), p. 79.

72. Stephanie Nolen, "Girls Just Wanna Have Fun," *Globe and Mail* (February 13, 1999), p. F1.

73. Ibid.

74. Hammond (1997), p. 31; and O'Sullivan (1994), p. 95.

TECHNOLOGIES OF PANIC AT THE MOVIES
Killer Viruses, Warrior Women and Men in Distress

Annette Burfoot

Introduction

In 1978, the test-tube child Louise Joy Brown was born as a result of "assisted conception," which for the first time took human fertilization outside women's bodies. In the next year, *Alien*, the first in a series of four popular science-fiction movies, was released. (The film introduces a bleak off-world view, where alien beings take over the human body to reproduce.) Three years after that, the Human Immunodeficiency Virus (HIV) and Acquired Immune Deficiency Syndrome (AIDS) were discovered, and a new era of fear of viral infection was born. I see these events as related because they all focus on the body as a problem. These events are also important examples of a new growth area in science and technology: biotechnology.

With biotechnology comes new political challenges. Feminists have been struggling with the new reproductive technologies, an early form of biotechnology, since Louise Brown's "miraculous" birth. More recently, developments in genetic engineering, such as the cloning of sheep in Scotland, have drawn criticism from feminists and others concerned with issues ranging from eugenics to safe food. The underlying issue is one of power. In the past, the practice of power has taken place with things we could easily understand and see: nation-states, corporations, armies, men and women. The new age of biotechnology, however, introduces us to microscopic beings in a largely invisible world that is difficult for most of us to access. We have to rely on how scientists and the media describe this world for us — we cannot go and take a look ourselves. This allows those who control biotechnology to also control its image and how we make sense of it. Because these microscopic beings may at the same time be a part of us (our test-tube embryos or our genetic code), the stakes are high.

This notion of creating and controlling life at the microscopic level is usually presented to us in a positive light. Despite terrible success rates, and after two decades of assisted-conception practice, the new reproductive technologies are continually represented in the media as evidence of scientific and medical progress. Genetic engineering, an extension of the principles of assisted conception to the level of DNA, also makes many promises of good things to come. One day we'll be able to get rid of genetic diseases such as multiple sclerosis and screen people to determine their chances of getting breast cancer, as well as genetically program plants to be immune to pests and alter animals to have desired food qualities. Some of these promises are hollow; there are very few diseases, for example, that can be recognized and found at the DNA level. Also, the implications of genetic engineering can be catastrophic — once a plant or animal is genetically altered, we do not know what will happen when it reproduces; we don't know how it may mutate. And no one knows what may result if and when native plants cross-fertilize with the genetically altered crops. Third-world countries are already protesting the forced growing of genetically engineered crops in their homelands because they are then bound to the companies who "own" the patented plants (which can often be fertilized and controlled only by products from the same companies). Finally, there is a real possibility of using genetic engineering in humans to discriminate, either by choosing "good" genes based on race, sex, and so on, or by "de-selecting" (i.e., aborting) fetuses with these "undesirable" genetic traits found through screening.

To understand why genetic engineering is allowed to continue despite the issues that form biotechnology's downside, we need to look at how the picture of the biotechnology world is created. To do this, we also need to investigate the underside of this microscopic world, and see what biotechnology seeks to protect and destroy. The focus of concern and the struggle for control have shifted in the biotechnological world to the body and its new point of origin, the DNA spiral. The body's boundaries are controlled within new fields of reproductive medicine and genetic engineering that effectively replace or correct reproduction in women's bodies with scientific reproduction and genetic replication. This control of origins provides comfort in a world that also contains microscopic monstrosities that threaten the body. The newly appreciated body is at risk of invasion by actual foreign and deadly enemies such as AIDS and its more violently deadly cousin, the Ebola virus. It is argued here that the construction of the biotechnological world as both promise and panic is based on the needs of a dominant white masculinity that sees itself under profound threat.

As part of this powerful climate of fear and horror, North Americans have been treated to one spectacle after another of human bodies under attack by simple-minded, relentless and very deadly viral enemies. The violent invasion of the body is also an image central to the highly successful *Alien* series. Like a recurring nightmare, the four films reenact the human struggle against an alien creature that first impregnates, then violently kills, its human host. Bleak images of reproduction and genetic engineering figure prominently throughout this sci-fi world as we watch the body fall under constant violent attack from alien impregnations. What is argued here is that these visions of the body encroached upon by a horrible reproductive threat mirror the public presentation of killer viruses, and that both represent a rising male panic over the loss of control of traditional male terrain, which includes the invincible body, institutional and state authorities, and the interests of women and other minorities.

Theories of horror help explain the link between gender and how bodies are presented. For example, Barbara Creed gives a convincing explanation of male panic as a form of womb-madness by analyzing recent images in horror and science-fiction films of "the ancient archaic mother who gives birth to all living things."[1] We will also see how this mother figure gets merged with "Others," particularly nature and non-whites, thus producing a combined sexist and racist effect: fear of the archaic (m)other.

Another response of masculinity in panic is to be found in the characterization of women. In the film series *Alien* the central character, Ripley, is female and powerful, and battles effectively against both the alien creatures and the patriarchy. In terms of honour and bravery, she usually outshines the men around her, who tend to sell each other out to corporate interests, or panic and die in the face of the monstrous alien. A similar characterization can be found in another popular and related sci-fi world, that of *The X-Files*. Dana Scully is an accomplished medical scientist who keeps her cool throughout a series of usually threatening alien encounters. Her male partner is the hysterical one who believes in monsters. These powerful female figures are rightfully welcomed as positive role models by many girls and women. However, it is also important to consider these characters in relation to male panic, and to contextualize this panic as one that arises just as some women gain social power and publicly resist patriarchy. Women who stand by men as they face their deep-seated fears over origins and ends (the archaic [m]other) may have gained the right to join the battle as equals, but the battle itself is profoundly sexist and racist.

To understand this fear of the archaic (m)other, we will look at the biotechnical world as it is presented in a variety of popular forms. The positive side of biotechnology (genetic engineering) as represented in a CNN production is examined here as a certain kind of success story. The presentation delights in a new world of procreation that is controlled away from women's bodies. One part of the fear, the inability to control origins, thus seems taken care of. Biotechnology's negative side, as represented in a selection of TV presentations on killer viruses and in the *Alien* series, provides a panicked venting of the other part of the fear: the force that can take life away; the end.

These popularized images also relate to feminist activism. Biotechnology has very real effects on women's lives, as more and more reproductive and genetic technologies are presented to us as being for our own good as well as for the good of society. We seem to be offered "starring" roles in this high-tech new world — roles that defy centuries of portrayals of women as the weaker, gentler and intellectually simpler sex. But as these new, powerful women emerge, so does a new era of social control through biotechnology. The "correction" and replacement of women's procreativity by reproductive and genetic engineering are being successfully "sold" to a public that tends to buy the promise of biotechnology. The downsides of biotechnology — sexism and racism — are carefully buried in dazzling presentations of technological potential. Women's liberation is also compromised, as hard-won reproductive rights are threatened.

Cleaning Up: Reproduction and Beyond

The gene is a fascinating object that has effectively transformed the human body from a brutish, natural material (traditionally associated with leaky female forms) into "cleaner" information more suited to apparently speedy and long-distance travel. Genetics is what science wants us to think we have become, and is what makes possible the shedding of the body as flesh. The mystery of nature has now been transported to the jungle of the Internet and the call of the fax. It is not a coincidence that TV images of transported humans as disassembled, e-mailed and reassembled information dominate popular culture. "Beam me up, Scottie" has become a common phrase, meaning, "Get me out of here," and is a symbol of a move away from the flesh as our selves. This *is* the information age and we are the information.

Genetics effectively breaks down the integrity of the body, reduces humanness to information and denies women's procreativity by turning reproduction into lab-based replication. Genetic information can be extracted, exchanged, stored and recombined to generate new information. A gene "library" is being developed at Livermore, an American military base in California. Scientists, meanwhile, seek patent protection for the life forms they mutate from existing genetic codes. And in 1984, Harvard University received a patent for the "oncomouse" (a mouse that is genetically altered to get cancer). Gene "therapy" now includes the transfer of genes from body to body, with viruses used as transportation devices. Genetics is a reduction of life to a language or code that can be translated and transferred from one being to another without pregnancy or birth. The information revolution has entered the artificial-reproductive age of genetic replication.

Besides being sexist, genetic engineering is also racist. The irony is not lost in the title of the documentary "CNN Presents: Perfect People," presented by the same American news network that reproduced the war in Kuwait as a highly entertaining and exclusive TV mini-series. "Perfect People," a highly polished production filled with computer-generated graphics and images, offers a positive view of the ability of genetic engineering to better the American way of life.

This use of information technology to manipulate our sense of what is good (and bad) is what Evelyn Hammonds calls "technophilic reproduction."[2] The term refers to computer "morphing," where images of real people can be carefully altered without the viewer being aware that the picture she ends up with is not a photo of a real person. In particular, Hammonds looks at morphed pictures of non-whites featured on the covers of recent American magazines that contain debates of what makes up racial difference today. She links the morphed, homogenized face of "SimEve," who portrays a desired mixed race (which — surprise, surprise — looks very white and Anglo-Saxon), with growing state fears over immigration rates of racial "Others." The morphed ideal (white and conventionally pretty), "SimEve" represents a measure of control over future immigration of non-white Others into the West and a continuation of racial discrimination between citizens.

In "Perfect People," the morphing of a perfect human identity is the result of a marriage between technologies of representation (visual culture) and the supposed creative possibilities of genetic reproduction (human identity, or DNA, in the culture dish). The nation in control of the ability to genetically create desired human types is the same that seeks to homogenize racial difference into as near white as possible. The show is typical of a science documentary: it's narrated by a calm and learned white person who orchestrates interviews with medical and scientific experts (equally calm and reassuring), as well as with real people suffering, in this case, from genetic disorders. The documentary also serves as a science show-and-tell, to encourage public consumption of scientific ideas. Such productions typically use computer images to explain basic genetics. In "Perfect People" images transport us from what we see and understand about life (trees, animals and people) to animations of the microscopic world of DNA and genes, the minute "building blocks of life." We are shown the microscopic frontier of genetic engineering, which is waiting to be "mapped." Genetic engineers are called "trail blazers," and the opening image of the presentation is of human explorers stepping into unexplored terrain (which reinforces senses of wonderment and excited anticipation).

Eugenics (choosing for desired genetic traits, which include sex and race) is not visible on the clean white horizon of this new world. Indeed, one of the few cautionary notes within the presentation deals, not with eugenics, but with a concern of the privileged: the protection of privacy and private property. As information, our genes not only fill genome libraries, but also can be traced and monitored. This raises the possibility of threats to individuals' prosperity, and of trespassing by the state onto fiercely guarded personal property. The traditional source of anxiety in the United States in regard to loss of personal privacy is the Federal Bureau of Investigation (FBI). In the CNN production we learn of the medical equivalent of the FBI, the Medical Information Bureau (MIB). The show provides an image of surveillance cameras lacing a windowless building as the voice-over asks, "But who is looking over our shoulder?" This segment informs us that millions of Americans' coded medical histories (very personal "property") are stored by the MIB in the windowless building (mostly for use by health-care insurers). In the American system of private health care, discrimination on the basis of genetic potential becomes a serious concern.

CNN serves as interpreter and guide in the foreign land of genetics. We learn and accept that the genetic-based control and regeneration of human life are possible but beyond our everyday reach, and that only a few will be entrusted to undertake them. Issues of racism, sexism and class difference are ignored, even though genetic engineering allows eugenic practices through pre-implantation diagnosis and sex selection, and through the economic exploitation of genetic information. Instead, control of life-threatening diseases seems assured: the body (and social order) is safe. But there is an underside to this world of promise: killer viruses that force genetic explorers to become microscope warriors.

The New Horror Movies

The downside of the microscopic world of life can be found in popular representations of a new and very serious threat to the human race: filo viruses, which are one category above HIV in terms of deadliness. Filo viruses invade human space with the simple and sole mission, we are told, to completely possess their hosts without any concern for the consequences. These microscopic foes wreak such chaos and destruction that formidable counter-measures are required. A military presence in the microscopic world is established, and war zones and military strategies are determined. In the process, the enemy is clearly marked and demonized as sexual and racial Other, and the body becomes a site of horror.

Many have studied the horror film for insight into the construction and fear of things considered Other. Among these studies are two that point to the meaning of femaleness in pictures of fearsome monsters attacking, consuming and destroying the body. Both Barbara Creed and Carol Clover use the language of psychiatry to analyze horror and its meaning for women.[3] Their views differ, though, in that Clover sees the role of the central female figure in most horror films, "the final girl," as a mask for masculine fear of the monstrous. "She" represents masculine vulnerability in the face of the unknown and treacherous, lasts to the final scene, and finally slays the horrific creature, thus returning masculinity and its world to safety and order. Creed provides more feminist insight into the meaning of the horror itself, and characterizes it, among other things, as a feared, all-powerful maternal figure or the archaic mother: "the point of origin and of end."[4]

In the first half of the 1990s in Canada and the United States, there were a number of broadcasts of news-show documentaries, news items and dramatizations of the threat posed to the human body by filo viruses. These included "Newsworld: Killer Viruses" (1994), *The Plague*

Monkeys (1994), "Understanding Viruses" (1995), *Monday Night Movie: Virus* (1995) and *Outbreak* (1995). Also in 1994 the docu-novel *The Hot Zone* was released in book form and on audiotape.

The world of viruses, like that of genes, is a microscopic one with the potential for exploitation (some viruses are used in genetic engineering to carry genes from one cell to another). But in the world of filo viruses, the terrain is violently hostile for humans (bodies are literally taken over by the virus and left as a bloody mass). As was the case with popular representations of genetics, TV shows that teach us about viruses use the same visual technique of zooming us from that which we can see to the luminescent green cartoon of the cellular world. But this foreign terrain is a war zone; it is not the exciting place of unexplored and potentially bountiful resources that the genetic trail blazers inhabit. Control is impossible, and even with extraordinary, militaristic strategies, the threat remains horrific.

In *The Plague Monkeys*, to ensure that we understand the degree of threat, a medical expert, himself visibly shaken loose from his professional demeanor, lists the symptoms of a filo virus in a human. A similar list is read very seriously in voice-over in "Understanding Viruses" as pictures of victims flash by:

- It begins with a headache and skin rash;
- The face then fixes into a zombie-like stare;
- The skin tears easily;
- Blood discharges from every orifice;
- Each organ fails at the same time, causing the patient to suffer terribly and then die;
- It takes only 10 days from the first symptom to death;
- AIDS is a level-3 virus; filo viruses, such as Ebola, are level 4;
- They are as contagious as a cold;
- There is no known cure or vaccine.

Fear of Other

In this characterization of terribly vulnerable human flesh, women share a place with other "Others." It is obvious in the construction of the body as a very vulnerable place that vulnerability is associated with being white and Western, and that the threat comes from a dark nature. Killer viruses do not discriminate among races, yet their threat is represented as an attack on the Western world from distant shores. In her investigation into the history of the monstrous body, Rosi Bradiotti describes how the dominant and ancient discussions centred on "the monstrous races at the edge of civilization ... or special lands where the monster races live."[5] Looking physically different from white Western men was, and still is, enough to generate monster status. In all representations of killer viruses, the African jungle and its nearby human inhabitants figure prominently as the source.

In all the tellings of the killer-virus stories, the "origin" of the Ebola virus is linked to monkeys, in several cases real ones temporarily housed in Reston, Virginia (another one is a dramatic character entering the United States without proper customs procedures in the film *Outbreak*). They are "patient zero," the term that refers to the first infected in a given epidemic. The construction of the viral threat as the enemy continues as the United States Army Military Research Institute for Infectious Diseases (USAMRIID) emerges as a key and common player in the dramas (real and fictionalized). USAMRIID is the silent military force posed for extreme action against biological threats, including an outbreak of a level-4 virus such as filo viruses. The voice-over in "Understanding Viruses" describes USAMRIID with military precision, as each part of the acronym is spelled out on screen in electronic pulses that fade to the sound of a fast-beating heart. It is this branch of the American military that responded stealthily to the outbreak of a filo virus among monkeys housed in the Reston containment facility near Washington, DC.

In *The Plague Monkeys*, various soldiers from the manoeuvre describe their heroic takeover of the Reston facility in a format that echoes tales of American soldiers in Vietnam dealing with the unfamiliar and unsettling lushness of the jungle and the deadly Viet Cong it hid. A camera walks us through the now-deserted and -stripped facility as the USAMRIID soldiers describe their furtive movements through darkened halls. Screams of the caged jungle creatures underscore the soldiers' descriptions of the incredible risks they took as they stalked and captured the volatile, sharp-toothed and potentially infected creatures. But the most horrific moment is reserved for the announcement that this jungle is just miles from the White House lawn. Visually, the animal containment facility is juxtaposed with the Montessori school across the street, where young mothers and their children played happily and innocently within yards of the outbreak. A volatile and murderous new neighbour has arrived from Africa and threatens to destroy the neighbourhood.

The connection of deadly immigrants with the "dark continent" continues. Every single presentation named earlier includes the pan from steamy African jungle (characterized by close-ups of primordial swamps and screaming monkeys) to first the radiant green of the petri dish and then the gentle swaying of the deadly, worm-like filo virus in North American labs. In the melodramatic context of *Monday Night Movie: Virus*, the jungle and screaming monkey are used to conclude the drama and to hammer home the real threat lurking in the lush African environment. In "Understanding Viruses," African drums thrum in the background as Candice Bergen articulates the nature of the threat: "So we stand locked in mortal combat with the simplest of foes ..." Footage of and interviews with medical "missionaries" who were present at the first outbreak of a filo virus — along the Ebola River, Zaire, in the 1970s — are also standard in both the documentaries and the dramatizations, and inspire the explosive opening scene of *Outbreak*. In all of these representations, scenes of white men in pressurized white hazardous-material suits contrast with the unprotected Zairians, whose near nakedness at the edge of the jungle keeps them closer to nature and posits both as dangerous in our view.

In the story of the filo virus, there is also a clear parallel drawn to another construction of the body (particularly the gay body) as a monstrosity: the AIDS scare of the 1980s. AIDS, initially called Gay Reduced Immuno-Deficiency Syndrome (GRIDS), is believed to have come from Africa and spread throughout the New York area in the early 1980s largely because of one sexually promiscuous, gay French Canadian, who was later defined as patient zero for AIDS. He was a flight attendant who had been in Africa.

In most depictions of viral invasion, the source is nature, while the racial Other is targetted as closest to the deadly contagion and as its means of transport into the first world. The clear implication of the streaming jets juxtaposed with representations of the African-originated virus is that that continent is where the problem lies and whence the trouble flies. The message is to sever such ties; suit up tight against the microscopic warriors and the dark bodies that carry them. Indeed, all popular representations dealing with the viruses emphasize the specially designed suits worn by the medical military personnel who deal with infectious diseases, in both their human and monkey hosts in the jungle and their microscopic form in the lab. Each of the documentaries and the dramatizations exploits the drama of suiting up and moving through the four levels of air-locked and secured labs to the area where level-4 viruses are handled. Mobile pressurized stretchers mark the transition between the archaic maternal and dangerous natural third world and the hermetically sealed, safe and rational first world as they are used to ferry the infected into the sterile: senseless body matter, bloody flesh of the female sphere, is moved to the site of sensible, scientific form.

Panic: But in Womb-Like Spaces, No One Can Hear You Scream

Sexism in biotechnology is less explicit than the obvious racism in pictures of the body under attack from African viruses, but, at the same time, that sexism is everywhere. The presentation of the body grotesque mirrors many scenes from horror films, where bodies are pierced or chainsawed, or explode and implode. It is this presentation of unknown yet all-powerful control over the body that Creed characterizes as the archaic mother. And as the archaic mother does not necessarily take a form but is the "vast backdrop for the enactment of all events,"[6] the world of deadly threat to the body acts as a hyperform of the feminine and is reason enough for a male panic.

Creed provides a convincing analysis of reproductive imagery in *Alien* as a horrifying perception of the archaic mother as that capable of denying, or "castrating," masculinity. This fear is the reaction of masculinity to what it perceives as not only the mutilator of the (male) body, but also the potential destroyer of its significance.

All four of the films in the *Alien* series take place in outer space on the margins of human settlement. The first three films open with similar scenes of a lonely, unlit spacecraft floating through cold, empty and dark space. The sounds of whistling wind, staccato high-pitched violins and eerie celestial music accompany these images. A pan of human bodies cocooned in frozen glass and metal cryo-tubes immediately follows in each of the first three opening scenes. Their "birth" from cryo-sleep to consciousness unfolds. Here is our first indication of a world of artificial reproduction. In a formulaic manner, each of the consequent films then proceeds to reveal the monstrous Other and also the only creature who actually reproduces using its body.

The most terrifying aspect of the alien in all four films is its use of the human body as an incubator for its young, which kill their host in the process of being born. Scenes throughout the films both appropriate and demonize reproduction. An embryo is placed by a scuttling, crab-like creature in its host through the mouth — the creatures who perform the task are called "face-huggers" by alien experts. In post-production interviews, the director of *Aliens*, James Cameron, describes them as more than biological; they are used as a plotting device to generate fear of the deadly Other as they attack, leap, scurry and react on their own. In unused portions of the original script for the same film, the central character, Ripley, is quoted as saying that the face-hugger "is essentially a sex organ ... It attaches itself to its victims and then it injects an embryo, detaches and dies." This sex role is active and male in terms of the injection through a penis-like protrusion that enters the mouth of the victim (the passive, stereotypically female "sex" partner). Again in the *Aliens* post-production notes, it is written that the face-hugger that attaches itself to one of the victims has "articulated testicle-type sacs that pulsated in order to appear to be feeding Russ oxygen ..." Face-huggers are also used by humans to force other humans to become impregnated (out of revenge in *Aliens* and for callous experi-mentation in *Alien Resurrection*).

Besides introducing on-screen male rape and the violation that represents, the alien life cycle also presents a particular and gender-biased view of reproduction. The face-huggers propel themselves from leathery and large eggs. In contrast to the agile, tenacious and penile "sex organs" that carry the entire embryonic alien, the eggs are repulsive, massive, immobile, defenceless, and simply containers. Once the alien embryo is incubated, it bursts through the chest wall of its host, killing it in the process. This happens to men first. In an initial screenplay for *Aliens*, the character Burke, caught in an alien cocoon, moans: "Ripley ... help me. I can feel it ... inside. Oh, God ... it's moving! Oh, Gooooooood ..." Pregnancy is no longer reserved for women; impregnation is rape, and birth is death.

Womb and birth-canal imagery are predominant throughout the series of films, and it is in these enclosed spaces that danger is most prevalent and the most intense battles take place. We first encounter the alien in a huge spaceship whose shape closely resembles two bowed legs. The human explorers enter at the crotch through a vulva-like opening. Darkness and disorientation are factors in creating suspense, and tunnels, long narrow corridors and cave-like places with light at the far end are common places for alien encounters. The air-processing station in *Aliens* becomes a nesting site for the queen, and is a horrific cave made up of alien secretions and found materials, including humans and their bones, and space station bits and pieces. It is warm and moist in the nest — people are immobilized and killed there. In *Alien Resurrection*, the nesting site is in the belly of the space station and is again made warm and moist. When our hero, Ripley, falls into it, she plunges through a mesh of dark, slimy, undulating alien flesh.

The queen, key to alien reproduction and the main reproducing female in the series, is described in promotional material for *Aliens* as the ultimate threat: "What's bigger, meaner, more terrifying than an alien? Its mother." To Ripley's horror, she learns in *Alien 3* that she is pregnant not only with an alien, but with a queen — the horror of horrors. In *Resurrection*, the half-alien Ripley smiles in a sinister way when she says to a man who was recently impregnated with an alien embryo, "I am the monster's mother." The battle against the aliens is also anti-reproduction. The horrific alien queen is presented as a massive, slow-moving, egg-laying creature. Her egg sac, filled with large, dark eggs, dominates her form. She also has the remarkable ability in *Aliens* to discard her reproductivity by detaching her torso from her sac to fight.

TV and Film Noir and the Woman Warrior

From these bleak, anti-(m)other worldviews emerge interesting female heroines who seem to contradict their anti-female backgrounds. Two of the most popular of these female characters are Sigourney Weaver's Ripley in the *Alien* series and Gillian Anderson's Dana Scully in the "TV noir" series *The X-Files*. However, despite their strength of character and their representations of women's gains (especially in workplace equality), both of these characters show how gender difference figures in a bleak worldview of masculine panic that is mostly bad news for women's liberation.

In *The X-Files* a form of male hysteria is characterized by Fox Mulder, the highly emotional forensic psychologist who believes that there really are aliens out there. He is teamed with the highly rational but emotionally distant doctor and scientist Dana Scully. Both are FBI agents working to solve cases involving the paranormal. Scully is to keep an objective eye on her partner, who is believed by many to be somewhat mad, and definitely biased, owing to his fast-held belief that aliens kidnapped his sister when they were young.

Gender roles are reversed: the male has become the hot-headed emotional carrier who is rarely believed, and the female is the cool professional who calmly brings her partner's ravings into question and dispels his claims of monsters and off-world visitors. But what is valued, as truth has shifted? All formerly legitimate forms of knowledge in this very popular series are not to be trusted. "Trust No One" and "The Truth Is Out There" are expressions that appear on-screen regularly, and Mulder's highly questionable beliefs form a popular anti-establishment quest. (In a recent episode, Mulder claims, "We all have our faith, and mine is the truth.") This X-generation attitude of general distrust of those over 40 and belief in conspiring governments places Scully, the cool scientist, in question and not in a position of gender equity. As Mulder's counterpoint, Scully is a suspicious character who has to be convinced of a higher, mysterious order than the one in which she has been schooled. And Mulder holds the key to unravelling that mystery.

Ten years ago, Julie Emerson noticed a trend in science fiction that allowed and validated a new (outer) space in which men could emote.[7] At the same time, the female action figure has become the source for considerable debate, especially among feminists. Undeniably, one of the most popular of these figures is Ripley. Like *The X-Files*, the *Alien* series presents a dark and bleak world that is filled with untrustworthy military and corporate interests, and hostile aliens. The films fall into various genres: the first is a classic horror film, with a single monster slowly revealed and not entirely visible until the very end; the second is a war film, where countless monsters meet a squadron of marines and do battle; the third is a British social-class satire, where the alien monster compares favourably with the brutalities working-class men face at the hands of the Corporation; the final film is a dark fantasy made by a French director who also made the grim fairy tale *La Cité des enfants perdus* (1995). The series follows the career and experiences of Ripley, who moves up the ranks from second in command on a mining freighter to outlaw expert on the aliens. Her character, unusually for women in Hollywood, dominates screen-time and is an active figure who is key to the story's progression. Her character also evolves over time from a challenged female authority figure and a good soldier to a fierce and canny guerrilla fighter.

In the first film of the series, Ripley, as the officer in command, attempts to keep the just-infected exploration crew from the ship but is overridden by a devious android whose instructions are to acquire new life at the expense of the human crew. This same android (a puppet of the evil Corporation) attempts to kill Ripley later on by ramming a rolled-up pornographic magazine down her throat. This scene has been analyzed by many as a profound feminist moment on screen and is a turning point for Ripley, a signal that she is not going to take "it" (patriarchal and corporate exploitation) any more. It is also at this point that she is victorious in armed combat (in her underwear) with the hostile alien. This final scene, which includes a striptease with the alien as Peeping Tom, has generated considerable debate over whether it undermines the feminist construction of Ripley up to this point and illustrates the limitations of Hollywood in producing feminist figures on screen.

In the second film, Ripley sports a huge and menacing flame-throwing weapon on one shoulder, and a young girl, whom she ferociously protects, on the other, as she confronts the alien queen. She also dons a heavy equipment loader like a suit of armour and fights the queen — her loader-grip against the creature's lashing tail and gnashing teeth — to the monster's death. Yvonne Tasker and others have pointed to these conflicting images of traditional female roles (Ripley as mother) and a masculinized female action figure as a powerful sign of crossover between normal gender boundaries.[8] As if to emphasize this point, Ripley dons lesbian chic in *Aliens 3*, with her shaved head and prison garb. She is stranded on an isolated prison planet with only male prisoners and ultimately wins the respect of this homo-antierotic group of "y-chromos." In the final film, the cloned and genetically engineered Ripley takes the ultimate form of a symbol of crossed boundaries; she is no longer afraid of the aliens because she has literally become one of them. In contrast to the image of Ripley as the triumphant warrior in the three previous films, her new mixed identity appears in the opening credits of the final film. Images of her human features and alien parts melt into each other across the screen.

Ripley clearly emerges in the final film as the only one who can effectively deal with the monsters (and save the remaining crew from certain death) by becoming one of them. She also provides the moral agenda by exposing the corrupt values of the ever-present Corporation, which is willing to sacrifice human lives for military and corporate exploitation of the alien creature as a highly effective weapon. It is this representation of female heroics in the face of brutish masculinity, callous and class-dominated societies, and hostile, isolated alien worlds that gives us the characterization of Ripley as a feminist figure capable of transcending sexism and classism. Despite the backdrop to her story — a fiercely negative view of femininity as deathly replication — many have claimed Ripley to be a woman of the 1990s and beyond. The armed warrior is no princess but a woman who befriends the lower-deck labourers, "grunts," "y-chromos" and space pirates — and embraces her Otherness to the point of becoming one with the dreaded alien. The image of the iron-clad Ripley mimicking the exoskeletal queen as she fights the monster to its death is how women can strategize in the face of masculine violence: know who your friends are and don the mask of that which is feared.

There is no doubt that the *Aliens* series presents rich and conflicting messages for debates of gender and the crossing of traditional boundaries. Ripley has become something of a feminist icon, and many women take pleasure in watching her triumphant battles over social inequalities. But her victories are also a sign of domination of the (m)other. As in the representations of deadly viruses and *The X-Files* (phenomenon), a male panic serves as the battle cry. This panic, in all three popular representations, is made up of a masculine vulnerability in the face of a deeply mysterious, deadly and fundamentally feminine principle. Woman-as-origin remains a profoundly scary thing for male-dominated societies.

In her analysis of Lacan's use of the feminine, "male feminization for feminine negation," Somer Brodribb helps explain the apparent paradox of the strong female character in face of extreme anti-femininity.[9] Part of this male feminization is a form of male hysteria typically illustrated in men's fearful fantasy of the feminine. Her explanation for this construction of the female as hostile and Other uncovers a male worldview that seeks transcendence from the material world to a spiritual plane in order to dominate, both actually (in terms of violence against women and recent interventions in human reproduction) and figuratively (in terms of the control of language).[10] There is a powerful example of the link between the world of language and women's material worlds embedded in both sets of representations of the biotechnological body.

Good and Bad Abortions: What Can Happen

The selling of genetic engineering is tangled up with current struggles over abortion and contributes to a disturbing and violent anti-abortion trend, especially in the United States.

Nowhere in CNN's pitch does a fetus appear, and so the very controversial issue of abortion as women's reproductive right does not block the progress of the clean, new science of reproduction and genetic engineering. At the same time, genetic science creates a new reason for abortion that could limit women's access by reducing allowable abortions to genetic "quality" control only. Meanwhile, people lose their lives in seeking and providing abortions as part of women's reproductive control. This paradox is partly explained by the power of imaging the biotechnological world.

Karen Newman makes a convincing case for how centuries of fascination with representations of the fetus (from crude drawings in the second century, to highly realistic wax models made throughout the European Renaissance, to 20th-century photographic "portraits" of fetuses in and ex utero) influence contemporary abortion debates. It is the long-term portrayal of the fetus as isolated and innocent that fuels the current hostility against women's reproductive control. "Despite a majority of voters who support choice, the right has co-opted the way abortion is framed in the US: as a modern slaughter of the innocents."[11]

This framing of abortion as manslaughter and women practising birth control as unfeeling murderers is also found in the *Aliens* films. Violent abortion imagery is scattered throughout the series. The triumphant killing of the monster by Ripley in the final scenes of the first two films involves her flushing it out the canal of airlocks as its body arches and whips against its inevitable destruction.

The final film, *Alien Resurrection*, represents the fetus as a slaughtered innocent in much the same way as many violent anti-abortion campaigns today. Because Ripley has been brought back from the dead as part alien, she has superhuman strength and her blood acts as acid. She gives birth to an alien queen, who in turn gives birth vaginally to a mutated alien/human (previously the queen only laid eggs). Ripley confronts her newly born "grandson" in the final scene and, despite her relation to him, flings a drop of her blood at a nearby porthole to dissolve the glass. After she positions the creature near the window, the mutant alien is slowly and agonizingly sucked out the tiny hole into the vacuum beyond. As it dies it screams, "Noooooooo" and "Heeelp meee."

This disturbing fictional image is reminiscent of the film *The Silent Scream*, made by anti-abortionists to scare women away from having abortions. That film creates an image of a screaming fetus as it is evacuated from the womb during an abortion procedure. Both images play on women's feelings ("You are a mother, not a woman making a reproductive choice"), place women as doing battle with their pregnancies, and intend to replace women's need for birth control with the needs of those who have constructed in pictures a new "person": the fetus.

Conclusions

It seems that to survive in its current form, white, Western masculinity needs monsters. To maintain its distinct identity, masculinity embraces a new world of "assisted reproduction" and genetic engineering. This alternative birthing site is a "clean," controlled and microscopic environment far away from women and other foreign bodies: (m)other. Meanwhile a "useful" tension between this brave new world of the DNA spiral and the fearful and horrific images of the effects on the body of its deadly viral counterpart continues. Genetic engineering is defended as a way of warding off the "monstrous" side of human reproduction (genetic anomalies). Despite a bright picture of genetics as an industrialization of the body and human flesh as both bountiful natural resource and efficient cellular factory, there are bad labour relations on the microscopic shop floor and the workers are revolting.

Frightening images of viral infection also create a new global threat. Racial distinctions are maintained in the telling of the horror story, in which African Blacks are identified as the primary transmitter of deadly viral outbreak to the white and Western world. The initial outbreak in Zaire is not construed as a threat; it is the jet-powered transmission to the first world, most notably Washington, DC, that is considered the most horrible. One solution is to prevent the flow of viruses from their source on the African continent; flights from Zaire were watched closely during the most recent outbreak of Ebola virus there several years ago. In short, the micro wars serve as an excuse for increased global ethnic and racial hostilities, first-world protectionism, and a reformation of the dichotomy between man [sic] and nature as interests in conflict.

These microscopic battles also create a view of natural reproduction as alien, brutal and deadly replication. For centuries, it seemed enough to treat women as nature, and to leave them both to their own devices. The new masculine science in the industrializing West was satisfied to focus its own attention on the more intelligent and important project: the working of the basic materials. Biotechnology, however, muddies these waters. Male bodies are now used as mere matter and as sites of deadly reproduction by invading aliens. The images described above, both fiction and science fiction, lament this loss of traditional masculinity.

Men seem to be trying on reproduction for size and are having a tough time with the fit. Biotechnologies, especially genetic engineering, offer the promise of a new form of reproduction in keeping with principles of patriarchal control (mind over matter). But the matter keeps getting in the way, and a fear of its uncontrollability plays out in various battles against masculinity's fundamental opponent: the archetypical mother, the point of all origin, the Other. *Aliens* is a very popular serial in this male psychodrama.

And what about women? We have not sat idly by as we have been portrayed as the weaker sex and mere reproductive containers. Women have struggled continuously for equity: education, career opportunities, fair pay, access to safe and effective birth control. So when Scully and Ripley show up on our screens as women capable of handling themselves as sexists, racists and corporate interests attack, there is no wonder many of us applaud. Yet when the Other is characterized as a hostile reproductive superpower, women remain compromised, and in the end, we are fighting ourselves. Closer to home, inadvertently or not, these images also play into a dangerous and violent anti-abortion campaign that could set back women's gains in birth control by decades. Finally, despite powerful representations of women in science fiction, they do not control the biotechnical revolution, which includes a new era of assisted conception that mutes or replaces our reproduction.

In the meantime, masculinity uncharacteristically becomes emotionally charged. This shift could be a welcome change in masculinity; however, it actually reconstructs the same gender hierarchy, just along different lines. Scientific truth seems to have lost its mystique and venerated status, and the paranormal has become the higher source of truth and value just when women become scientists. At the same time, the crossover between media presentations of science-as-fact and popular science fictions reasserts rationality, since masculinity needs it to defend its interests (genetic reproduction, first-world protectionism and female domination) and to justify its panicked reactions to male bodies in a vulnerable, female-like state. This promise-and-panic Ping-Pong match keeps women symbolically rooted in a worldview of reproduction as threat.

The challenge for us in the next millennium is to watch carefully where battle lines are drawn, to discern whose fight it is and what role we, as women, are expected to play. We need to remember while enjoying ourselves at the movies that daily battles over reproductive control continue worldwide, and that citizen populations of privileged countries are watched closely for "alien" invasions. Genetic engineering is real, and many women face increasing pressures to use it and the new reproductive technologies as improvements over — and in some cases, replacements — of their reproductivity. Women's health groups need to consider carefully what they think about that. Also, the larger issue of eugenics (sexism, racism, ableism) in genetic engineering has to be addressed by feminists — surely we do not want to participate in this kind of social pruning through high-tech health care? To begin the difficult task of breaking down conceptual barriers that attempt to either transcend birth or deny it altogether, we need a feminist culture and politics of reproduction.[12] We should start fantasizing for ourselves and reproduce the world: Grab Sigourney Weaver's Ripley character from the alien zone and have her join the feminist network against genetic engineering and spray-paint the subway!

ENDNOTES

1. Barbara Creed, *The Monstrous Feminine: Film, Feminism, Psychoanalysis* (London: Routledge, 1993), p. 24.

2. Evelyn M. Hammonds, "New Technologies of Race," in Jennifer Terry and Melodie Calvert (eds.), *Processed Lives: Gender and Technology in Everyday Life* (London: Routledge, 1997), p. 120.

3. Creed (1993); and Carol Clover, *Men, Women and Chainsaws* (London: BFI, 1992).

4. Creed (1993), p. 17.

5. Rosi Bradiotti, "Signs of Wonder and Traces of Doubt: On Teratology and Embodied Differences," in Nina Lykke and Rosi Bradiotti (eds.), *Between Monsters, Goddesses and Cyborgs* (London: Zed, 1996), p. 142.

6. Creed (1993), p. 19.

7. Julie Emerson, "Control of Biotechnology and How We Lost It at the Movies," *Resources for Feminist Research* 18 3 (1989), pp. 44-46.

8. Yvonne Tasker, *Spectacular Bodies: Gender, Genre and the Action Cinema* (New York: Routledge, 1995), p. 151.

9. Somer Brodribb, *Nothing Mat(t)ers: A Feminist Critique of Postmodernism* (Melbourne: Spinifex, 1992), p. 17.

10. Ibid., pp. 140-141.

11. Karen Newman, *Fetal Positions: Individualism, Science, Visuality* (Stanford, CA: Stanford University Press, 1996), p. 21.

12. Mary O'Brien, *The Politics of Reproduction* (Boston: Routledge & Kegan Paul, 1981) and *Reproducing the World* (Boulder, CO: Westview, 1989).

PART FOUR

WOMEN IN CYBERSPACE

JACKING IN TO THE VIRTUAL SELF

m.c. schraefel

A Context

Recently, I was interviewed for the "feminist perspective" about a group of women called PMS: Psycho Men Slayers, who play as a clan (a team) against any other clans in a networked game called Quake. In Quake, team members stalk virtual representations of other team members on-line through levels of mazes of various degrees of difficulty. The goal, of course, is to kill kill kill. When the other team is wiped out, your team wins.

The Psycho Men Slayers group's Web page proclaims, "Under every floral print dress lies a lady wearing black garters, carrying a big f*cking gun!"[1] Members' individual pages list iconography, from male fantasy comic books, of stiletto-heeled women with big guns. I read an interview with one of the PMS members in *HotWired*, which quotes the PMS founder as saying, "It's always going to be boys versus girls. It's something that's been with us since grammar school." Indeed, both members of PMS and the only other all-female clan, Crack Whore, complain about the sexist treatment of women in that environment: "The fact that we are mostly girls just seems to pile on the sexism. Everyone wants to play us, and wants to either talk sex or give us shit." Playing well, they claim, has a certain mitigating factor on the sexism: "When you get to the top of the scoreboard and they're at minus one, suddenly they show a lot of respect."[2] In the interview, I was asked to speak about what was positive for women in what these women were doing and what was not so positive.

There is nothing new in these young women finding solace in the belief that they are beating men at their own game and gaining respect for this. Many of these women go to university, where they learn every day how to do malestream thought, how to write malestream essays, how to compete with men, how to deny they are being harassed while doing so.

There is nothing new in the image these women use to dress up their competition: the femme fatale. The stereotype comes prefabricated with what Freud referred to as "castration anxiety" — the dangerous fear of, and attraction to, the seductress, who of course only wants to cut off a man's balls.

There's nothing new in a woman's actions regularly being taken to be about a man rather than for herself. This misogynist icon runs the gamut of historical pop culture, from Medusa to Nikita. While it is compelling that these women want to foreground their gender, to challenge assumptions of how women can play or behave, it is problematic that they use male-defined images of women to attempt to make their point. In this game, their representation of their strength is relative only to the men they overpower. These women use the femme-fatale image without irony or contradiction, which begs the question: What are they trying to prove? That they are this stereotype, rather than another? That they are the sexual killer (in a game where there is no overt sexual intrigue, only Rambo-esque blood and guts), rather than the Madonna?

Where the players do break with their chosen stereotype is through their willingness to acknowledge much male attention as "sexual harassment in the form of put-downs or requests for virtual sex." The women acknowledged that they are not treated as equals in this environment until they have "proved" they are the male players' equals or betters. The lesson here seems to be that if they can be seen to be as good as, or better than, men in this game (i.e., can shoot a virtual gun, can pound a keyboard very quickly), they will no longer be treated as women.

They note that many women who do play Quake do not identify themselves as women because of the harassment. When the PMS group put out an invitation for women players to join their clan, it did not receive many replies. The members put this down to the harassment, too. But maybe the lack of response is because not all woman who play Quake identify with this version of what it is to be constructed as a woman who plays Quake. What if one is a woman in Cyberia without a gun or a dress? It is hard to be a woman in Cyberia.

The Discussion Proper: Jacking In

Estimates are that the number of persons jacking in to the 'Net is growing exponentially. This means as that population grows, so (it is

men set the standard

hoped) will the number of women on-line. Currently, women represent a third of the on-line population. But these statistics reflect only the most recent period of the Internet's almost 50-year history.

The Internet has been around eight times as long as the Web, and for that entire length of time the dominant group on the network has been white males between the ages of 25 and 50. They have been researchers, academics, telecommunications experts and members of the military. In fact, the Internet, until 1995, was funded by the U.S. government, with special interest by the U.S. military.[3] In 1995, just after the explosion of the World Wide Web onto the scene, the government sold the main backbone, the main line of Internet traffic, to the telecommunications company MCI. Prior to that, however, the 'Net had been the domain of the military and academics. It is important to note, for instance, that in the United States, computer science departments came into being largely through military initiatives and funding. It is only with the coming of the World Wide Web and large-scale Internet Service Providers (ISPs), which made access to the Internet possible in private homes, schools and businesses, that women, along with the rest of the population who can afford to do so, have been going on-line in more significant numbers. Despite this opening up of access to this resource, however, we come not to a brave new world,[4] but to a space that has decades-old protocols for exchange and decades-old prejudices about who may exchange what and how.

Our initiation into these protocols is immediate. To access the 'Net and its resources — like electronic mail, the Web, discussion groups and file transfers — we must "log on." We must identify ourselves to the system. Our log-on identity determines how we are perceived by the system, that is, what our privileges are within that system: what information we can see and, perhaps more important, what information can we change.

This is only the first wave of self-construction we engage in on-line. Identity for the system is simply authorization. It is not, in most places, a fingerprint. It is like a key that anyone can carry. If you have my log-on name and password, you *are* me for that system, or at least you are all the system needs to know about me. The construction can be extremely limited: on-screen name; password; real e-mail address. In some spaces, a user will enter the second wave of identification, which is not for the system, but for other users. Users are asked to create a personal profile of likes and dislikes, occupation and so on. It can all be true. It can all be false. That is, once within the system — once the system has allowed you to access it on its terms — further identity construction has little to do with the system's authorization for the purposes of entry and tracking for surveillance. Quite the contrary, in fact. Identifying oneself to other real users within the system is about commodification, not authorization. Who we are, as demographic entities, is highly valuable and prized information to the global economy gone digital. This information is bought and sold among collectors at an increasing rate. As we reach the coming millennium, as more and more of our (always already logged) transactions take place on-line, as the source for informational exchange becomes increasingly limited to the digital domain, the nature of identity (and how or why it is constructed on-line) is of critical moment.

On the 'Net, after log-on, there are two main places in which identity construction is focused: a self-created identity, for use in electronic exchanges such as e-mail or live, real-time textual exchanges; and a form-based identity, for marketing purposes. This discussion is most concerned with issues around the first type of self-construction, but I will make the following point about the latter, since the two intersect.

Companies that use the Web to sell things (especially virtual things such as software or information) have changed the way they do business. In the early days of the Web, a user could go to a company site, look for the most recent version of a software program on the site and download it. Increasingly, however, companies are blocking direct access to both software and information downloads with forms that request information about the downloader. As well as name, postal code, e-mail address and sometimes physical address, sites will ask about occupation, annual income, where you will use the software, how many people are in your organization and whether you are male or female. On some sites, not filling in age or gender is not an option. If you want the software, you have to fill in something. On other sites, like Microsoft's, if you want to access the software support areas, you must allow them to track your computer or you will be denied access to their help files. Similarly, if you wish to get the "free" version of New York Times On-line, you must take out a virtual subscription. Your age, gender, country, name and e-mail address are mandatory before you can access the site. In this case, the news becomes a wrapper for capturing, and likely selling, your stats to other vendors. We will give you some news, but first you must surrender your demographic valuables. As the NYT Web customer-service writer puts it, responding to an e-mail query about their policy for collecting age, gender, e-mail and country information:

"Different news organizations on the Web do different things in order to earn enough revenue to provide their services. The *Wall Street Journal*, for example, charges $59 a year for access to its site. Several others request a zip code or a birth date in order to use a particular service, or gather information about readers and their viewing habits gradually through 'cookies' as they travel a site. Some sites do nothing at all; many of those sites are losing not insignificant amounts of money.

"In our case, asking a few questions of our readers is the 'price' we charge for access. As stated in our Privacy Policy, linked from the bottom of our home page http://www.nytimes.com, the information we gather from our individual readers is kept strictly confidential. The major use of this information is to allow advertising banners on our pages to be shown to the readers for whom they are most pertinent. This means that readers see advertising that is most likely to interest them, and advertisers send their messages to people who are most likely to be receptive, improving both the viewer's experience and the effectiveness of the ads.

"The information we gather also allows us to learn how various types of users respond to the features we provide, helping us to improve our services."[5]

In the corporate Web, the mall of the next millennium, this is identity: a marketing survey that denies anonymous transactions, that insists on categorizing us according to its terms. "Types of users" are defined by age, sex, country and income for both initial survey and future monitoring. This is the price of admission. If you don't provide the information, you cannot get the product.

These details are power and currency. Through these questions, a corporation will represent us to ourselves, market us and, of course, sell us to other corporations. There is little room in such exchanges for identity constructed as other than age/gender/country/e-mail/address/income-optional. On-line, it doesn't matter if you're Black or white, but it does matter if you are male or female, young or old, and, increasingly, what you do and what you get paid for doing it. I am not sure what is worse: a future where all other aspects of cultural affiliation are reduced to income bracket, so that a site can be pitched to that user's price range; or a future where more refined information is required, where whether you are Black or white, blue- or green-eyed, is part of the form, without which, nothing. It won't mean that you will not be served, but it could make a very big difference in what you are served.

Such scenarios as the above do not surrender their rationales to their users. While many sites have so-called Privacy Policies that protest that the information you give them is confidential, you will not be told what "confidential" ends this information will be put to within the organization. And unless the policy explicitly says so, your information can be sold to other companies with whom you may wish never to do business. This type of profile-gathering is not new. Coupons, rebates, subscriptions do much the same thing. But the type of questions have become more intrusive and more restrictive: unless you give us your e-mail address and gender and occupation, we will not give you this product. In the real world, you can still buy a subscription to a newspaper without providing this kind of information. Such is not the case within the hidden workings of the on-line commercial identity trade.

With the above *caveat emptor* in place, this discussion now turns to the other highly structured zones of virtual transaction, such as e-mail, chat rooms and other forms of "personal" exchange. It's in this well-defined space that the other form of identity construction is situated, the self-identity construction. In each of these spaces, we are asked over and over, before entering the space, to construct an identity for ourselves.

This free-floating nature of the name in cyberspace has been hailed as one of its liberating qualities; outside of the e-commerce forms described above, the Web is "neutral." It does not perceive race, nation, age, physical ability, gender, because there are no bodies, no flesh, in cyberspace. But just because we can't see it, does that mean the body, and all the cultural markers and prejudices that go with it, disappears? More to the point, what happens when there are no fleshly anchors to an identity, or when another claims to speak from that identity? If identity is supposedly so fluid on the 'Net, what is the future of women in Cyberia?

To look at this question, we need to consider first how communication is constructed in cyberspace/cyberia.[6] Cyberia is the scene of the new literacy; it is the publishing medium *du jour*. Despite the emphasis on multimedia content — the combining of interactive images, sound and video in one Web page or in a single e-mail — for the foreseeable future, the virtual world of the 'Net will remain largely text-and-icon-based for the exchange of information and the publication of ideas. In this invisible, burgeoning[7] zone, identities are communicated through textual descriptions or icons that represent some text. Currently, text-only dominates web-based transactions. In the near future, one will be able to enhance text with icons and avatars — graphic representations of a character representing "you" in an exchange. There is no guarantee that the more representational options available, the more "truthful" the representation of self to system or self to other will be. On the contrary, the tools are there for your construction of an identity, not necessarily the representation of an identity. As such, in this world of words and icons, anyone can claim to be anybody.

In Cyberia, claiming to be anybody has, according to many, become simply the way of being on-line. It is taken for granted, for instance, that gender-bending is part of the fabric of many on-line fora. As Amy Bruckman states regarding her research into multi-user domains/dungeons (MUDs):

> "Without makeup, special clothing, or risk of social stigma, gender becomes malleable in MUDs. When gender becomes a property that can be reset with a line of code, one bit in a data structure, it becomes an 'object to think with' to use Seymour Papert's terminology.[8] In public forums like rec.games.mud, people reflect the values that our society attaches to gender. In private experiences, people can explore the impact of gender on their lives and their construction of themselves."[9]

Rather than critiquing the implications of such identity claims, Bruckman sees these on-line fora as an "identity workshop."[10] And intense work it is, according to Sherry Turkle in *Life on the Screen*. Playing at another gender is an energy-intensive exercise that demands attention to a variety of details: speech mannerisms, interpretation of experience, consistency of presentation over time. There is also anxiety about whether or not one is successfully passing as the Other.[11] But, despite these anxieties, Turkle and Bruckman maintain that gender-swapping on

Or the opposite: let's strictly enforce these gender stereotypes

MUDs can be a safe way (one will not get arrested for cross-dressing on-line) to learn about identity. As Turkle states:

"MUDs are proving grounds for an action-based philosophical practice that can serve as a form of consciousness-raising about gender issues. [For example, when] men playing females on MUDs are plied with unrequested offers of help on MUDs, they often remark that such chivalries communicate belief in female incompetence. When women play males on MUDs and realize that they are no longer being offered help, some reflect that those offers of help may well have led them to believe they needed it."[12]

Indeed, in the literature exploring so-called on-line gender-bending or gender-swapping, the oft-cited markers of gender that men notice are that women get hit on a lot; and that when they get offers of help, it is usually in expectation of some kind of favour (tiny sex,[13] usually). And according to this research, women notice that they receive less help when they present as men.

Both Turkle and Bruckman (as well as other researchers in this area) believe that, based on such observations as those noted above, life on the screen does indeed provide the opportunity to "explore" (undefined) gender issues through this on-line "embodying" of personae of the opposite gender. The fake identity becomes a "vehicle of self-reflection."[14] But to what end? Does the man who gets hit on on-line become a more caring and sensitive man in real life (RL)?

In one of Turkle's interviews in *Life on the Screen*, she speaks with a man, Garrett, who says he goes on-line as a woman to "know more about women's experience ... I wanted to see what the difference felt like ... I wanted to be collaborative and helpful, and I thought it would be easier as a female."[15] Turkle notes that Garrett as an on-line female "could be collaborative without being stigmatized." While Turkle talks about Garrett's RL history, however, she never mentions if Garrett in RL tried to be collaborative as himself with other men, or even what "being collaborative" means to him.[16]

How these men presume to construct virtual gender goes unproblematized. In the only other case that Turkle gives much consideration to, she sums up another male's (Case's) take on why he gender-bends: "[F]or Case, if you are a sensitive man, it is coded as 'being a bastard.' If you are assertive as a woman, it is coded as 'modern and together.'"[17] In whose universe? Turkle does not comment on Case's incredibly reversed perception of gender attributes. As has been recited over the past 30 years in arenas from feminist scholarship to pop women's magazines, if women are assertive they are bitches; if men are aggressive they are confident. Furthermore, women aren't praised for being caring and sharing; they are simply punished if they are not. Men, on the other hand, are praised for any turn of seeming sensitivity.[18] One wonders if it is simply not easier to play at being a stereotypical woman, to move as such within the company of women, than to attempt to challenge male identity patterns?

Turkle's presentation of this mode of gender-bending as self-reflection also does not consider that the person who has been evolving himself through stereotypical role-play for his own ends in a "safe space" — safe for him — has been contributing to the propagation of a gender stereotype, not to the social challenging of it. Neither Turkle nor Bruckman considers what happens to women who present on-line as women in ways that challenge these swapping stereotypes — who do not behave as men playing women do, for instance. Quite the contrary.

On-line gender-appropriation assumes that playing at stereotypes of gender is actually exploring gender, rather than redrawing again and again the stereotypes so helpful to male domination. Turkle, however, insists that these on-line personae are "serious play" and have RL repercussions. She points to a singularly reiterated occurrence of on-line rape, one man's take on it anyway,[19] to raise the "question of account-ability for the actions of virtual personae who have only words at their command."[20] Julian Dibble tells of how one character in a MUD "took over" another player's character and described raping the character in front of the other participants. The MUD community was in a state over how to treat the offender. One might think that the actions that provoked redress in this on-line community were the rape itself. Not so. Debate ranged around the realness or seriousness of a "verbal only" action. Nothing, in fact, is done until one member's virtual robot dog is also "possessed" by the rapist and returned dismembered to the MUD. The player's character, it is decided, will be terminated. The consequences? The shunned member returns in another identity. There is no concern expressed for the laissez-faire way in which gender and identity are presented as an appropriatable, abusable commodity either within the original story, or within Turkle's retelling of it. Those who view gender as such a transferable commodity, and those who practise this commodification, do not consider the logical conclusion to be drawn from this for race and other specific sites of agency.

A man who wants to present as caring and sharing, Turkle notes, finds it natural to present as a "woman." Would someone wanting to appear evil go on-line as small-bodied and Austrian? Would someone wanting to be seen as musical or athletic go on-line as African American? Turkle's and Bruckman's investigations into the "serious play" of on-line identity construction are limited to their accounts of gender-bending. They are either unaware of, unconscious of, or uninterested in similar appropriations of race and class. Perhaps it is less easy to make claims about the nature of "play" when culture, race and class are at issue, rather than gender alone. But where these two academic women (both from MIT) may be afraid to tread, *Wired* magazine boldly goes.

Race in Cyberspace

At the end of 1995, *Wired* ran an article by Glen Martin entitled "Indian Wars on the Internet." The point of the article seems to be that the actions of a white man claiming to be a Native American shaman spurred a group of Native Americans into developing a tele-communications network. While the argument that the fakery of a white man was the genesis of an all-Native network seems spurious, the article does address the issue of cultural appropriation on-line. The writer of the article asks whether, in a culture (on-line) where all information can be translated as zeros and ones, anything can be sacred. "How do you upload holiness?" In other words, because a technology enables the appropriation of all things that can be digitized, then everything is available for the taking by everybody. To deny this, the article suggests, is to be a narrow-minded fundamentalist.

The author of the article implies that the ability to wear multiple identities on-line is liberating to enlightened Native Americans but threatening to traditionalists. He does not, however, quote or otherwise identify any actual Aboriginal persons who espouse the belief that it is okay for a white man to claim he's an Aboriginal shaman practising authentic Aboriginal rituals. Of course, by labelling as "traditionalists" those Aboriginal persons who find such practices to be cultural appropriation, he discredits their having anything meaningful to say in a supposedly non-traditional, on-line world. The article gives the last word to the white man, too, who says all he wanted was for more Natives to be communicating on-line.

The Native Americans quoted in the piece, however, state that to be spoken for — for a white man to claim as his the little left to a people from which so much has already been taken — is too much to bear. They resent the stereotyping and misrepresentation of their practices as well. They also referred to the act as fraud: the man was claiming to practise actual Native spiritual rights when he wasn't. To make matters worse, America On Line (AOL), the company hosting the man, was making money from the exploitation. AOL users had to pay an additional fee beyond AOL membership to enter the chat room where this pseudo-shaman presided. But despite numerous tribal council protests to have the man's platform pulled because of the damage such appropriation does to their cultures, AOL stalled. One of the Native women involved in the efforts to block the fake states in the article:

> "But anger [on the part of the Native Americans], says [Susan] Miller, was the dominant emotion — especially when [Native] protests were repeatedly stonewalled by AOL. 'I was e-mailing a Sioux friend about it, and we came to the conclusion that the company didn't want us disturbing the fantasy,' said Miller. 'It doesn't want real Indians — we're not "Indian" enough. It wants the buckskin fringes and the feathers.'"[21]

Dionne Brand, in her book *Bread Out of Stone*, refers to the protection and propagation of such stereotypes as part of the cultural-appropriation agenda: "It confirm[s] and reinscribe[s] that colonial representation so essential to racial domination."[22]

From incidents like that described above, we can see that the multiple but actual identities of all women on-line are also blocked from virtual acceptance in preference of male fantasy and its perpetuation of female stereotypes. Unlike the Native resistance mounted against AOL, women's groups have not petitioned any Internet service providers (ISPs) to stop supporting the appropriation and misrepresentation of women's voices on-line. The terms have been set: it's "gender-bending," after all, not "cultural appropriation." The activity has become far too much a part of 'Net culture to be questioned as anything other than what the 'Net's dominant culture says it is: just fun, just a game, just a joke.

One may suggest that, as a group, women are far more heterogeneous than Native Americans, and therefore have no particular identity to be threatened, misappropriated or lost by such virtual cross-dressing. That assumes that women want to protect some imaginary homogeneous identity. That there are so many voices also marked as "women" is exactly the point. There is a multiplicity of women's voices. For some time, those voices have asserted the basic feminist challenge to stop reading women in terms of stereotypes (from earth mother to nymphomaniac)[23] that only subjugate the real differences between them. But the dominant 'Net culture is about as interested in the actual voices and experiences of any women as it is in actual Native Americans. Despite claims that the 'Net is the embodiment of postmodern play, where identity is entirely subjective,[24] the Wild Wild Web, the male-dominated state that produces MUDs and MOOs (MUD oject-oriented), is, as Margie Wylie observes, "male territory." As Wylie states: "Far from offering a millennial New World of democracy and equal opportunity, the coming web of information systems could turn the clock back 50 years for women."[25]

With popular emphasis like Bruckman's and Turkle's on gender-bending through stereotype, women's presence on-line becomes even more entrenched as either the traditional domestic caretaker or a sex object. Yet Turkle, who has done research specifically on women's reluctance to engage computers in part because of the machine's macho image,[26] makes no comment on the propagation of these very stereotypes in the supposedly gender-liberating explorations that her research subjects enact (for their own self-reflection), and that she seemingly extols.

The result of this ready acceptance of stereotyping that passes as meaningful, "self-reflective" gender-bending is the continued silencing of women, a reiteration in this brave new world of the same old, same old. Indeed, the very old. As Karen Coyle points out in "How Hard Can It Be," her article on women's perceived relations to the computer, the majority of computer ads currently on the market equate the machine with power: if women are present at all, they are either on the sidelines, cheerleading male prowess as measured in MIPS or MHz, or they are very obviously replaced by the Tower of Power as the preferred sex object (or, at best, compared with it, such that having the technical object is equivalent to having the organic one).

But ads are not the only place Coyle points to where computers are equated with heroic brawn and brain. Such is the history of computing.

Coyle deftly describes how both *Wired* author Stephen Levy and George Gilder, the influential futurist of the anti-gay, anti-feminist, arch-conservative Discovery Institute, effectively erase women from the annals of computing heroics, both going so far as to suggest that women don't hack and don't "compete" with men in computation because we're not genetically up to it.[27] As Coyle points out, Levy's celebration of the early days of MIT male hackerdom misses other possibilities for women's supposed absence:

> "[Levy] never considers relevant that this hacking took place in a campus building between midnight and dawn in a world where women who are mugged at 2 a.m. returning from a friend's house are told: 'What did you expect, being out at that hour?' Nor does he consider that this hacking began at a time when MIT had few women students. And though he describes his male hackers as socially inept, he doesn't inquire into their attitudes toward women and how those attitudes would shape the composition of the hacking 'club.'

> "But most of all, he never considers the possibility that among the bright women attending MIT at that time, none were truly interested in hacking. What if the thousands of hours of graveyard shift amateur hacking weren't really the best way to get the job done? That would be unthinkable."[28]

With this frame of mind — the belief that the computer and computer jock must be heroic — it's no surprise that Levy and most other writers of computer history erase the significant and substantial contributions of women (like the notion, design and implementation of the first computer programming language).[29] Coyle speaks to the disparate social status of computation as yet another reason for excluding women's voices from computer science. "The assumption in our society is that men's activities are difficult, and that is why women can't or don't engage in them. Women's activities are, of course, inferior, which is why men don't engage in them."[30] Not until the computer is reduced to the level of appliance, like a refrigerator, will it be acceptable for women to be visibly involved in computing (again):

"But it is doubtful we will be able to demote the computer to appliance status in the near future. The inevitable march toward the development of the 'information superhighway' means that we are depending on the power and mystique of computers to provide new markets for our economy for the foreseeable future. And a machine with all the fascination of a toaster won't motivate the consumer market."[31]

We can see that unfounded, stereotypical presumptions about women erase their real achievements in computing. Presumptions about the masculinity of the computer also erase us from the marketplace of "serious" computer users,[32] and these same presumptions operate in on-line fora, where identity is appropriated and the stereotype becomes the only allowable version of women on-line. The scene is grim for female would-be participants in the great information revolution. It gets worse when actual women resist this erasure.

It's All Just a Game

Any criticism of activities practiced on MUDs, MOOs and chat rooms is often dismissed by their participants with the "it's just a game" response. This response acts as a carte blanche excuse for a range of behaviours, from cross-dressing to virtual rape. Indeed, Rapp, the man faking shaman status on AOL, has the typical chauvinist response to criticism from a subordinate group. He is described as somewhat bemused by all the heat and bile generated by his on-line persona. "Basically, what we did was done in fun," he observes. "We certainly didn't intend any disrespect."

It was a joke; I didn't mean it. Of course these very familiar rationalizations do not modify the behaviour critiqued. Instead, they become the rationale for its perpetuation: because it is a game, I can do what I want. Even if one was to accept that rationality for chat room-like on-line environments, there are other places on-line where these same behaviours take place and do not have the excuse of being "just a game." These are on-line newsgroups and mailing lists.

When speaking about off-line conversational exchanges in her book *The Writing or the Sex*, Dale Spender noted that if women generate more than 30 percent of an exchange, they are considered to be dominating it.[33] Retaliation, often aggressive, ensues to reclaim the margin, with arguments that, for example, freedom of speech has been impinged. The same statistics have been reaffirmed in on-line newsgroups and mailing lists — even those with titles such as alt.feminism and SWIP-L (the Society for Women in Philosophy list).[34] In her extensive research in the area of computer-mediated communication (CMC), Susan Herring cites regular use by men of aggressive on-line behaviours such as flaming and personal insult. She notes that this behaviour is validated by "netiquette," as codified by published texts such as *Towards an Ethics and Etiquette for Electronic Mail* by Norm Shapiro and Robert Anderson, who advise, "Do not insult or criticize third parties without giving them a chance to respond." In other words, flame away, as long as the attackee has a chance to flame back. The flames themselves, when directed at women (something Shapiro and Anderson do not consider), are more often than not framed as rape threats, and are sometimes mailed not only to the attackee but also to the rest of the list.[35] Unfortunately, threats like these, which would otherwise be grounds for legal action, are regularly practised on-line, where arrest is difficult: it is hard to arrest someone from across a provincial or national border, assuming the threat is even taken seriously in the first place.

I never realized how amb-iguous internet is...

Stephanie Brail discovered that women in particular are the victims of retaliation that goes beyond the caustic flame. She cites especially e-mail harassment of a graphic and threatening nature, and system administrators unsympathetic to pulling the on-line privileges of the perpetrator. Pornographic writings were posted across various newsgroups and attributed to Brail. Another woman was harassed at work and nearly lost her job as a result of false accusations made about her to her boss by men rubbed the wrong way by her challenging them — politely — on-line.[36]

Netta "grayarea" Gilboa relates similar off-line terrors levelled at her when she inadvertently upset certain hackers on an Internet relay chat (IRC) channel. She found her phone number changed regularly; her phone calls monitored and broken into; various confidential data accessed and published on-line.[37] All were acts over which it is very hard to exercise any control.

Ironically, Herring's CMC research found that men dislike flaming and related behaviours as much as women do.[38] Despite their stated dislike for these practices, however, they still perpetrate them and dominate on-line exchanges. Women do not; when turned off by a climate of flame or silence, women frequently leave. Be flamed or be ignored — both are the normal, abusive responses to women's postings. Herring insists that we do not read this scene as simply two different cultural approaches to conversation not getting along. As she states:

> "[T]hese cultures are not 'separate but equal' as recent popular writing on gender differences in communication has claimed. Rather the norms and practices of masculine net culture, codified in netiquette rules, conflict with those of the female culture in ways that render cyberspace — or at least many 'neighborhoods' in cyberspace — inhospitable to women. The result is an imbalance whereby men control a disproportionate share of the communication that takes place via computer networks."[39]

This violent chauvinism of the on-line world is not restricted to on-line exchanges. Coyle raises the question of how off-putting it might have been for an MIT female student to engage with the nerd culture of the early hackers. Spender takes this question further in her description of computer labs where men regularly outnumber women, where activity from networked war games to shared pornography to macho conversation can poison the working atmosphere for women.

The 'Net (and the RL environment that fosters it, from research and undergrad computer labs[40] to *Wired* magazine) is not a gender-neutral space. Communication may be disembodied, but it is not disengendered or politically neutral. In "Gender Issues in On-line Communications," Hoai-An Truong states:

> "Despite the fact that computer networking systems obscure physical characteristics, many women find that gender follows them into the on-line community, and sets a tone for their public and private interactions there — to such an extent that some women purposefully choose gender neutral identities, or refrain from expressing their opinions."[41]

In *Technologies of the Gendered Body*, Ann Balsamo cites the above observation and adds:

> "Thus we see an interesting paradox in action. Cyberspace is a place where bodies aren't supposed to matter, but many women discover that they do matter. The false denial of the body (mainly by male

users) requires the defensive denial of the body (mainly by female users) so that communication can occur. For some women, this denial of the body is simply not worth the effort. Most men apparently never notice."[42]

This is why research so involved with images of gender and the (predominantly male) practice of so-called gender-bending, like Turkle's and Bruckman's, is so frustratingly naïve. Far from making a space for women's voices, their uncritical acceptance of these stereotypical reenactments of gender only further enables the erasure of women's agency on-line.

What is more distressing in this simultaneous denial of gender and the ready acceptance of the appropriation of gender on-line is the misrepresentation and conflation of political and philosophical positions to support it. Turkle, for example, points to Donna Haraway's "Cyborg Manifesto" and its founding principle of irony to support what she sees as the multiple identities that are the way of being in *Life on the Screen*. What passes for on-line gender-bending is just one more way of articulating that multiple, postmodern self. What Turkle fails to consider is that Haraway does not contextualize that irony as the playtime exploits of a group of mostly white male individuals who can play at being a stereotype of a woman for "self-reflexive," self-serving ends. On the contrary, Haraway's Cyborg entirely resists just this type of presumption around patriarchally defined categories of gender (woman = nurturing). In fact, her Cyborg specifically exists to resist any attempts to situate a "woman" category, or any identity that does not recognize the layers of political and social construction, the standpoint of that Cyborg identity's articulation.[43] Turkle's men, who play at being women, are very much removed from Haraway's demand to take the politics of complex identity structures into consideration (especially those identities that are constructed "negatively," like "woman of colour"). Indeed, from Haraway's Cyborg position, MOO/MUD gender-bending — the presumption that this naming of oneself as a woman is actually bending gender — is only the entrenched erasure of difference, of otherness, since it is that actual otherness that threatens the comfortable assumptions of such privileged "serious play."

'Net culture, then, like dominant RL culture, actively resists alterity (otherness, difference) when that alterity seeks to name itself and the terms of its difference in ways that challenge the 'Net's racist, sexist status quo. It is little wonder that many women go on-line with gender-ambiguous or male pseudonyms. These women do so, not to "explore" another gender, but to protect themselves, at least somewhat, from the various forms of on-line harassment they regularly experience when they identify themselves as women. We also do so for the reason Spender points to in historical women's writing. Maryanne Lewes (George Eliot), Charlotte and Emily Brontë, to name a few, all published under male names, not only in order to be published to begin with, but also simply to be heard. To be taken seriously with less fear of reprisal.[44]

But such camouflage is only temporarily and situationally feasible, and is clearly no answer to making it possible for women to be safe speaking on-line as our actual, heterogeneous selves for more than 30 percent of the bandwidth.

In Other Words

Many possible solutions have been put forward to facilitate women's communication on-line. One is that we should learn the tools of the 'Net. To that end, a new publishing niche is forming — on-line guides specifically geared to women by women, with the provocative titles of *Surfer Grrls* and *Net Chick*, with the hope that knowing a little UNIX can make a gal feel pretty empowered, and that finding like-minded chicks is even more empowering. Such knowledge is not only empowering, it is essential for the informed critique of these systems by women who bring to bear their expertise from other fields, from psychology to literary theory. All aspects of the 'Net and its deployment are in need of such *informed* feminist critique from the inside out.

From the outside moving in, where the user meets the system, *Women'space*, a paper-based magazine and companion Web site from Nova Scotia, seeks to use the 'Net as both an information resource and a tool for empowerment for women. It states that "*Women'space* aims to promote accessibility to the Internet, its tools, information and resources; enhance the effectiveness of women's organizing through national and global connections; bring global on-line resources to local community actions; support the exchange of ideas and experiences amongst women."[45]

Toward these ends, *Women'space* organized the Women's Internet Conference in Ottawa in 1997 and, in the same year, published the resource volume *Virtual Organizing, Real Change: Women's Groups Using the*

Internet. Predating these publications, other on-line strategies in mailing lists have been to form women-only lists that, though not impervious to impostors, still attempt to construct a safe space for women to network or communicate specific concerns.[46] On women-centred lists where men do post, there's a growing strategy to identify and name the behaviours of dominance to the rest of the group, so that the group can and will (usually) pull the plug on them. While these groups can be, and often are, as ethnocentric as mixed lists, there is a higher likelihood these attitudes will be identified and dealt with in some manner.

Outside these specific net neighbourhoods, however, it is simply a continual risk to be a non-status quo woman on-line (if you're not a woman, please, don't try this at home). The same sexism, homophobia, racism prevails on the Wild Wild Web as in RL, but is often allowed to express itself unchallenged by any 'Net sheriff. While the price of naming one's alterity to male, white, heterosexist discourse on-line is a continual risk, however, even within the rare women-only lists, what is the price of not naming one's alterity on-line? Several years ago, Audre Lorde spoke out to academic women at an MLA conference to say, "Your silence won't protect you." This is a point worth remembering in on-line discourse as well. Do we silence our selves and our sisters if we do not risk speaking as ourselves? As attorney and Arapaho Native American Tamera Crites Shanker states, "If we don't define who we are on the 'Net, other people will do it for us — And when that happens, part of who we are disappears."[47] But in our silence, part of who we are does not simply disappear; it is erased.

It is not in the interests of those in power ever to acknowledge alterity. It will not be in the interests of patriarchy[48] to allow women to speak as ourselves on-line. Perhaps part of the radical solution to halting the fixed erasure of alterity from the 'Net is to increase the number of neighbourhoods where the specific agency of a woman's identity is valued and encouraged. We can also intervene in the structures themselves. There could be such a thing as what I've called *feminist engineering practice*, research and development of the systems themselves from a perspective that listens to alternative voices and perspectives. In other research work,[49] for instance, I have proposed how to use this understanding in software systems that generate documents based on user interaction. The design is grounded in these studies of difference, of conversational difference and of valuing these differences.[50] As an outgrowth from her work on the Systers Mailing List for Women in

Computer Science and the Grace Hopper Celebration of Women in Computer Science conferences, Anita Borg founded in 1998 the Institute for Women and Technology at XeroxPARC (www.parc.xerox.com/iwt.org). The express mission statement of the institute is:

n To increase the impact of women on technology, in education, design, development, deployment and policy;
n To increase the positive impact of technology on the lives of all women; and
n To help communities, industry, education and governments accelerate and benefit from these increases.[51]

No doubt these virtual neighbourhoods and actual interventions will be small initially. But if there are enough of these spaces, or at least if these precious exchanges are frequent enough, the results on the entire system, like increasing the tiny air bubbles in a brakeline, can be significant.

ENDNOTES

1. Taken from the Psycho Men Slayers Web page at: www.underramp.com/~pms/. See also the other main women-only Quake Clan page at: www.crackwhore.com/. Much of the same femme-fatale imagery applies.

2. Taken from: www.wired.com/news/story/1885.html.

3. See chapters 2 and 3 of: Douglas. E. Comer, *The Internet Book*, 2d ed. (Englewood Cliffs, NJ: Prentice-Hall, 1997).

4. "Oh brave new world that hath such people in it," says Miranda to her father in Shakespeare's *The Tempest*. The brave new world to which Miranda, isolated on an island since childhood, refers is of course the very old world from which her father was driven by corrupt politicians. Hence her father's not un-ironic response: "It is new to thee." For most of us, this is the reality of the Internet: seemingly wonderful, but only because new and unknown. Wait until you log on.

5. E-mail from the NYT Web customer service department, April 19, 1998.

6. I prefer the term "Cyberia" to "cyberspace" because of what it implies homonologically: Siberia is a particular place on a map (not unlike Manitoba, weather-wise) with a particular culture. The name seems more grounded than the amorphous ether of "cyberspace."

7. I use the term "burgeoning" with caution. While thousands of Web pages are added to the 'Net each month, recent North American stats (Canadian Librarian Association, 1996) show that only 7 percent of the population use the Internet. Of that 7 percent, approximately a third are women.

8. Seymour Papert, *Mindstorms: Children, Computers, and Powerful Ideas* (New York: Basic, 1980).

9. Amy Bruckman, "Gender Swapping on the Internet," from proceedings of INET '93 (The Internet Society, 1993).

10. Ibid., p. 13.

11. Sherry Turkle, *Life on the Screen: Identity in the Age of the Internet* (New York: Simon & Schuster, 1995), p. 212.

12. Ibid., p. 214.

13. "Tiny sex" refers to on-line real-time, text-based sex "acts" by typing.

14. Turkle (1995), p. 219.

15. Ibid., p. 216.

16. In work/play relations with men, collaboration is not the normal practice for women.

17. Turkle (1995), p. 219.

18. The sensitive man has become a media imperative, from films such as *Sleepless in Seattle* to top-ten sitcoms such as *Friends*.

19. Julian Dibbell, "Rape in Cyberspace," *The Village Voice* 38, 51 (December 21, 1993), pp. 36-43.

20. Turkle (1995), p. 254.

21. Glen Martin, "Internet Indian Wars," *Wired* 3, 12 (December 1995), pp. 108-117.

22. Dionne Brand, *Bread Out of Stone: Recollections on Sex, Recognitions, Race, Dreaming and Politics* (Vintage Canada, 1998), p. 129.

23. Sheila Ruth, "Talking Back: Feminist Responses to Sexist Stereotypes," in Sheila Ruth (ed.), *Issues in Feminism: An Introduction to Women's Studies* (Mountain View, CA: Mayfield, 1990), pp. 123-137.

24. Turkle (1995), p. 202.

25. Margie Wylie, "No Place for Women," *Digital Media* 4, 8 (January 1995), pp. 3-5.

26. Sherry Turkle, "Computational Reticence: Why Women Fear the Intimate Machine," in Cheris Kramarae (ed.), *Technology and Women's Voices: Keeping in Touch* (New York: Routledge & Kegan Paul, 1988), pp. 41-61.

27. Karen Coyle, "How Hard Can It Be?" in Lynn Cherny & Elizabeth Reba Weise (eds.), *Wired Women: Gender and New Realities in Cyberspace* (Seattle: Seal, 1996), pp. 42-55.

28. Ibid., p. 44. In a fourth-year software engineering course I teach called "Computers and Society," one of the male students made the observation that there are no known women virus writers or arch-hackers. He and his male colleagues asked why. "Women are busy," I replied.

29. Women put the numeric keypad on the keyboard; a woman came up with the idea of programming memories and textual program representation (i.e., programming languages) over plugs and dials to make programming more manageable (see: Thomas Petzinger, Jr., "History of Software begins with the work of some brainy women," *Wall Street Journal* 228, 98 (November 15, 1996), p. B1.

30. Coyle (1996), p. 53.

31. Ibid., p. 54.

32. According to a 1997 *USA Today* survey, women are the majority buyers of the household/family computers.

33. Dale Spender, *The Writing or the Sex? Or Why You Don't Have To Read Women's Writing To Know It's No Good* (New York: Pergamon, 1989), pp. 9-11.

34. I have been told by computer scientists who were there in the early 1980s ('Net prehistory) and the very early days of Usenet newsgroups that one of the fiercest flame wars to break out was over the establishment of comp.women, a newsgroup meant to discuss women's issues as they pertained to computer science. There are clear rules for establishing new newsgroups, rules based mostly on demonstrating demand. The request to see if there was demand went out and was flamed immediately by those who claimed all the comp.whatever groups had to have something to do with computer science. Comp.women plainly did not. And if you look today, you will not see comp.women. You can find comp.society and five subgroups, though, such as comp.society.folklore.

35. In many sources, such as Dibbell's "A Rape in Cyberspace" (1993), this kind abusive language/pornographic narrative supposedly describes "sexual acts" or "unwanted sex." Sex has nothing to do with it. Sex is not a crime. Rape, or the threat of a man using his penis as part of the humiliation or overpowering of a woman, is an assertion of dominance, not sex.

36. Stephanie Brail, "The Price of Admission: Harassment and Free Speech in the Wild, Wild West," in Cherny & Weise (1996), pp. 141-157.

37. Netta Gilboa, "Elites, Lamers, Narcs and Whores: Exploring the Computer Underground," in ibid., pp. 98-113.

38. Susan Herring, "Bringing Familiar Baggage to the New Frontier: Gender Differences in Computer-Mediated Communication," in Victor J. Vitanza (ed.), *CyberReader* (Toronto: Allyn & Bacon, 1996), p. 149.

39. Ibid., pp. 151-152.

40. I was recently asked to comment on an argument between a faculty member and her grad students regarding the naming of a new networked printer that she had purchased for her lab. She had asked for suggestions from the (predominantly male) research group for the printer's network name. Failing to receive any, she and the only woman grad student in the group called the printer "Daisy." Then the men in the group reacted, saying they wouldn't use a printer named Daisy. One said quite loudly that his colleague had said he would never approve of such a name. What did they think he was? Gay? This is when I was asked for a possible solution. I suggested that since the professor bought it with her research money, she could call it anything she wanted, and if the male students wouldn't use it, that was their loss. "Use your power to name the thing. Quit letting Adam do it." "But I want to be democratic." Some democracy. Sometimes it may be appropriate for a woman to lead. The example may seem small, but I was surprised to see that sexism was alive and well at such a high level of scholarly work and at such a trivial level of exchange. Even the name of a printer could be an affront to a grad student's masculinity.

41. Hoai-An Truong, "Gender Issues in On-line Communications," CFP 93 (Version 4.1), ftp.eff.org.

42. Ann Balsamo, "Feminism for the Incurably Informed," in chapter 6 of her book, *Technologies of the Gendered Body* (Durham, NC: Duke University Press, 1996).

43. Donna Haraway, "A Manifesto for Cyborgs: Science, Technology and Socialist Feminism in the 1980s," in Elizabeth Weed (ed.), *Coming to Terms* (New York: Routledge, 1989).

44. Dale Spender, *Man Made Language* (London: Routledge & Kegan Paul, 1980).

45. Taken from the masthead of *Women'space* (Spring 1998).

46. There are a host of unfortunate examples of men crashing women's lists, claiming that to be excluded is bigoted or violates their rights to freedom of speech (see: Dale Spender, *Nattering on the Net* {Toronto: Garamond, 1996}; or L. Jean Camp, "We Are Geeks, and We Are Not Guys: The Systers Mailing List," in Cherny & Weise {1996}, pp. 114–125).

47. Martin (1995), p. 117.

48. Read, especially in this case, as white, middle-class, heterosexual, middle-aged males, the dominant group currently in Cyberia.

49. m.c. schrafel, "ConTexts: Intensional Document Creation, Delivery and Retrieval," proceedings of the Pacific Rim Conference on Communications, Computers and Signal Processing (Victoria, BC: IEEE, 1997), pp. 417-419.

50. Dr. Anita Borg, of Parc:Xerox and founder of the Systers mailing list, has recently initiated the Institute for Women and Technology as a space to explore women's needs and interests in the development of technology.

51. Taken from the Institute for Women and Technology Web site at: www.parc.xerox.com/oct/projects/iwt.org/mission.html.

BODY(E)SCAPES

The Politics of Embodiment in Virtual Reality

Allison Whitney

Developments in computer-based communication technology in the past decade have contributed to a popular interest in "virtual" phenomena, from virtual cafés to virtual pets. These developments have also led to the creation of virtual spaces, which immerse their users in a seemingly all-encompassing world of auditory and visual stimuli. This type of virtual reality (VR) technology has applications in diverse fields, including entertainment, medical instruction and military training. The emphasis on the virtual suggests a binary opposition with the real, or the actual — a division that supports the distancing of the material world of bodily existence from the intellectual, abstract realm of data. This article addresses some of the practical and philosophical issues concerning the position of the body in relation to VR technology, and how factors such as gender and race are, and might be, articulated in virtual worlds. I will argue that the agenda of separating the material from the informational is related to gender ideology, and has its roots in Western notions of the relationship between the body and the mind and the binary division of nature and technology. Artists and theorists are working to counter this agenda, as they grapple with the difficult task of envisioning and designing the future of communication technology.

Feminist scholars have frequently addressed the role of gender in the development and application of communication technologies, and VR provides a particularly interesting case for speculative study because it is often associated with the hype of a "gender-free" medium. Computer-based communication technologies can create the illusion of a space in which the social hierarchies of the real world no longer apply. In fact, many people claim that cyberspace provides a domain in which gender, race, age, class, sexualities and other social distinctions cease to be relevant, a utopian space where one can leave behind the reality of one's embodied existence in favour of a forum where all persons are valued for the contents of their characters and the quality of their ideas. In practice, however, it is clear that, rather than providing an alternative world, virtual spaces simply recreate the power imbalances of the real world. Even so, the hype continues, and therefore it is important that feminists reveal the gendered dynamics of VR technology and dispute its claims of distancing the virtual from the actual. Since VR often presents itself as a means of escaping the body, this article addresses the role of embodiment in VR, not only in an effort to defeat some of the utopian claims, but also to demonstrate the significance of bodily existence in VR immersion and how that existence is articulated through gendered bodies.

My focus is the potential for VR systems to alter individuals' experiences of embodiment, the representations of bodies in VR, and the ways that contemporary artists use VR technology to address changing notions of the body and its role in subjectivity. VR technology is still in its infancy, and therefore we do not yet know how economic, corporate, historical and social forces will shape its creation, distribution and use. As a result, this article is in part a project of speculation, an anticipation of the ways VR technology may relate to concepts of gender and embodiment. I consider the theories of a number of scholars working in the field of gender and technology, and describe how their theories are, or are not, made manifest in artists' installations. I also refer to the work of cyberfeminist activists, who are striving to create a more powerful role for women in the production and use of VR systems. My primary interest is in so-called immersive VR (that which incorporates head-mounted displays providing visual stimuli) and other interface devices, such as datagloves, bodysuits and the 3-D mouse.

G.L. Mallen argues in "Back to the Cave: Cultural Perspectives on Virtual Reality" that VR has until now been developed in ways that privilege visual stimuli, a trend that has its roots in the 19th-century obsession with optics, which gave rise to vision-based technologies such as the photographic camera, the stereoscope and the cinema. Mallen argues that contemporary VR designers belong to one of two distinct schools of computer-graphics development. The first is preoccupied with "graphics as simulated optics," where realism and suspension of disbelief are the main objectives; the second is concerned with "using the computer as a tool to help understand the structure and behaviour of the world around us."[1] The first school, in other words, wants to create virtual spaces that simulate environments in the real world (i.e., flight simulators), while the second works to represent the otherwise invisible (i.e., a large-scale model of a molecule or a virtual map of the human body). These two schools — one which views VR as a substitute reality, the other which uses VR as a tool for envisioning actual reality — are both relevant in terms of gender analysis. We are as much concerned with the representation of the female body in VR environments that claim realism as we are with issues of embodiment in more abstract applications.

Mind/Body — Male/Female

Allucquere Rosanne Stone's "Will the Real Body Please Stand Up? Boundary Stories about Virtual Cultures" proposes a number of theoretical approaches to the development and use of VR technology, with particular emphasis on the location of the body in such equations. She begins her article with the story of Julie, a male psychiatrist who developed Internet relationships with a number of people while using the persona of a disabled woman.[2] This anecdote flies in the face of one of the major fantasies associated with VR: that it renders the body irrelevant. Initial reactions to the revelation of Julie's true identity ranged from amusement to outrage; some people felt violated and cheated by Julie's "deceit and trickery,"[3] while others saw on-line gender-swapping as an opportunity to broaden one's human experience. The implications of on-line impersonation are numerous and complex, but for our purposes this anecdote indicates that, in social interaction, the bodily existence of the individuals involved remains important.

The VR agenda of decoupling the body and the subject has a long cultural history in the West, but it is most clearly articulated in the work of Descartes, who claimed, "I am not that set of limbs called the human body."[4] As we make the transition from the industrial age to the information age, and start to discern virtual modes of existence, the split between mind and body may become even more pronounced. At the same time, however, Stone suggests that the divide is starting to collapse, because the body as a symbolic system is undergoing major revision. This re-definition of boundaries is related to the disintegration of patriarchal systems that position the feminine as the negation of the masculine.[5] Stone cites the work of Donna Haraway, whose *Simians, Cyborgs and Women* explains how the division between nature and technology is collapsing. Haraway describes her work as an "argument for *pleasure* in the confusion of boundaries and for *responsibility* in their construction."[6] Her vision is one where the traditional systems of categorization that divide the world into binary opposites are replaced by a new system that allows for multiplicity. She calls on feminists to take responsibility for the creation of a new coding of subjectivity.

This confusion of boundaries is directly related to the position of the body in VR, for the body itself can be understood as a "boundary figure" that belongs to "at least two previously incompatible systems of meaning — the organic/natural and the technological/cultural."[7] Stone suggests that "Nature" is a fairly recent concept, put in place as a way to "keep technology visible" by standing in opposition to it.[8] The body is shaped by both natural and cultural forces, and VR technology presents us with further means of dismantling the binary distinctions between systems of meaning.

The mind/body and nature/culture divisions are significant in a discussion of VR because they are bound up with gender ideology. Stone refers to David Tomas' "The Technophilic Body," a text that describes the experience of immersive VR as one of enormous "freedom."[9] This "freedom" is achieved through a feeling of the mind's detachment from the confines of the body. The gendered nature of this technology-mediated mind/body split is made explicit in Katherine Hayles' "Embodied Virtuality: Or How to Put Bodies Back into the Picture." She explains that the idea of transcending the body and existing entirely in an intellectual/spiritual realm is very powerful in Western culture. She refers to a work entitled *Mind Children* by Hans Moravec, head of the Carnegie-Mellon Mobile Robot Laboratory, an institution involved in the research and development of artificial-intelligence technology. Moravec's futuristic vision is one where:

> "The age of the protein-based life forms is drawing to a close, to be replaced by silicon-based life forms. Humans need not despair, however, because they can have their consciousness downloaded into a computer. In the fantastic scenario in which he imagines this operation, Moravec has a robot surgeon cut away a human brain in a kind of cranial liposuction until all the information ... is inside the computer ... Once human consciousness is safely ensconced inside a computer, it is effectively immortal. If the computer begins to wear out, consciousness can simply be transferred to a new machine."[10]

Moravec's fantasy, which is not unusual in the realm of VR and contemporary science fiction, positions the subject as information. If human essence can be reduced to pure data, then it can be transferred from machine to machine indefinitely; thus, we escape not only the social significance of the body, but also its mortality. Hayles' analysis of Moravec's arguments claims that, if technology allows the subject to be independent of the body, then it implies a new state of being "not born of woman."[11] Feminists have documented the long history of attempts by social, medical and religious institutions to control and usurp women's sexual and reproductive powers.[12] The desire to create VR technology that allows an illusion of disembodiment may be interpreted as yet another effort to evade the troubling reality of female reproductive power and place the role of subject-creation in the hands of male technicians.

The dualistic concept of mind versus body closely mirrors that of male versus female, where maleness equals reason and intellect, and femaleness equals body, material and biology. Such thought patterns have had great implications for the oppression of marginalized groups throughout history; there is a long-standing tradition of defining otherness and inferiority in bodily terms. For example, a common argument in support of women's exclusion from positions of power is that their biological characteristics are an impediment to leadership, that their reproductive powers make them psychologically unstable, mentally feeble or physically weak. Similarly, the oppression of people of colour, lesbians and gays, the poor and the mentally ill is consistently linked with, and rationalized by, their real or imagined bodily differences from a patriarchal norm. Members of these groups become closely identified with physicality itself, for their identity and social position are inextricable from the body. If marginalized persons are more "body" than those in power, then it follows that a binarized social system will fail to attribute the characteristics of intellect and spirituality to these hyperphysical groups. Katherine Hayles clearly explains that "the dualities line up as follows: mind is superior to body; silicon technology is superior to protein organism; man is superior to woman."[13]

This gendered relationship between embodiment and power is illustrated in the work of William Gibson, a cyberpunk writer whose work has great popular appeal and has attracted the attention of many feminist critics. His novel *Neuromancer* is about the exploits of a male protagonist named Case who is a professional hacker and spends most of his life in cyberspace as a disembodied agent operating within the world-wide computer network. His companion is a female bodyguard named Molly. It is interesting to see how physicality and virtuality are designated as gendered concepts in the ways that these characters use technology. Case uses it to enter cyberspace and thus transform himself into pure data and leave the "meat" of his physical body behind. But Molly uses technology in the form of implanted devices that enhance her physical abilities and make her a better cyberwarrior. Case also has the ability to transplant his consciousness into Molly's body and share her physical sensations. What is particularly interesting is that while Molly is presented as a "warrior," Case's experience while inhabiting her body is described as one of "passivity," which suggests that even while Molly's profession might constitute a reversal of gender roles by today's standards, her female identity remains associated with passivity and physical weakness.[14] In fact, physicality itself is equated with weakness and vulnerability, for when Molly is injured, Case can extricate himself from her body and flip back into a disembodied state but she has to endure the pain. As a female, Molly's personal and professional identity is based on her physical existence, so she must remain forever stuck in the "flesh prison" of her body.[15]

Gibson and other cyberpunk writers create scenarios based on technology that does not actually exist, but it is nevertheless interesting to look at how VR is being conceptualized, as the visions and agendas set down in the culture today will influence the ways VR technology is designed and marketed in the future. Issues of gender and ideology in cyberpunk fiction are very complex and cannot be fully explored in this article, but it is important to note that some feminist literary critics have discussed the work of writers such as Gibson as part of an anti-feminist backlash, not only in the realm of science fiction, where the work of female writers is consistently undervalued, but also in the general context of Western culture. These critics position cyberpunk as a reaction to "the emergence of feminist concerns regarding the technologized body and the resultant boundary confusions that occurred in both science fiction and in the culture at large."[16] In spite of the prevalent cyber-hype, which heralds the advent of a post-gender world that promises the elimination of bodies and their political significance, cyberpunk narratives tend to reassert the body/mind dichotomy and ensure that the accompanying gender categories remain intact.

Synners, a cyberpunk novel by Pat Cadigan, offers an example of how alternative narratives informed by a feminist sensibility might describe and critique these fantasies of disembodiment. In Anne Balsamo's analysis of *Synners*, she suggests that it operates on the premise that bodies are always gendered and racialized in cyberspace; rather than envisioning virtual reality as a means of jettisoning the culturally inscribed body, Cadigan's narratives position the hyper-embodied status of women and people of colour as a desirable characteristic.[17] Cadigan's women, including a woman of colour, use cyberspace as a tool of collaboration and connection, while the white male characters use it to separate themselves from their bodies, to the point where their bodies disappear. Rather than describing the materiality of woman as a burden or a "flesh prison," Cadigan presents the thoroughly embodied status of women and people of colour as a welcome alternative to the disintegrating white male body.

Cadigan's reevaluation of the desire for disembodiment is significant in that it suggests how the disappearance of the white male body may in fact represent a destabilization in white male hegemony. The apparent desire of white men to leave their bodies through VR may be related to the ways that North American social movements of the past 30 years have challenged white male privilege. Cathy Peppers suggests that deconstructionists' "eagerness to embrace a 'dissolved' subject" is a ploy to avoid addressing feminist concerns about gender and subjectivity.[18] Anne Balsamo notes that VR technology emerged in the 1980s, a time when the body (specifically the white male body) "was understood to be increasingly vulnerable ... to infection [HIV/AIDS], as well as to gender, race, ethnicity and ability" social movements.[19] The VR fantasy is one where technology can neutralize the physical body and offer white men "an enticing retreat from the burdens of their cultural identities" and the increasingly transformed social order.[20] It would appear that the encroachment of social movements' redefinitions of subjectivity, along with their gradually successful attempts to assert and affirm the experience of women, people of colour, lesbians and gays, and other marginalized groups, threatens the authority of the white male body. What follows are patriarchal fantasies about a virtual space where the body vanishes, thereby rendering moot any further discussion of social injustice against those whose oppression is supposedly based in bodily difference. Of course, these fantasies rest on the assumption that while the virtual body may pretend to be free of real-world coding, all but white males are relegated to the category of "other," and therefore can never attain the power of subjectivity. It is vital that feminist thinkers and practitioners counter these fantasies, for there is a danger that VR and cyberspace will be understood only as sites where the body no longer matters, making it easy to silence those who criticize the existing gendered dynamics of such technologies.

Bodily Experience of VR

Anecdotal evidence suggests that men and women experience VR immersion in different ways. For example, women tend to report more motion sickness and disorientation than men. Katherine Hayles suggests that "the cultural constructions that identify masculine subjectivity with the mind, female subjectivity with embodiment" are responsible for these differences.[21] She argues further that, since men are encouraged to distance their sense of self from the body and imagine themselves as abstract entities, they may be quite comfortable with technology that separates point of view from bodily experience. By contrast, females are accustomed to identifying point of view with the body, and would therefore find the illusion of disembodiment highly disturbing. Hayles emphasizes that her analysis is based on anecdotal evidence, and it is still too early to conduct far-reaching studies on individuals' reactions to VR immersion, but these reports suggest the extent to which cultural constructions inform the way an individual inhabits his or her body.

If men and women experience their day-to-day embodiment in distinct ways, then it follows that gender will be a crucial factor in VR's potential to alter bodily experience. Catherine Richards is a Canadian artist whose work explores the power of electronic art to challenge conventional notions of embodiment. While in residence at the Banff Centre for the Arts in 1991, Richards conducted a series of experiments, documented in a video entitled *Spectral Bodies*, that focused on the manipulation of proprioception. Proprioception is a function of the nervous system that enables people to sense the boundaries and position of the body. Proprioception allows you to know, for example, that your legs are bent or that your arms are swaying, and allows you to coordinate your actions. People whose proprioception is damaged or altered through illness or brain injury are unable to sense the location of their body parts, and can literally forget how tall they are and must relearn how to move and control their bodies. Some have described it as feeling as though they no longer inhabit their own bodies, losing the sense of location in the body that we take for granted.

Richards' experimental subjects wore blindfolds (so visual stimuli would not interfere with other sensations), and she then applied vibrating devices to specific areas of the skin. These vibrations interfere with the proprioceptive system, and the subjects reported that their bodies felt like they were changing shape, as if the boundaries of the body were being "remapped":

> "One woman reports that she feels her neck shrinking and then thickening, becoming like a bull's neck. The process continues until her head retreats into her chest, her shoulders forming an unbroken line across the top of her body. Another woman remarks that her arms are growing longer and longer, stretching six feet or more away from her body."[22]

These experiences were extremely powerful, such that the subjects genuinely felt as though their bodies were undergoing a metamorphosis. Although Richards' experiment did not seek to directly apply these experiences to VR, her work invites speculation that, if VR technology could be refined to the point that its sensory inputs could alter proprioception, users might operate in a virtual environment in a different physical form. In other words, the subject who felt that her arms were six feet long could exist and function in a virtual world as a person with six-foot arms, all the while unable to distinguish the sensations and characteristics of her virtual body from those of her actual body. Assuming that VR technology could manipulate a user's proprioception in a sophisticated way, one might envision programs that allow users to virtually inhabit the body of a seven-foot-tall basketball player, an infant or a dog. Such notions have enormous potential to destabilize conventional categories of gender, race, age, and so on, and raise questions about what constitutes a "human" body. But they also make it clear that such explorations of subjectivity are closely linked with bodily identity.

VR's destabilizing potential rests in its ability to alter the way we feel "at home" in our bodies, to openly question the relationship between bodily and psychological identity. While people have long tried to assume the identities other than their own, whether through masquerade or the appropriation of cultural practices, the implications of proprioceptive manipulation are that one might operate in a virtual realm with unfamiliar physical features and limitations with an unprecedented degree of verisimilitude. If this were indeed possible — if a user could literally feel that she were a foot taller, or 50 pounds heavier, or a different race or gender — then the notion of the body as the stable, concrete seat of subjectivity will come under challenge. Not only would a user present herself in VR as a body different from her own, but she would in effect represent herself to her own nervous system as such. It is important, therefore, that feminists continue their philosophical consideration of the nature of identity and the position of the body in that equation.

Representing and *Recognizing* Bodies

Considering how the creation and application of VR will relate to the politics of embodiment, a great deal of ideological work needs to be done before we enter the realm of complete VR immersion. It is important that the aesthetic, social and cultural factors that inform VR production be analyzed and understood so that individual users, and society in general, can be prepared for the technology and its possible implications. Such factors will have considerable impact on how VR is designed and used, particularly in the realm of gendered bodies. Stone makes reference to Judith Butler's idea of the "culturally intelligible body," which theorizes the way social codes influence our relationships to our own bodies and those of others.[23] Butler would argue that much of our bodily experience is culturally defined, and that each of us employs a specific set of criteria for identifying bodies and placing them into social categories. Information about gender, race and social class is condensed into a set of codes that are then *recognized* by the receiver. The degree to which we rely on these codes in everyday life is evident in instances where one encounters a body that is in some way "unintelligible" or "illegible."[24] For example, people are generally very uncomfortable when they meet a person whose gender is ambiguous. Many of our conventions of behaviour and communication, including body position, gesture, tone of voice, and even syntax, depend on gender, so it is very difficult to interact with a person without perceiving her or him as gendered. Since it is inevitable that codes employed in the real world will be carried over into cyberspace, likely to women's detriment, we must consider the ways that criteria of intelligibility will be inscribed onto representations of the body in VR.

Stone's research into how the body is represented in virtual worlds is grounded in an examination of the ways bodies are encoded in the phone-sex industry. In phone sex, physical characteristics and actions are made manifest through an established repertoire of phrases, expressions and codes that the worker, usually a woman, uses to construct a scenario, and the listener, usually a man, interprets, or re-cognates, into a fantasy of physical presence. This repertoire is constrained by a number of social, linguistic, economic and cultural factors, and therefore the "bandwidth for physicalities in phone sex is quite limited." Stone cites a worker who says that "on the phone, every female sex worker is white, five feet four, and has red hair."[25] This is an ironic comment, but it points to the ways in which cultural codes surrounding gender, sexuality, race and body type are embedded in the criteria we use to construct human subjects. It also suggests that in virtual environments, stereotypes can become even more potent than in real life because, as Margaret Morse explains, while "in physical reality, it's not so easy to become He-Man or Barbie … in a virtual world, stereotypical ideas about gender and sexuality can be brought to bear without the inevitable contingencies and imperfections that plague the act of physically embodying a gender identity."[26]

Therefore, it is easy for the phone-sex customer to believe that he is talking to a white, five-foot-four redhead because he does not have to contend with the phone-sex worker's actual bodily presence, and it is unlikely that the customer will ever be asked to acknowledge that the notions of female appearance and sexuality manifest in this "virtual" woman are in fact an illusion.

A primary reason that gender roles must be reinforced in so many ways in any society, through everything from children's toys to public washrooms, is that the strict and exclusive categories of masculinity and femininity are fundamentally unnatural. Morse's comment points to the fact that to live life as a human being is to possess physical, psychological and intellectual characteristics associated with both masculinity and femininity, however they may be defined in a given time and place. If we do not appreciate the ways the contingencies of the actual body operate, then we may make dangerously limiting worlds in VR. If the codes of bodily *recognition*, both external and proprioceptive, are based on a "Barbie and He-Man" model, then there is a danger that the complexities of embodied existence will not find expression in VR, and that the environments created in cyberspace will prove even more limiting than those in the real world.

Sexist and racist coding practices are very much alive in the construction of VR avatars. (An avatar is a representation of a user in cyberspace.) Women Entering Avatar Virtual Environments (WEAVE) is an organization dedicated to facilitating women's involvement in VR. On their Web site, they explain that in contemporary VR, the active avatars are primarily white, male and able-bodied.[27] Anne Balsamo concurs, stating that "in VR applications, cyberspace heroes are usually men, whose racial identity, although rarely described explicitly, is contextually white."[28]

VR scenarios generally operate on a heterosexual dynamic, and are focused on the exploits of male subjects. It is the observation of WEAVE members that, when females are represented, it is often in a sexualized context, and they tend to be a "blonde and nubile" stereotype. It is true that in many cases, avatars are represented as stick figures, or with green skin, or as supposedly genderless animals, which might make it seem problematic to describe them as "white and male," or indeed to attribute any human characteristics to them at all. However, it is dangerous to assume that a green stick figure does not carry social coding, since VR environments already function on the assumption that their users belong to a particular category of intelligible bodies.

In his 1996 article "Virtual Skin: Articulating Race in Cyberspace," Cameron Bailey claims that, in cyberspace there is a white male norm, and that one is assumed to be a part of that norm until one self-identifies as a woman or a person of colour. Bailey's research includes an interview with a Black man who says he prefers to hide the fact that he is Black when he's on-line because he finds it interesting to see how people interact with him when they think he's white.[29] It is significant that Internet users assume that other users are white males unless it is stated otherwise. It is clear that, at this point in our history, there is no such thing as a truly genderless, raceless, or indeed bodyless, subject. Rather, subjectivity is restricted to white males, and everyone else is designated to the category of "other."[30] A similar set of assumptions operates in VR environments, and therefore the green stick figure may not be as neutral as it first appears.

Codes of *recognition* also reflect social class, which may in turn be inscribed onto the virtual body. Lev Manovich's "The Aesthetics of Virtual Worlds" includes insightful arguments about how economic power might be expressed in a VR context. Much of the debate about gender and class in relation to technology concerns issues of access.

Access is a complicated concept, but basically it means that, if one is denied the knowledge to operate a technology, or if one cannot afford the technology itself or the time to use it, then one cannot participate in a given mode of communication (or at least not as easily as a more privileged person). In the case of VR, financial constraints may limit the technology to a privileged few. But even if the technology is made widely accessible, an individual's power to use it as a means of communication may be closely related to social class. Manovich points out that, in the realm of digital imagery, resolution equals wealth. The word "resolution" refers to the clarity of the image, which is directly related to the amount of coding used in the image's composition. The fact that resolution is quantifiable in terms of bits and bytes makes it easy to commodify. It is not uncommon to download a picture from the Internet, only to find it accompanied by a notice that promises higher resolution, as long as you are willing to pay for it. "Realism has become a commodity ... It becomes possible to automatically adjust the appearance of a virtual world on the fly, boosting it up if a customer is willing to pay more."[31] In theory, the quality of an avatar and its powers of navigation in the VR environment could be determined by the user's financial resources, thus re-inscribing economic status onto the virtual body, keeping in mind that "representations of virtual bodies in VR systems affect how users interact with the virtual world — and what they can do in that world."[32] Representations are therefore very important within VR environments, as they may dictate the capacities and roles of their users in much the same way that gender codes direct behaviour in society. Since women tend to have less economic power than men, it follows that women's avatars may have lower resolution, and therefore less freedom to function in virtual worlds.

In response to the troubling potential of VR to exclude or impede users and their experiences, cyberfeminist artists take care to explicitly address the position of the body and its codes of intelligibility in their work. Eva Wohlgemuth, an active cyberfeminist artist based in Vienna, addresses the codification of the virtual body in her 1997 *Bodyscan* project, where she scanned a high-resolution 3-D image of her actual body into a computer database. She has since used this data in a number of installation works. For example, she developed a VR environment at the Ars Electronica Center in Linz entitled *In/Out*, in which the user navigates through the interior of her digital body.[33] Through this project, Wohlgemuth asserts the importance of women constructing their own representational models in cyberspace. The *Bodyscan* Web site includes images of this virtual body, and when one clicks on each of its parts, one receives "personal" information about Wohlgemuth — everything from details of her daily routine to her passport and telephone numbers. Here, Wohlgemuth literally inscribes the specificities of her actual experience onto her virtual body, making it clear that it is possible to create VR environments that represent the complex relationships between the body and life experience.

Representation from Within

While the visual representation of avatars is a primary concern, what is even more intriguing is the possibility that codes of *recognition* may operate on a deeper physical level. The observation that men and women tend to react differently to VR immersion points to the possibility that cultural coding goes beyond the visible surfaces of the body into the ways people interpret and experience the body as a whole. As was noted previously, William Gibson's cyberpunk narratives describe the experience of inhabiting a female body as one of passivity, imprisonment and pain. This type of description suggests that the cultural construction of gender encodes not only the visible (hair, skin, clothing, gesture) and the audible (tone and pitch of voice, speech patterns), but also the realms of haptic response (touch) and proprioception. This is not to suggest that female experience is in actuality anything like Gibson's patriarchal fantasy, but if VR technology has the potential to transform one's sense of embodiment, then one suspects that cultural notions about masculinity and femininity will inform the ways VR technology is constructed and employed. One can speculate that without considerable deconstruction of body ideology, VR environments could reinforce patriarchal structures through all the senses, including touch.

The incorporation of touch, or haptic response, into VR interface is of major interest to the industry. For example, a 1996 article in the *International Journal of Human-Computer Interaction* states: "It is quite likely that much greater immersion in a VE [virtual environment] can be achieved by the synchronous operation of even a simple haptic interface with a visual and auditory display, than by large improvements in, say, the fidelity of the visual display alone."[34]

This means that the introduction of texture, temperature, pressure and other bodily perceptions into the VR experience will make it all the more convincing and useful in many applications, some of which include entertainment, surgical training and military training. Possible instruments for haptic feedback include "inflatable bubbles ... materials that can change from liquid to solid state under electronic charge" and vibrating coils that might be installed in datagloves, helmets, bodysuits or other interface devices.[35]

There remains great interest in vision-based VR, of course, but industry experts are increasingly aware of the variety of bodily experience and the relevance of embodiment in VR immersion, and there are major incentives for VR producers to create increasingly sophisticated bodily-interface technology. At this time, such technology remains limited, and it is anticipated that it will be another 30 years before there exist fully immersive VR environments. While it is true that many of the fantasies associated with VR involve distancing the mind from the body, the interest in including more sensory interface with the machine may be related to what Stone describes as "cyborg envy," a desire to jettison the frailties of the "meat" body in favour of a level of physical competence available only in a virtual world.[36] This is perhaps the ultimate expression of the mind/body duality: the abstract mind of the computer creates a new, immortal and impermeable virtual body, free of the contingencies of actual bodily existence. We may read the promise of "greater immersion" as an enhancement of a user's suspension of disbelief to the point where virtual environments possess a level of authority comparable to the real world.

The ideological significance of haptic response and bodily distortion is underexplored, largely because cultural theories, from Marxism to psychoanalysis, have placed their focus on the visual and auditory senses. This neglect of touch and proprioception is related to technological history — before VR immersion became an issue, such questions would not have seemed relevant in the analysis of cultural phenomena. Moreover, sight and touch have been constructed in the modern West as oppositional because, while the former is often positioned as a "disembodied" sense, the latter remains thoroughly embodied.[37] More work needs to be done in the study of how touch is socially constructed if we are to guide the development of immersive VR toward a feminist-informed realization.

Media such as television, cinema, radio, sound recordings and video games have allowed us to become accustomed to isolating our auditory and visual senses and differentiating the real from the representational. For example, when you listen to a CD recording of a piece by Mozart, you never believe there is an orchestra present in the room with you; rather, you understand that you are hearing a recording of a musical performance. This is because we have, in the visual and auditory realms, an established tradition of representation. However, we do not have a representational tradition for haptic sensations, and certainly not for proprioceptive manipulation. There are no established conventions in place to differentiate the real from the virtual when it comes to such bodily sensations.

The VR industry is acutely aware of this lack of a cultural tradition, which is why it claims that haptic response will create a greater sense of immersion than visual stimuli alone. For example, if a VR user wearing a dataglove picks up a "cold" object in a virtual space and feels a temperature change in the fingers of the glove, is that sensation "real" or is it a representation of coldness? We know how to distinguish an apple from a photograph of an apple, but is it possible to define a semiotic difference between virtual and actual cold? It is possible that, in time, people will develop a system akin to "spectatorial distance" in the realm of VR, but this is problematized by the fact that much of the technology's potential power comes from the creation of seamless and totally immersive virtual environments.

The potential for confusion in the case of haptic response points to the disintegration of boundaries between nature and technology that is the basis of cyborg culture. Artists such as Catherine Richards suggest through their work that technology places the body in an ever more troubled relationship with the subject. The woman in *Spectral Bodies* who feels that her head is sinking into her chest is faced with the question of how her body represents itself to her mind, which in turn raises the question of who "she" really is — a body or a mind? — and whether either of these entities is in any way stable. This question points to the ways the subject is connected to the body, and how "being a body constitutes the principle behind our separateness from one another and behind our personal presence ... Both law and morality recognize the physical body as ... an absolute boundary, establishing and protecting our privacy."[38] The notion of the body providing stable boundaries for the subject is questioned in VR, much in the way that Haraway claims cyborg culture destabilizes the binary world order.

It is the intention of many immersive VR designers that the user will be similarly unable to distinguish the boundary between real-life sensation and virtual sensation. For example, in an article on flight-simulation technology, John Vince explains, "Immersion is an important feature of virtual reality systems as it is central to the paradigm where the user becomes part of the simulated world, rather than the simulated world being a feature of the user's own world."[39] When the boundary between real and virtual worlds becomes indiscernible, there is danger that a user who is not aware of the ways his or her virtual experience might be informed by chauvinistic norms will take the virtual sensations for granted and accept, for example, that female embodiment really does entail passivity. Therefore, the question to be posed when examining a VR environment is not so much whose reality or point of view is represented, but whose reality is "created" in the virtual space and how does that reality articulate "relationships between technologies, bodies and cultural narratives."[40]

Cyberfeminist Responses and the Promise of Resistance

Stone would explain the biases and power imbalances in VR representation as indicative of their creators' interest in gendered models of desire, although she questions to what extent users will go along with these models. In spite of the burden of gendered VR dynamics, there is room for resistance, and it is likely that VR users will make use of this technology in unexpected ways. VR technology is not yet in common use, and we do not yet know exactly what forms it will take, but there are already feminist responses to the maleness of virtual environments and the sexist representations of women who inhabit them. These responses involve computer-based communication on many levels (e-mail, Internet chat groups, computer games, software and hardware design, etc.), and are concerned with female subjectivity, safety, representation, and equal opportunity for use and design of virtual environments.

As I have mentioned, WEAVE is an Internet-based organization of cyberfeminists (and feminist-friendly men) who are working to encourage women to participate in the use and design of VR systems. WEAVE conducts reviews of on-line virtual worlds; holds on-line conferences on women's interests and needs in cyberspace; and forms affiliations among cyberfeminists, programmers and engineers. Such groups can raise awareness of gender issues in computer technology and ensure that the agenda of VR development is not dominated by male interests and desires.

A major concern of cyberfeminists is that the interface technology used in VR take the characteristics of female bodies into account. On the most basic level, some of the difficulties women encounter in their relationships with technology have to do with the fact that many machines are "designed by men with men in mind."[41] For example, many women experience problems when using machines whose weight and dimensions are appropriate to typical male users, who are tall and broad-shouldered and have large hands. Even when machines are designed for female users, male engineers customarily base their design decisions more on their own biases about female behaviour than on the actual needs of women. VR technology, particularly that which incorporates haptic response, promises to offer even greater challenges in terms of compatibility with a variety of human body types, and cyberfeminists want to ensure that women are not faced with literally trying to fit their bodies into a male mould. This is a valid concern, considering the fact that virtual spaces already tend to presume and favour a white, male, heterosexual user.

One of the most articulate responses to issues of interface design is found in the work of Canadian VR artist Char Davies. Davies' most recent work, *Éphémère*, is a gallery installation of a fully immersive VR system. The interface devices include a head-mounted display helmet that fills the field of vision and a vest that monitors the immersant's breathing and balance.[42] Thus, the immersant navigates the virtual space through subtle changes in breath and balance: you move up as you inhale, down as you exhale, and control direction and velocity by leaning. *Éphémère* is deliberately designed to enhance a sense of embodiment by using the torso, rather than bodily extremities such as hands or feet, as the site of communication with the computer. At the same time, however, the floating sensation that accompanies immersion in a 3-D space creates a sense of disembodiment. These contradictory sensations are kept in careful balance, and thus *Éphémère* manifests the ideological struggle to define bodily experience in cyberspace. Although the experience is relaxing and meditative, the virtual environment poses questions to the immersant on a physical level, challenging her to consider her bodily position and identity.

Davies avoids using the hands as interface tools because she views them as "instrumental and manipulative," and she wishes to avoid the aggressive conceits of driving, flying and shooting that are the basis of most video games and other VR systems. In an earlier Davies installation entitled *Osmose*,[43] immersants who moved too quickly or aggressively were "punished" by the VR system — the computer would return them to the least interesting part of the virtual space until they learned to behave themselves.[44] In both *Osmose* and *Éphémère*, forms of arguably masculine interface that value speed and destruction are supplanted in favour of what Davies describes as an "intuitive" interface, one that reasserts the centrality of embodied experience.

The virtual space of *Éphémère* is divided into three levels: landscape, earth and body. Each of these spaces evolves through a set of temporal cycles; the landscape undergoes seasonal change, the seeds under the earth germinate, and the body passes through an aging process whereby living organs and bone are reduced to ashes and dust. These gradual transformations are not directly related to the immersant's location or activity, so while she has a degree of control over navigation, the virtual environment evolves in ways that are independent of her actions. Whereas masculinist VR fantasies focus on mastering one's environment and realizing a specific goal, Davies' immersant has control over her own subject, but also understands that the surrounding world has a life of its own.

Davies chooses not to use avatars or "body icons" to represent immersants in her VR works, because in her view they only objectify the body, while her project is to affirm the body's subject position. In avoiding any visual representation of the immersant's body, Davies forces us to use more embodied modes of perception to navigate in the virtual space. As I mentioned previously, vision is commonly regarded as the form of perception that is most distanced from the body.[45] Breathing, by contrast, which is crucial to navigation in *Éphémère*, is physically located in the interior space of the body. More specifically, breathing is the most basic form of interface between the body and the outside world — a constant exchange of gas molecules between the human bloodstream and the earth's atmosphere. By locating the very idea of interface at the body's core, Davies demonstrates how VR technology might conflate bodily experience with representation by manipulating haptic and proprioceptive response. Davies' interface technology is already in contact with the body's interior, and therefore it directly addresses notions of how the body might be employed and transformed in VR.

Visitors to the *Éphémère* installation can share in the immersant's experience by watching a video projection of her field of vision and by listening to the sounds she encounters in the virtual space. At the same time, the visitor/spectator can see the immersant silhouetted against a back-lit screen and watch as she moves her body to navigate the virtual environment. The visitor/spectator is therefore continually reminded that the images and sounds are directly related to bodily action and experience. For both the immersant and the spectator, the body is constantly reasserted in the course of the *Éphémère* experience. Davies' work is an excellent example of how artists can create alternatives to the conventions of objectification, aggression and disavowal of the body in VR.

Conclusion

As Judy Wajcman eloquently argues in *Feminism Confronts Technology*, "Technology is ... a cultural product which is historically constituted by certain sorts of knowledge and social practices as well as other forms of representation."[46] Although much of the existing VR hardware and software is already loaded with masculinist ideology, it is still possible that VR can develop in a way that is informed by feminist concerns. This would entail the collaboration of feminist artists, cyberfeminist activists and feminist engineers who are willing to produce technologies that are based on women's practices, knowledge and bodily experience.

ENDNOTES

1. G.L. Mallen, "Back to the Cave: Cultural Perspectives on Virtual Reality," in R.A. Earnshaw (ed.), *Virtual Reality Systems* (London: Academic, 1994), p. 268.

2. Allucquere Rosanne Stone, "Will the Real Body Please Stand Up? Boundary Stories about Virtual Cultures," in Michael Benedikt (ed.), *Cyberspace: First Steps* (Cambridge, MA: MIT Press, 1991), p. 83.

3. Ibid.

4. Cameron Bailey, "Virtual Skin: Articulating Race in Cyberspace," in Mary Anne Moser (ed.), *Immersed in Technology: Art and Virtual Environments* (Cambridge, MA: MIT Press, 1996), p. 33.

5. Judy Wajcman, *Feminism Confronts Technology* (University Park, PA: Pennsylvania State University Press, 1991), p. 158.

6. Donna Haraway, *Simian, Cyborgs and Women: The Reinvention of Nature* (New York: Routledge, 1991), p. 150 [italics in original].

7. Anne Balsamo, "Forms of Technological Embodiment: Reading the Body in Contemporary Culture," in Mike Featherstone & Roger Burrows (eds.), *Cyberspace/Cyberbodies/Cyberpunk: Cultures of Technological Embodiment* (London: Sage, 1995), p. 215.

8. Stone (1991), p. 103.

9. Ibid., p. 107.

10. N. Katherine Hayles, "Embodied Virtuality: Or How to Put Bodies Back into the Picture," in Moser (1996), p. 2.

11. Ibid., p. 3.

12. Wajcman (1991), p. 66.

13. Hayles (1996), p. 4.

14. Cathy Peppers, " `I've Got You Under My Skin': Cyber(sexed) Bodies in Cyberpunk Fictions," in Deborah S. Wilson & Christina Moneera Laennec (eds.), *Bodily Discursions: Genders, Representations, Technologies* (Albany, NY: SUNY Press, 1997), p. 171.

15. Michael Heim, *The Metaphysics of Virtual Reality* (New York: Oxford University Press, 1993), p. 102.

16. Peppers (1997), p. 169.

17. Anne Balsamo, *Technologies of the Gendered Body: Reading Cyborg Women* (Durham, NC: Duke University Press, 1996), p. 144.

18. Peppers (1997), p. 165.

19. Balsamo (1995), p. 229.

20. Balsamo (1996), p. 144.

21. Hayles (1996), p. 12.

22. Ibid., p. 22.

23. Stone (1991), p. 111.

24. Ibid., p. 112. Note that Stone italicizes the "re" to emphasize that intelligibility is an ongoing process of coding.

25. Ibid., p. 105.

26. Margaret Morse, "Virtually Female: Body and Code," in Jennifer Terry & Melodie Calvert (eds.), *Processed Lives: Gender and Technology in Everyday Life* (London: Routledge, 1997), p. 27.

27. WEAVE Website at: www.ccon.org/weave/index.html (1998).

28. Balsamo (1996), p. 130.

29. Bailey (1996), p. 43.

30. The idea of subjectivity as the exclusive domain of the white male is explained in: Judith Butler, *Gender Trouble: Feminism and the Subversion of Identity* (New York: Routledge, 1990).

31. Lev Manovich, "The Aesthetics of Virtual Worlds" (1997), accessed at: http://jupiter.ucsd.edu/manovich/text/virt-space.html.

32. Ralph Schroeder, *Possible Worlds: The Social Dynamic of Virtual Reality Technology* (Boulder, CO: Westview, 1996), p. 61.

33. See her Website: http://thing.at/bodyscan/XXXXX/index.htm.

34. Grigore Burdea, Paul Richard & Phillippe Coiffet, "Multimodal Virtual Reality: Input-Output Devices, System Integration, and Human Factors," *International Journal of Human-Computer Interaction* 8, 1 (1996), p. 12.

35. Michael Gigante, "Virtual Reality: Enabling Technologies," in Earnshaw (1994), p. 23.

36. Stone (1991), p. 108.

37. Donna Haraway, *Modest_Witness@Second_Millennium.FemaleMan _Meets_Oncomouse: Feminism and Technoscience* (New York: Routledge, 1997), p. 174.

38. Heim (1993), p. 100.

39. John Vince, "Virtual Reality Techniques in Flight Simulation," in Earnshaw (1994), p. 137.

40. Balsamo (1996), p. 125.

41. Wajcman (1991), p. 21.

42. Davies refers to users as "immersants."

43. *Osmose* appeared in 1995 at the Museum of Contemporary Art in Montreal.

44. Char Davies, "*Osmose* and *Éphémère*: Landscape, Body, Earth and Time in Immersive Virtual Space," installation at the National Gallery of Canada, Ottawa (June 1998).

45. Davies has cited her severe myopia as a source of inspiration for the visual style of her works, which are characterized by translucent and indiscrete forms. One might speculate that it is problematic for visually impaired persons to displace visual experience from embodied experience. This question of the bodily location of vision may inform the way Davies addresses issues of representation in her VR work. I suggest this connection because I have always felt that my own myopia has served as a reminder of the bodily foundations of visual perception in my day-to-day experience of the world.

46. Wajcman (1991), p. 158.

PART FIVE

KNOWLEDGE & POWER

GIVING WOMEN A VOICE IN THE FACE OF GLOBALIZATION

A Case Study of Alternative Feminist Media in Costa Rica

Margaret E. Thompson & María Suárez Toro

Introduction

Globalization has been hailed as a panacea for all the world's problems, a means to fuel worldwide economic activity, with benefits trickling down to all countries and peoples. For many developing countries, structural adjustment programs (SAPs), which are designed and implemented by the World Bank (WB) and the International Monetary Fund (IMF), have been lauded as the key to boosting national economies. These strategic plans are designed to make countries more competitive in the global market economy; they promote growth and reduce poverty levels by eliminating large external debts through massive cuts in state spending and through privatization.[1]

Basically the changes wrought by the SAPs represent an ideological shift from a state-centred system focused internally on providing some social services, as well as local agricultural and industrial production, to a market-oriented economic system focused externally on foreign investments and non-traditional export production. The increased emphasis on producing agricultural and industrial exports has led to a loss of local control and self-sufficiency, because many consumer goods that were at one time produced locally must now be imported. The results have benefited the national elite and transnational corporate interests at the expense of the less powerful, particularly women.[2]

Costa Rica has historically been a strong liberal democracy with considerable political stability and a relatively high standard of living compared with other countries in Central America. Thus it has been hailed worldwide as a "best-case scenario" in Central America for implementing SAPs to boost the economy and curb international debt. Unfortunately, the best case appears rather bleak in a variety of ways, with a deterioration in economic and social conditions for most people, and women in particular, becoming the norm in recent years.[3]

Costa Rica was once a society of small farmers and entrepreneurs, but those people cannot compete with today's larger producers and foreign transnational corporations (TNCs), especially in terms of prices and also access to credit. In rural areas in particular, small- and medium-scale farmers who used to grow food crops for local markets have been driven out of business. Forced to sell their land to the larger landowners, they become workers themselves or migrate to urban areas. As a result, resources such as income and land ownership have become more concentrated among large local businesses and foreign commercial interests. These larger businesses have easier access to credit, and in turn receive massive government subsidies and tax breaks for export production in agriculture and manufactured goods, as well as for tourism. Thus agriculture, for example, has become dominated by large-scale production for export of commodities such as bananas, macadamia nuts, cut flowers and pineapples.[4] Because of this, the country is more dependent on outside interests for import of consumer goods and employment in foreign-owned businesses. This has had disastrous effects. For example, Costa Rica was relatively self-sufficient for food during the 1980s; today it has to import half of all cereals, as well as corn, beans and wheat. The country's trade deficit increased by 400 percent in the six years between 1984 (US $134.9 million) and 1990, from $134.9 million (U.S.) to $568.7 million (U.S.).[5]

By requiring massive cuts in state spending, the SAPs are designed to reduce the external debt burden. In 1997 in Costa Rica, the foreign debt amounted to 27.8 percent of the gross national product (GNP), which was the lowest level in 10 years, but this mainly represented a shift toward the national internal debt, which then amounted to 29 percent of the GNP.[6] According to the Costa Rican government, "every year over one-fourth of the public expenditures are spent on paying the [debt] interest, and this is money that could be used for social services."[7]

Although the GNP in Costa Rica increased by 6.2 percent in 1998, this was mainly because of high foreign investment, especially in the areas of construction, transportation, communications and utilities (electricity and water services). Historically, when a nation's GNP increases, there is generally a similar decrease in unemployment and poverty, but this has not occurred in Costa Rica (unemployment was 5.7 percent in 1997 and 5.6 percent in 1998; poverty levels were 20.7 percent in 1997 and 19.7 percent in 1998). Some Costa Rican economists believe the reason for this is that the GNP increase was mainly a result of an expansion of bank credits rather than a real increase in production.[8]

Contrary to the optimistic predictions of SAP supporters, the number of people living in poverty in Costa Rica climbed from 21 percent in 1989 to 28 percent in 1991.[9] And more recently, according to the Costa Rican Statistics and Census Office, 19.7 percent of citizens didn't have enough money to meet their basic needs.[10] The poorest 20 percent of the population spend most of their income on food, leaving very little for clothing, transportation, communication, education or health.[11]

As in many countries worldwide, poverty among women is far higher than among men. SAPs have had an impact on the growing feminization of poverty in Costa Rica and throughout Central America, for four major reasons:

1. Women have always been the poorest of the poor, with lower wages and less ownership of land, so declines in real wages and jobs have a particularly strong impact on them.

2. Increased privatization has led to higher costs in health care, such that a growing number of families cannot afford proper medical treatment. Government spending on health declined from 29.7 percent of the budget in 1980 to 20.5 percent in 1992-95.[12] It is women who make up for this shortfall, taking on extra tasks as substitute nurses or caretakers, often in addition to working at paid jobs. And as with other domestic unpaid work of women, these tasks have no economic value in a market economy. Cuts in daycare services and support also create additional burdens for women.

   Public education is universally available in Costa Rica, and spending on education has decreased only slightly, from 23.7 percent in 1980 to 22.9 percent in 1992-95.[13] However, increases in the "hidden costs" of schooling, such as books, uniforms, lunch money and transportation, make it more difficult for a growing number of poor children to attend school beyond the elementary level. Of course, preference is given to boys if a family cannot afford to send all its children to school. It is most often girls who end up staying home to help with domestic work, and in many cases it is the mothers who end up serving as substitute teachers, trying to teach these girls at home. Literacy rates in Costa Rica are relatively high, compared with other Central American countries, but of the 5.2 percent in the population who are illiterate, 96 percent are women.[14]

3. SAPs have not only fuelled a widening gap between rich and poor, but also contributed to higher unemployment and lower wages, all of which

have taken a greater toll on women. In sectors where employment levels have actually increased, particularly for women, the positions tend to be low-paying, with few benefits and no job security. In Costa Rica, women comprise 59 percent of the public-sector workforce. With the cuts in state spending, 85 percent of the public-sector workers who have been fired were women. Overall, real wages declined 16.19 percent between 1980 and 1991.[15]

4. Women are more likely to put themselves last, focusing more on their families when it comes to food, education and health care, and so are far more likely to be malnourished, illiterate and have chronic health problems that go untreated. For example, between 1998 and 1999, there was a 26 percent increase in alcoholism among women in Costa Rica (versus an 18 percent increase overall in the country).[16]

Declines in economic prosperity have also contributed to a deterioration in social conditions, with widespread increases in crime and violence, particularly against women. Crime rates in Costa Rica climbed 3.9 percent annually between 1987 and 1995,[17] and there has been a 24 percent increase in homicides between 1998 and 1999, as well as a 20 percent increase in suicides (33 percent increase among women) during that same one year period.[18] Likewise, reports of domestic violence increased 216 percent between 1994 and 1998, according to the Costa Rican Women's Commission.[19] In 1994, the commission received 1,736 reports of violence against women by men; this increased to 15,007 in 1998.[20] Although these changes may be a result of increased awareness and better record-keeping efforts regarding domestic violence, rising levels of violence in society in general tend to have a disparate impact on women.

The Environmental Impact of Globalization on Women in Costa Rica

In general, globalization places greater environmental pressures on the South as a source of cheap natural resources and labour for the production of agricultural and consumer goods, which are in ever-increasing demand from consumers in the North.

The increased emphasis on agricultural-export production required by SAPs has provided jobs but has also led to greater pollution and environmental damage. Banana plantations, which are major exporters in Costa Rica, generate large volumes of plastic waste. And bananas, along with coffee and vegetables, rely on massive amounts of chemical fertilizers, which affect not only groundwater, but also the health and well-being of workers and residents in the area.

The three Tribunals on the Violations of Women's Human Rights in Costa Rica between 1995 and 1998 included testimonies of women banana workers, whose health and fertility had been severely damaged by the toxins used at their jobs. In the 1980s, male banana workers who had become sterile as a result of exposure to the pesticide PBDC received, in a non-judicial arrangement made when their case was brought to the courts in Texas, indemnization from the companies that produce and distribute it. However, although women have long provided evidence of the impact of these toxins on their own health through testimonies and personal experience, they were not included in the men's case because of the lack of "scientific" evidence of the effects on their health. And no official medical studies have included women until very recently in Costa Rica.

Philosophy of FIRE: Feminist International Radio Endeavour

Major media organizations in many countries have become increasingly globalized in recent years, merging to form ever-larger mega-transnational corporations. Not surprisingly, this trend brings no change in the tendency of most major news outlets to focus primarily on political and economic elites, rendering invisible those who are less powerful, including many women. And women of the Global South, including Central America, are even more invisible because much of the Global North's limited news coverage about this region falls under the "coup and earthquakes syndrome" (i.e., it focuses only on major disasters and catastrophes). Thus many people outside of Central America know little about the women who live there, beyond the Carmen Miranda-type stereotypes of Latinas presented in many Hollywood movies and TV programs.

Because of this, a primary dimension of Feminist International Radio Endeavour (FIRE) has been to give priority to individual women's lives and perspectives — to "give a voice to the voiceless" — on a variety of issues and events. FIRE is a radio program broadcast by the Associación de Comunicaciones Feminist Interactive Radio Endeavor (AC FIRE), which is a non-profit non-governmental organization (NGO) based in Ciudad Colón, Costa Rica. Among its numerous activities, FIRE has conducted live broadcasts from local, regional and global conferences and events, including the United Nations World Conference on Human Rights in Vienna in 1993, the World Conference on Population and Development in Cairo in 1994, and the NGO Women's Forum '95 and Fourth U.N. World Conference on Women in Beijing, China, in August/September 1995. In addition to international events, FIRE has also broadcast from local and regional events throughout Latin America, the United States, Africa, Asia and Sweden. These events have focused on, among other things, issues facing indigenous women, Black women, women with disabilities and women in journalism.

Since 1991, FIRE has been broadcast in Spanish and English over international shortwave radio to more than 100 countries worldwide, including those in Scandinavia, western and eastern Europe, Japan, South America, North America and the Caribbean. FIRE also rebroadcasts women's radio programs produced for local AM and FM stations around the world, thus "amplifying their voices." FIRE programs have been re-broadcast by women producers in local radio stations on all continents. Recently, FIRE began broadcasting on the Internet by uploading recordings of live broadcasts onto its Web site; it has plans to eventually do real-time live broadcasting over the Internet and establish a women's Internet radio station. Thus FIRE has developed a strategy of connecting multiple voices, technologies and actions by combining traditional and modern media.

The programs of FIRE address diverse themes, from a gender perspective. These include women's opinions on neo-liberal policies and SAPs, women's human rights, sexual and reproductive rights, the environment, sustainable development, racism, militarism, sexuality, education, and art and culture. FIRE is produced by a permanent staff of two Latin American and Caribbean women (Katerina Anfossi Gómez from Chile, and María Suárez Toro from Puerto Rico and Costa Rica). Other temporary staff members have in the past come from Costa Rica, the United States, Spain, Chile, Puerto Rico, France and Germany.

A primary dimension of FIRE has been the priority given to women's individual testimonies about their human rights and other life experiences. FIRE has organized or co-sponsored five tribunals on violations of women's human rights, including the Global Tribunal on Violations of Women's Human Rights in Vienna during the U.N. World

Conference on Human Rights in 1993. This event featured more than 40 women telling stories of forced marriage, lack of access to education, spread of fundamentalism, rape and other violence. Another tribunal organized by FIRE was the Latin American and Caribbean Radio Tribunal on Violations of Women's Human Rights at the Sixth Latin American and Caribbean Feminist Encuentro in October 1993 in El Salvador. More than 350 women listened to 19 women from the region describe violations of human rights, including violence; violations of economic and social rights and the right to a safe and health environment; persecution and repression during war and internal conflict; persecution and discrimination on the basis of race or ethnicity, disability, political choice or sexual preference; and violations of reproductive rights. Women who attended or heard FIRE broadcasts of these events said that the strength and courage of the women who testified inspired them to raise their voices to demand recognition of women's human rights and to continue the struggle for the respect of those rights.

Case Studies of FIRE as an Alternative Feminist Media

Since 1991, FIRE has broadcast hundreds of women's voices from around the world. In a number of situations, these broadcasts have led to policy, political or social changes that empowered women. What follows are four case studies of FIRE's actions at the local, regional and international levels — all illustrate the power of giving a "voice to the voiceless."

AN INDIGENOUS WOMAN'S FIGHT FOR HER LAND

On January 19, 1995, FIRE received a phone call from a Bribri-Cabagras indigenous-*campesina* woman from the province of Puntarenas in southwest Costa Rica. Death threats by a local transit policeman had prompted Paulina Días Navas to call. Paulina said that she chose FIRE because two years earlier, in 1993, she had been on a live broadcast at the Fifth Interdisciplinary Congress in Costa Rica, and she'd seen how word spread very quickly on shortwave.

"This is Paulina Navas calling FIRE from the town of Bolas in Buenos Aires, Costa Rica," she began. "I want to go live on the air on FIRE because I have received a death threat." Paulina, a single woman, told

FIRE and its listeners that the policeman had threatened her with a gun because he wanted to take her inherited land away from her. She told the story of her family's 70 years of resistance to keep their land.

"When I was 12 years old, my father was put in jail through blackmail so that, in the meantime, the land could be taken away from us. He was a Bribri who did not even speak Spanish. It did not work, and now when [my father] is dead, they are after me."

Paulina's father and brother left the land to her when they died. "Nowadays, my land is surrounded by land belonging to big owners. Because my land belongs to me, a single woman, they feel I am vulnerable enough to have it taken away by them." She had tried to take her case to the local court, but the policeman had intimidated her neighbours to try to convince them not to testify on her behalf. Women in the town who supported her cause were sexually harassed. "They are afraid to leave their houses or testify," she stated. "I want the case to be denounced beyond the community."

Paulina told her story on FIRE in 1995 during a live broadcast. FIRE took the report to the ombudsperson's office in Costa Rica, and also sent information to women's groups and human-rights organizations worldwide, asking for letters of support.

A year after the original broadcast, FIRE contacted Paulina for an update and learned that the policeman who had threatened her was now in prison. "Today, my ownership of the land I inherited from my family is mine and is respected! We indigenous women have to be respected; our right to our lands, our indigenous women's rights to work the land, have to be respected."

Paulina described how the campaign launched by the FIRE broadcast resulted in an outpouring of support from around the world, which in turn prompted the minister of security to order an investigation and demand that the local police protect Paulina's rights to her land.

"I am thankful to these organizations, because they accompanied me and a little path to justice was opened for me to tell people what I was going through. Today I am respected in my land rights, and no police can harass me. Mine is a voice that, so long as I am alive, no one will silence in denouncing this and other violations of our rights."

Paulina's case illustrates one major impact of globalization, which is the accumulation of land, power and wealth among a few powerful elite, with less for the poor. Pressures to sell land to large landowners are common in many countries. Thus women, who often are left out in land-redistribution schemes by governments, may own land only through inheritance, and even then are pressured to sell out to large landowners. Such pressures are particularly acute for indigenous peoples.

FIRE helped counter this power imbalance by giving Paulina a voice on international media, which enabled her to mobilize support for her cause, and ultimately end the threats and harassment of local officials. Through networking and building solidarity with national and international women's and human-rights groups, this indigenous woman was able to break through the isolation and silence that disempowers many women.

"FIRE is very important for the lives of women around the world," said Paulina, "because through FIRE's international communication, our rights are recognized." Paulina noted that she and other indigenous women are planning to ask FIRE to help them start an indigenous women's radio program.

In the past few years, Paulina has played an ever-more-active leadership role in the struggle for indigenous women's rights. She is head of the National Indigenous Women's Commission and the president of the Association of Indigenous Women Agriculturists in Costa Rica. In 1996, she was awarded the Women's Creativity Award from the Women's World Summit Foundation in Geneva, Switzerland. And recently she received an award in Nicaragua for her work with indigenous and *campesina* women in the Central American region.

A LOCAL ENVIRONMENTAL CAMPAIGN

In February 1994, the Costa Rican government decided, without consulting the local communities, to build in a rural area about 25 kilometres west of San José a large waste-disposal site that would handle all of the garbage from the capital city. However, the area selected is near El Rodeo Reserve, a protected environmental zone that includes the last forest of its kind left standing in the Central American region, and that represents a borderland between the Atlantic and Pacific ecological zones. It contains flora and fauna that can be found only there, including species that are near extinction. Placing a dump site in the area would have a major detrimental impact on the environment.

Such attempts that clearly affect environmentally protected lands have become more common in many countries, including Costa Rica. Under market-economy models, "development" is too often defined in terms of the political and economic interests of governments and businesses, rather than the preservation of natural areas. In addition, large-scale migration to the larger cities has fuelled increased waste and environmental degradation, and rural areas are viewed as dumpsites for nearby urban areas.

In response to the Costa Rican government plan, a local female environmental activist led the efforts of other women in the communities around the El Rodeo Reserve to fight against the proposal. They felt that a garbage dump would present a severe threat to the environment and the health of the families in the communities in terms of both food production and living conditions.

As part of the local community of El Rodeo, FIRE became involved in the fight and decided to do what it could using the power of radio. To promote the campaign to both a local and an international audience, FIRE conducted, on horseback, a radio "eco-tour" of the forest in the area, using walkie-talkies to transmit live back to the station. The FIRE staff felt that this strategy would enable them to bring to an international audience in more than 100 countries the natural environment that was the site of the controversy, thus giving listeners a chance to hear the birds and animals in the forest. During the eco-tour, FIRE staff also interviewed villagers who were working in their fields or homes and stopped to make comments about the campaign on the radio. "My ancestors lived here for ages … [The government is] selling out our health, our environment, and our peaceful living," said Doña Elida Quiroz of the village of El Rodeo.

In addition to the eco-tour, FIRE organized a call-in show, broadcast both on the air and by loudspeaker in the streets of a small town nearby. This enabled local citizens, including many women and schoolchildren, to talk about their concerns over the proposed dumpsite.

The results of the FIRE broadcasts were dramatic: listeners from both the local area and around the world started calling FIRE to find out more about the campaign. The novelty of the "first-ever radio eco-tour on horseback" prompted other media outlets worldwide, including the BBC, to pick up the story. By getting the voices of the women out to the local and international communities, FIRE was able to link their concerns with others', and that helped to put pressure on government officials, who eventually dropped their plans for the waste-disposal site. Ofelia Quiroz Azofiefa, one of the leaders of the campaign, noted that FIRE was a very important asset for the community, and particularly for women. "FIRE gave women a place in the world through communication," she said.

BRINGING GENDER AWARENESS TO THE ZAPATISTA MOVEMENT

In February 1996, guerrillas in the indigenous Chiapas-based Zapatista movement were heavily attacked by the Mexican army. Indeed, the invasion was so massive and so unexpected to the Zapatistas that, for a few days, they were isolated from one another, not knowing one another's fate. In an effort to find out what was really going on in Chiapas, Commandante Marcos, who was hiding in the bushes together with two other Zapatistas, pulled his shortwave radio out of his backpack (he had only a gun and the radio). He wanted to try to listen to international media coverage about what had happened, assuming that, as had often been the case, the local Mexican media would only repeat the army's press release about the results of the combat operation.

In scanning the shortwave band, Marcos came across a woman talking at length (in Spanish) about "las Zapatistas." He zeroed in on the program and for the next half-hour listened to this woman with a Mexican accent describing the historical struggle of women in the political movements of Latin America, and also their political participation in building the very same movements that excluded them. Marcos and his *compañeros* also heard her speak about how in a patriarchy there can be no real revolution unless gender is made a part of the agenda of social transformation and women are included in the decision-making process. The Zapatistas, frustrated because they weren't able to catch the woman's name and had missed the first half of the program, tuned in to the same frequency a half-hour earlier the next day for a repeat broadcast. Marcos learned that the program they had listened to was FIRE, broadcasting from Costa Rica, and that speaker was Marcela Lagarde, a Mexican feminist who was well known throughout the region for her reconceptualization of gender in social transformation. Lagarde's talk had been recorded six months earlier at the National University of Costa Rica in Herredia, but it was being replayed as part of FIRE's coverage of the latest assault on the Zapatistas.

A few months later, once their situation was stabilized, the Zapatistas asked Marcela Lagarde to come to the Selva Lacandona for a special meeting, the purpose of which was unknown to her. At the meeting,

Lagarde was asked by Commandante Marcos to become the "gender adviser" to the Zapatista movement. She accepted. Afterwards, Marcos told her that he had learned about her from the FIRE broadcast, and that she had helped him realize the importance of bringing gender issues into the Zapatista agenda.

These direct and indirect actions by FIRE illustrate another example of the radio program's efforts to combat globalization. Most major media outlets in Mexico, as in many countries, are controlled by local elites, so that the public rarely receives news of the Zapatistas outside of the perspective of the Mexican army and government. And with globalization, these same elites are combined with the international mainstream media through increased monopolization of ownership. So again, the perspective on issues such as the Zapatista movement remains limited. Thus the role of FIRE as an alternative voice is critical in bringing forth issues that are often silenced, especially in counter-insurgency warfare.

This case also showcases the fact that in women's media, unlike the traditional patriarchal formula, news is not only what is happening at the movement, the focus is not only on the immediate coverage of "hard news" events that is so common in mainstream media. Also, because women's voices and perspectives have been made so invisible, a talk such as Marcela Lagarde's, which took place months before, was news to a Mexican political leader, but he listened to and came to understand the importance of a gender perspective previously unknown to him. Marcos's willingness to listen to the FIRE broadcast is even more remarkable, given that the Zapatista women themselves had been struggling since 1995 to be included in the movement's agenda and decision-making. Perhaps, as reception-report studies by FIRE have shown, the intimacy of radio allows men to listen to women's perspectives without feeling threatened, giving them an opportunity to learn about new perspectives.

UNITED NATIONS FOURTH WORLD CONFERENCE ON WOMEN

About 31,000 women (and some men) from 185 countries around the world travelled to Beijing, China, in 1995 to attend the Non-Governmental Organizations (NGOs) Women's Forum, as well as the U.N. Fourth World Conference on Women. Participants met to discuss and strategize a platform for action that focused on 12 issues, including the feminization of poverty, violence against women, access to education, health care, the impact of armed conflicts on women, the participation and advancement of women in political and economic decision-making roles, women's human rights, media and communications, and access to new technologies. The document was designed to be used to press national governments to take action on these issues on behalf of women in their respective countries.

Despite such widespread participation and efforts on a vast array of issues, the mainstream media rendered practically invisible the work of the thousands of participants at both the NGO Forum and official U.N. conference. They instead focused on U.S.-China geopolitics, human-rights abuses in China, and sexual and reproductive rights as confronted by the Vatican and other religious fundamentalists. They also gave voice almost exclusively to "important" women, including heads of government delegations and controversial women such as Hillary Clinton, who talked about human-rights issues in China in her speech at the conference.

Such limited and homogeneous coverage, which is becoming ever more the norm in the globalized media, served to render invisible the diversity of women, both at the conference and worldwide, in terms of race/ethnicity, sexual orientation, nationality, disabilities and age. And major media audiences also do not hear about the central concerns and strategies of the international women's movement on a vast array of economic, social and political issues.

Fortunately, FIRE was a major presence at the conference, organizing 52 hours of live broadcasts as a joint endeavour with 24 other women's media organizations from all over the world. FIRE democratized the communication venues by giving voice to more than 200 women in Spanish and English, an achievement that reflects the diversity of not only the women present at the conference, but also the strategies and actions of the international women's movement. And FIRE gave voice to ordinary women, as well as to the "big stars."

Through this strategy, FIRE helped build connections not only among the conference participants, but also between these women and international audiences, who were eager to get more than the shallow and homogeneous view of the conference offered by most mainstream media. As one FIRE listener later wrote in a feedback letter, "I will never forget the daily broadcasts you made … uniting the women worldwide, and keeping their agenda alive in the midst of the intergovernmental negotiations. Thank you for the roads you have opened and the links you are weaving between women in the North and South."

FIRE also served as a catalyst for other women's media organizations, which developed mobile radio stations and grass-roots radio programs for women in many other regions of the world. In addition, many portions of the FIRE broadcast were made available on tape to be re-broadcast on radio stations throughout the world.

Thus again, FIRE's feminist efforts served to combat the influences of globalization on women. In the context of the conference, FIRE's broadcasts provided far more indepth and diverse reporting of events, but also served as a major catalyst for creating and enhancing connections among women both at the event and around the world.

Conclusions and Implications

Globalization is bringing major changes to many parts of the world. In theory, global economic and social trends should encourage greater diversity through market competition. But, in fact, this diversity is only superficial, because dominance of the competition by ever-fewer transnational corporations means that the global homogeneous message is that we should all eventually eat the same foods and wear the same shoes.

And the global media is no exception. Mainstream media outlets may present different voices, but a closer examination reveals that most represent the same overall perspective, which is supporting the status quo and the forces of globalization. And women's voices and perspectives are rarely present in great number unless featured within a patriarchal advertising, entertainment or news framework.

As the four case studies in this essay illustrate, FIRE puts into action a feminist communications strategy of connecting voices, technologies and actions as a counterforce against the negative impacts of globalization. The producers of FIRE use a popularization strategy developed through their many years of experience in Central American social and political movements. This democratization involves putting the power of the media in the hands of women in terms of both content and production, using both the traditional medium of radio and, more recently, the Internet, a new communications technology.

FIRE first started broadcasting from Costa Rica in 1991, and for many years it was the only feminist shortwave radio program. The medium of radio has a long history in Latin American social and political movements, particularly during dictatorships that maintained strict control over the press. As a relatively inexpensive and simple technology, radio, and particularly shortwave radio, could be broadcast from many different locations and under many different conditions. As described in the case studies, FIRE staff have found creative ways of using technology to meet specific objectives. For these reasons, FIRE has deliberately used very simple, portable and accessible technology for its radio programs.

As part of its feminist popularization strategy, FIRE has often invited women to become "radio women" at various events, providing them with simple, on-the-spot training on the use of the tape recorder or broadcast equipment, which enables them to interview other women on their own for FIRE programs. These new "radio women" have often been very young or much older women, who will offer unique perspectives on the event or issues, thus adding to the diversity of voices in FIRE coverage. The result is that FIRE puts the control of the production in the hands of women themselves, which is far different from the actions of most traditional mainstream media.

Reception-report studies of FIRE have provided considerable evidence of the success of their feminist communication strategies in using radio to "give a voice to the voiceless" and in making connections with women, as well as men, around the world. This research has shown that radio has been a very effective way of reaching women, for a number of reasons. First of all, radio is the least expensive medium, and women are a majority of the poor. Second, radio is often used as a secondary medium to be listened to while doing something else, and women are frequently busy with multiple tasks, both at home and in the workplace. (Women employed picking crops or engaged in industrial work, such as in the *maquilas*, are often allowed to listen to the radio for entertainment while working.) And third, radio is an important companion medium for women, and is a readily available source of advice, with local call-in shows and the like.

Another important factor is that radio provides an intimacy and a certain sense of freedom that is not found in other media. Women feel more comfortable calling a talk show or be interviewed on the air, because they know that they will be judged first by what they say, rather than how they look. And FIRE's reception-report studies indicate that many of their male listeners say that they are often more willing to listen to women's, and even feminists', perspectives on radio, because they have the power to turn it off. Thus the intimacy of radio may help bridge the gap between men and women.

Presenting a diversity of women's perspectives on various issues and events is just one aspect of FIRE's feminist communications strategy. These perspectives often come in the form of testimonies from women, gathered via interviews, speeches or discussions at events. Some FIRE programs are produced by the staff with edited cuts and narrations, but a majority of FIRE programs are made up of unedited interviews and live broadcasts that enable women themselves to frame the issues and events from their own perspectives. In addition, many broadcasts utilize tapes sent in by women who wish to contribute to the diversity of voices presented on FIRE. In contrast, most mainstream media outlets impose restrictive patriarchal frameworks on issues and events, often rendering invisible (or at minimum, distorting) the voices and perspectives of women, particularly those from developing countries.

These patriarchal pressures are also evident in the mainstreaming of gender and feminism that is now occurring in institutions such as the United Nations; many feminists run the risk of being mainstreamed into the status quo, especially when they begin using U.N. jargon and talking primarily to the U.N. establishment. The feminist media keeps the multiplicity of alternatives alive by bringing to the audience the realities and struggles of women's lives, which often contradict "advancements" being made in the law and in the system. The feminist media helps keep open the connection between the grass-roots, local, regional and international arenas, a connection that too often is lost in the process of mainstreaming. For example, women negotiators in the mainstream may "soften" their demands or language to make them acceptable to the status quo, while in feminist media women speak frankly and with their own language, keeping the alternative frameworks alive. If Paulina Díaz Navas had not had access to FIRE, she might still be pounding on the doors of mainstream radio stations. And if FIRE had not opened its microphones in Beijing to grass-roots women who were there, only the voices of "celebrity" and "famous" women would have been heard by the international community.

Recently, FIRE has expanded its media venues to include broadcasting over the Internet. The staff felt that this shift would enable them to reach more and different kinds of audiences, including many young people. But merely providing text summaries of FIRE's programs on its Web page was not enough. Because of their years of experience in radio, the staff believed that women's perspectives could best be expressed orally, so audio clips are a central feature of the Web page.[21] Also, Internet access and production are relatively democratic, in that the producers do not need to register or otherwise ask permission to make material available in most countries (once they have access to a computer, phone line and Internet account, which are admittedly expensive). Also, this form of international communication is far less expensive than those requiring satellites, ISDN lines, and so on. By linking its Internet broadcasts to radio, FIRE can re-broadcast on traditional radio, thus providing greater access to the programs, particularly for women.

In the future, FIRE plans to start a women's Internet radio station that will bring a combination of both traditional and modern media venues together. Thus FIRE plans to continue its feminist communications strategy of giving a "voice to the voiceless" and "empowering the disempowered," in order to provide an important counterforce to the negative impacts of globalization, particularly as they affect women.

Finally, after nearly nine years of fostering connections among women worldwide via various types of media, FIRE staff have launched an effort to link women through face-to-face meetings at the Institute for Community Development and Communications by Women (ICDCW) in Ciudad Colón, Costa Rica. Students from around the world come for two- to four-week sessions to live with families (primarily single women heads-of-households) and work on community-development projects with rural and indigenous women in the area. They also take a course entitled "Central American Women through Communications," which is taught by ICDCW professors as well as visiting faculty, and focuses on issues and actions of the Central American women's movement at the local, regional and international levels. Local women are hired as staff leaders in their particular area of expertise, which they teach to the students. The students then make a contribution by giving the local women a voice in the international media through interviews, and then write feature stories with video and audio excerpts, which they post as multi-media productions on the Internet. The result is that each side contributes to the exchange, and this often leads to a breaking down of the stereotypes that each had brought to the situation — stereotypes developed through globalized mainstream media.

Thus ICDCW and FIRE, with their feminist progressive efforts to subvert the negative impacts of globalization on women, both serve an important purpose for the new millennium. Using a combination of traditional media, new communication technologies, and intercultural exchanges, FIRE presents a variety of women's perspectives on issues and promotes women's connections at the local, regional and international levels. Such efforts represent the cutting edge of feminist action for the next millennium.

ENDNOTES

1. Shea Cunningham & Betsy Reed, "Balancing the Budgets on Women's Backs: The World Bank and the 104th US Congress," *Dollars and Sense: What's Left in Economics* 202 (November/December, 1995), pp. 22-25; and L.A. Lorentzen & J. Turpin, "Introduction: The Gendered New World Order," in L.A. Lorentzen & J. Turpin (eds.), *The Gendered New World Order* (New York: Routledge, 1996), pp. 1-12.

2. Cunningham & Reed (1995), pp. 22-25; Lorentzen & Turpin (1996), pp. 1–12; and "Defending the State, Empowering the People: An Interview with Ottó Solís," *Multinational Monitor* 17, 9 (September, 1996).

3. Karen Hansen-Kuhn, "Structural Adjustment in Costa Rica: Sapping the Economy," adapted from Karen Hansen-Kuhn, "Structural Adjustment in Central America: The Case of Costa Rica," *The Development GAP* (June 1993).

4. Hansen-Kuhn (1993).

5. Ibid.

6. *State of the Nation in Sustainable Human Development*, No. 4 (San José, Costa Rica: Editorama, 1997), p. 98.

7. Ibid.

8. "Incremento del 6.2% del PIB en 1998, Aumento Produccion," *La Nación* (February 17, 1998), p. 31A.

9. Hansen-Kuhn (1993).

10. "Listening to the Fire's Message," *Tico Times* (September 18, 1998), p. 2.

11. Espinoza, Mauricio, "Ups, Downs in Human Development: Ticos are `Richest Among the Poorest,'" *Tico Times* (September 18, 1998), p. 11.

12. United Nations Program for Development (UNDP), *Extracto Centroamericanodel Informe Sobre Desarrollo Humano 1997* (San José, Costa Rica: UNDP, 1997).

13. Ibid.

14. Ibid.

15. Hansen-Kuhn (1993).

16. "Otra sacudida: Informe de Desarollo Humano: sin tiempo que perder" (editorial), *La Nación* (July 13, 1999), p. 13A.

17. Hansen-Kuhn (1993).

18. *La Nación* (editorial; July 13, 1999).

19. Ana Carolina Mora, "Delegacion de la Mujer publicó libro: Se duplicaron las agresiones," *La Republica* (August 13, 1998), p. 10A.

20. "Nuestra cara invisible," *La Nación* (August 12, 1998), p. 13A.

21. Margaret Thompson, "Internet FIRE Spreads its Flames Into Cyberspace," *Tico Times* (April 16, 1999).

WOMEN AND THE UNIVERSITY AS CORPORATION

A Call for Feminist Response

Mary Beth Krouse

As we approach a new millennium, there are trends in higher education that are escalating the exploitation of those who work as academics, especially women and members of racialized groups.[1] Several scholars have emphasized that these trends can be linked to the fact that more and more universities are being structured in accord with the capitalist, patriarchal bottom line of cost-efficiency.[2] Cary Nelson and Barbara Ehrenreich point out that all the buzzwords of hyper-capitalism are fitting; universities are downsizing, outsourcing, subcontracting work, converting full-time labour with benefits to temporary and part-time labour without benefits, and cutting costs through the use of technology. Bill Readings explains that the move in these directions coincides with the changing role of the university as an institution within the transnational global economy. He argues that because capital now reproduces itself at a transnational level, rather than at the level of the nation-state, it is no longer necessary for the university to uphold national culture as it once did. One general implication is that there is less importance placed on the traditional humanistic disciplines and on the content of what is being taught. Instead, the university is becoming a consumer-oriented corporation. Consequently, as Readings points out, it now makes sense for Ford Motors to partner with The Ohio State University to attain "total quality management in all areas of life on campus."[3] This quality control is maintained in the name of "excellence," *the* watchword within the university these days. But Readings emphasizes that this term is especially useful precisely because of its emptiness of meaning. The word "excellence" masks the fact that it is the logic of capitalism that guides decisions about university policy. This term justifies the mounting pressures on academic labourers to work ever longer hours and to turn out more and more "products," such as published articles and books.

The increasing exploitation of labour on campuses is the first of three trends in higher education that I examine more closely below. Another is the greater control over education and "knowledge" exerted by administrators and non-academic powerholders, which more and more involves turning knowledge into a commodity. And the final trend is the intensified promotion of surveillance of labourers in higher education. In addressing each of these, necessarily in broad strokes, I emphasize that the forces driving these developments are the patriarchal and Western imperialist forces of capitalism, and that "knowledge" produced in higher education increasingly serves the interests of domination. Meanwhile, the university is being rebuilt particularly on the exploitation of women, racialized groups and those who are not economically privileged, both within and outside the university. The practices and mind-sets that make this possible are misogynist, racist, (hetero)sexist and elitist, and their effects reach well beyond university campuses. Therefore it is crucial that women and men committed to feminist social change together resist these trends.

Toxic Trends in Higher Education

THE INCREASING EXPLOITATION OF LABOUR ON CAMPUSES

WORKING-CLASS SERVICE WORKERS:
Academic labour must be seen within the larger network of labour that creates the conditions for its existence in the first place. Therefore my discussion of the increasing exploitation of labour on campuses begins with a focus on working-class service workers. Robin Kelley highlights the important point that as the number of service jobs has increased dramatically, universities and hospitals have become two of the largest employers of service workers. Citing a U.S. Department of Education statistic,[4] she reports that colleges and universities directly employed more than 2.5 million workers in 1991. She notes that among these workers is "a vast army of clerical workers, food-service workers, janitors, and other employees whose job is to maintain the physical plant," emphasizing that "these workers are more likely to be brown and female than to be the good old blue-collar white boys we're so accustomed to seeing in popular culture."[5]

As "cost-efficiency" has become the watchword for the corporate university, staff and faculty have been downsized, resulting in layoffs, wage freezes, and speed-ups. Kelley stresses that service workers are the lowest-paid and most exploited labourers on campuses, that racialized groups and women are concentrated in these service jobs, and that racism and sexism are used to justify their treatment. Universities have also increasingly used non-unionized and temporary part-time labour. As Kelley recognizes, subcontracting to outside firms not only allows for the reduction of wages and benefits for service workers, but also disguises the degree of exploitation actually occurring on campuses and blocks local unionized labour. Meanwhile, divisions between women on campuses grow as female faculty and administrators remain ignorant of, or indifferent to, the heightened exploitation of working-class labourers. Some even have a direct hand in that exploitation. Divisions also grow between academics and local communities whose economies are directly affected by "cost-efficient" university practices. These practices include not only the hiring of non-unionized labour, but also the buying of local properties for conversion to businesses that cater to students' and universities' interests, all in the name of development. What can result is the displacement of affordable housing and alternative sources of employment, and the increased burden on communities when universities bargain with local governments to avoid property taxes.

Even though the forces working against all labourers on campuses are often the same, both Nelson and Kelley suggest that elitism, racism and sexism keep many faculty members from identifying with working-class labourers and learning from their struggles against exploitation. Dorothy Smith and Adrienne Rich each claim that it is the labour of women that makes possible the privileges of men in academics — both their economic advantages and their control of knowledge production.[6] This analysis needs revision to highlight the fact that any privileges that still exist within the university are held in place by a network of exploited labour that extends through the entire global economy. This exploitation is not only gendered, but also racialized and elitist, and is hidden behind catchwords such as "accountability," "academic planning" and "excellence."

GRADUATE STUDENTS:
The labour of graduate students is one of the primary targets of increased exploitation on campuses. To put this in context, it is important to look at some of the most recent trends effecting students in general. There is the assault on affirmative action, which is threatening to

exaggerate even more how much access to higher education is linked to race, gender and class. Due to the passage of Proposition 209 in California, a bill to end affirmative-action programs in the state, offers of admission at U.C. Berkeley's law school were down 81 percent to African Americans, 50 percent to Hispanics, and 78 percent to Native Americans for the 1997-98 academic year.[7] Similar trends are appearing in other California schools. The rising costs of education continue to limit its access to privileged groups, with the government replacing grants with loans and terminating tax deductions for student-loan interest.

Bearing in mind, then, that discrimination selects those who have access to graduate education in the first place, those who do receive graduate appointments can expect to provide academic labour for the least possible compensation. Graduate students are teaching a growing percentage of course offerings, with pressures to teach sometimes keeping them from completing their own degrees. According to the American Association of University Professors, graduate students teach more than half the introductory offerings at many large U.S. universities. Earning usually between $1,000 and $3,000 per course, graduate assistants are paid well below living wages, forcing them to shoulder substantial debt. As Cary Nelson, Stanley Aronowitz and several others maintain, the fact that graduate- student labour is absolutely strategic to the workings of universities is cloaked in the language of opportunity. The labour of graduate students is framed as an "apprenticeship," which justifies the minimal pay, and the unionization of graduate students is fought on this basis. The use of paternal (or maternal) or sexualized language by faculty sometimes further hides the exploitation of graduate students. For example, this happens when faculty suggest to students that tasks such as running library errands or calculating grades provide important career preparation or will earn the student special favour with the faculty member.

PART-TIME AND ADJUNCT FACULTY:
Nelson refers to part-time and adjunct faculty as the "permanent underclass" in academia, and clearly it is women who are most concentrated in this underclass. The extent to which these faculty are exploited is difficult to overstate. Like graduate students, part-time faculty receive an appalling $1,000 to $3,000 per course, wages that change very little year after year. As Linda Ray Pratt notes, even when

these faculty teach six courses per year or more, they are still called part-time.[8] Some are legendary "highway flyers," or "gypsy scholars," who attempt to piece together a livelihood by travelling between part-time appointments. Pratt fills in the grim picture that results for part-time faculty: outrageously low wages; no job security; no retirement benefits; no research or travel support; inadequate office space; no representation in decision-making; no eligibility for teaching awards; and the added stress, energy and expense of applying for jobs year after year. When these conditions are contrasted with the privileges enjoyed by faculty who are in the highest ranks in universities, ranks that are still overwhelmingly populated by men, the gendered structure of higher education becomes obvious. Further, as so often happens when exploitation takes place, the very labourers who are most exploited are also most blamed for their own situation. For example, when full-time positions are open, those making the hiring decisions (including women faculty and administration) often assume that anyone who has been job-searching for consecutive years is less competent or less desirable as a candidate.

Pratt reports that the percentage of faculty holding part-time positions in the United States is growing dramatically, from 22 percent in 1970 to nearly 45 percent in 1992,[9] which well exceeds the rate of increase for the United States overall, even though that increase is quite high. From the logic of cost-efficiency, the reasons for the prevalence of this trend are clear. The costs saved in the salaries of part-time and adjunct faculty are what allow the university-as-corporation to function, since these faculty do about 45 percent of all the college and university teaching in the United States.[10] The common practice of turning to the spouses of (white, male) tenured faculty to fill these positions has heterosexist, racist and patronizing implications. Yet, again, the language of opportunity often is used to cloak this exploitation.

TENURE-TRACK AND TENURED FACULTY:
Tenure-track and tenured faculty encounter some of the same types of exploitation that other academic labourers experience. For example, it is not uncommon these days for colleges and universities to advertise positions as tenure-track, but terminate after a few years those who are hired so that the wages for these positions can be kept low. Ever-higher standards of productivity are used to justify this practice. A parallel trend involves the appearance of positions that are created from the outset to

offer tenure but not promotion. These are low-paying, teaching-only positions that are designed to staff low-level courses and are targetted at those who are structurally positioned to fill them — mostly women.

At the other end of the scale, there is momentum toward the creation of highly rewarded "superstar" research positions. Leon Anderson and Mara Holt note that access to these positions depends on conditions that are more likely to be enjoyed by white males. Such conditions include having fewer courses to teach; less involvement with students outside the classroom; greater freedom from some types of service responsibilities, such as committee work; and the greater likelihood that a partner is freeing them from responsibilities at home. They add that the move toward superstar positions as a means for universities to gain academic prestige reinforces publication productivity as the overriding criterion of academic merit and ups the competitive ante for all in higher education. All this contributes to a sense of failure among those who do not enjoy the resources or the workloads that allow such "productivity." We might expect that superstars also are more likely to act as the gatekeepers of their fields, making critical decisions about whose work gets published and what counts as reliable "knowledge." If this is true, there are implications for even more dismissal of the work of academics who are not white, male and economically privileged.

Of course, these trends contribute not only to a sense of failure but also to the actual failure of those who do not receive tenure. And as Shelley Park reminds us, those who are granted tenure are still more likely to be male and white.[11] For those who are fortunate enough to be in tenure-track or tenured positions, workloads are swelling in service, teaching and research. Leon Anderson and Mara Holt point to a number of reasons for these increases.[12] Administrators' efforts to restructure and downsize universities result in fewer full-time faculty having to shoulder the increasing burden of service. This potentially cultivates divisions between tenure-track and tenured faculty when pre-tenure publishing pressures collide with expectations that all full-time faculty share heavier service loads. Anderson and Holt observe that one reason why service expectations have increased is because administrators, equipped with technology that can manage ever more information, have escalated demands for "accountability" from faculty, resulting in dramatically more labour-intensive paperwork. They note that greater service expectations also are accompanied by the "speed-up" of academic research and pressures to increase full-time faculty teaching loads. For example, in 1997 the Ohio Board of Regents directed Ohio universities to increase their faculty teaching loads by 10 percent. Again, Park reminds us that the heaviest teaching and service loads tend to fall to women from racialized groups and white women. She notes that one of the reasons for this is that women, especially women of colour, are sought out as positive role models for individual students, student groups and community organizations. She also observes that women, as well as men, of colour are often sought for university service to insure minority representation and to signal university commitment to diversity.

LESBIAN, GAY AND WORKING-CLASS FACULTY:
Although not enough research has been done to give the following point the attention it deserves, heterosexism in universities does operate to systematically exclude lesbian, gay, bisexual and transgendered scholars from the more rewarded positions in higher education.[13] Verta Taylor and Nicole Raeburn show that lesbians and gays in sociology, especially those perceived to be engaged in political resistance, face "discrimination in hiring, bias in tenure and promotion, exclusion from social and professional networks, devaluation of scholarly work on gay and lesbian topics, harassment and intimidation."[14] William Norris and Toni McNaron find similar evidence of discrimination against lesbian and gay faculty. Norris's research also documents the abuse suffered by staff and students, even at one of the most liberal campuses in the United States. His and other campus studies reveal that this abuse includes physical violence, property damage, threats of exposure, verbal and sexual harassment and social ostracism.

Those of us who are lesbians suffer particular forms of discrimination and abuse.[15] When faced with the financial stress that many women in academics encounter along their career paths, lesbians have no male income to cushion the blow. Financial and emotional support from family is in question when lesbians who are out are not accepted or when closeted lesbians are threatened with exposure. Fear of reporting sexual harassment or other forms of abuse is especially heightened for lesbians attempting to avoid exposure. The struggles with invisibility and finding voice in male-dominated literatures and departments are all the more complicated for women who are closeted or for those who are out and targeted for abuse. Sometimes the very work for which lesbians should be credited and promoted is what remains hidden, as when articles on lesbian topics are left off vitas and long hours spent in support of lesbian, gay, bisexual and transgendered organizations and students are not claimed. Many lesbians face barriers to research and teaching focused on lesbian topics, barriers that are grounded in both misogyny and homophobia. And we who experience these forms of discrimination and alienation are often isolated or hidden from one another, moving through professional or personal crises without vital social support.

Also receiving far too little attention and research is the impact of class in the experiences of academics. Yet some authors have documented that, for working-class people in higher education, class has everything to do with institutional barriers to upward mobility.[16] These barriers affect access to such things as Ivy League education; current books and journals; research and conference sites; and money for initial, uncompensated professional expenses or to get through periods of financial stress. Michelle Tokarczyk and Suzanne Sowinska, as well as bell hooks, discuss the fact that many working-class academics feel torn between their professional lives and their roots, without a sense of belonging in either setting.[17] Under severe pressure to conform to the demeanor of the privileged, they sometimes feel it necessary to surrender all class-identifying traits — such as mannerisms, forms of speech, ways of expressing emotions and intellectual curiosities — and ways of locating themselves in the world. All these factors, and many more, keep working-class academics among those who are most marginalized and exploited in the corporate university.

CORPORATE CONTROL OF HIGHER EDUCATION AND "KNOWLEDGE"
Several authors have emphasized that, especially in the last decade, there has been a marked power shift within the university that has displaced academic decision-making from faculty to larger administrative bodies, boards of trustees and state legislatures — central locations of patriarchal power. Corporate logic, which is focused on downsizing and the job market, dominates decision-making and replaces academic priorities. Virtually all realms of the university and its mission are affected. Decisions from these sites of power have everything to do with how the university is structured, who staffs its positions at all levels, who attends universities, what is taught and published, how teaching and writing take place, and how "knowledge" gets defined.

The structure of the university is controlled through crucial decisions made about such issues as funding and its allocation, who occupies the most powerful positions in universities, what departments and programs are created and cut, how tasks are assigned and evaluated, what directions job security and tenure take, and how technology is used. All these decisions are effected by top administrators, university trustees, government legislatures and grant donors — corporate, government and private. How the university is structured then directly influences who is hired, and who and what is taught and researched. For example, control over who attends universities is exercised through decisions about funding of education, costs to students, admission standards and affirmative action. As we have seen, these decisions continue to privilege white men. We also have seen some of the (hetero)sexist, racist and elitist patterns that emerge in regard to who is hired to teach and do research. However, for a fuller understanding of the workings of power in higher education, it is important to see how domination takes place through defining "knowledge" as a commodity.

The more the university becomes a corporate enterprise, the more knowledge is approached as a commodity that is to be produced, packaged, advertised, sold and consumed. Under these conditions, knowledge is deemed to be relatively scarce, and therefore something that should not be accessible to just anyone. Control over the definition of knowledge and its value is maintained in part by the Western patriarchal power structure of science. Western science still requires that knowledge of the highest value be objective, analytical, specialized and instrumental — capable of accomplishing desired effects. Knowledge by this definition is a zero-sum game. One either has it or not. Universities sell it. Students consume it. And those of us who are faculty are trained to compete with one another to produce it.

Furthermore, strict criteria for "objectivity" and "rationality" strip knowledge of its connections to personal lives and to the political forces that create oppression in people's lives. Therefore, as hooks, Patricia Hill Collins and many others express, those of us who come to academics hoping to understand the pain in our lives actually undergo severe pressure to disconnect from and deny those experiences — and to approach ourselves and one another as objects.[18] When scholars such as hooks and Collins resist this pressure and expose the workings of power that create oppression, their work is dismissed. When they offer new criteria for knowledge that are consistent with the lives and knowledges of Black women, criteria that emphasize women's experiences, community dialogue, accountability and caring, often they are not taken seriously. Those who buy into Western patriarchal definitions of knowledge, male and female alike, use phrases such as "not rigorous enough" or "not theoretical enough" to discard their work. This is not to suggest that anyone's scholarship is beyond critique, but that one of the fundamental ways that domination happens in academics is through limiting critique to white male standards.

How these standards are developed and enforced depends, in part, on whose work gets promoted and published in academia, and publication is closely linked to the funding of research that often comes from corporations and the government. It is white men who are most strategically positioned to grant such funding, as well as to receive it and to publish as a result of it. But the effectiveness of patriarchal criteria for knowledge also depends on the extent to which all of us, inside and outside academia, buy into and enforce Western scientific prescriptions for credibility. The "objectivity" that is fundamental to Western science requires that subjects be approached as objects, and objectification is a central move in all forms of oppression.[19] This insistence on objectivity can be found to underlie many instances of oppression in universities.

Dorothy Smith discusses how what is required for an objective stance is a distancing, or abstraction, from everyday lived experiences. She demonstrates that it is possible for men in academia to remain so distant only because the exploited labour of women keeps them from having to deal directly with such things as dirty dishes and diapers in the home, and clerical and service chores at the office. Smith emphasizes that as men then dominate in the realms of research and publishing (knowledge production), the abstract and objectifying view they promote is what erases evidence of the gender oppression that holds their privilege in place. She also points to the rage from men that results when women challenge male "rationality" or defy their subservient placements.[20] And in some of her most recent work, Smith shows that by framing reports of sexism in the objectifying, courtroom language of "allegations" and "evidence," men in academics distract from the substance of these reports and hide the gender order from which they take their privilege.[21] It is especially important to note that these are techniques of oppression used both inside and outside academia, with effects that are at once (hetero)sexist, racist and classist.

There are many other techniques like these used in academia. For example, Berenice Carroll explains how the slippery notion of "originality" is used to credit men's scholarship and to discredit women's, even though the term is empty of meaning.[22] However, hooks makes it clear that such moves are made not only by men, and not only in regard to gender. She shows that when those who resist oppression of various types do write as subjects, the authority and credit for their work is more readily given to the privileged who attempt to speak for them or who present these ideas as their own.[23] Many feminist writers who address and resist multiple structures of domination point to the objectifying practices of scholars, including feminist scholars, who deny subjects their voices and perspectives. Mohanty, for example, explains how many Western feminists "re-present" women in the Third World in contrast to an assumed first-world norm, suggesting a notion of an "average Third World woman."[24] Writing or teaching in this way characterizes all women from Third-World countries as the same poor, uneducated victims. These practices erase the complex material realities of these women's lives, by defining them as objects and ignoring their self-representations. Mohanty also shows how objectifying effects are created in classrooms when "differences" are reduced to characteristics of individuals and are not recognized in relationship to larger contexts of power, history and knowledge. She exposes how this treatment short-circuits awareness of racism in multicultural programs in all levels of education and in many corporations and businesses.[25] Roxana Ng explains that this reduction of "difference" to the individual level makes it possible for those with privilege to subvert and trivialize feminist statements with their own claims of "not feeling safe" or "feeling silenced."[26]

These are just a few of the critical ways in which oppression operates through cultural representations in classrooms. Arlene Stein and Ken Plummer give another example, showing how heterosexist assumptions organize social theories as well as classrooms and other social spaces. This results in the invisibility and oppression of those who identify with sexualities that challenge the dominant sexual order. The exercise of imperialism through culture shows up in university settings in countless ways to silence and commodify the self-representations and perspectives of those on the margins in the corporate university.

Knowledge that resists commodification and challenges the status quo tends to involve scholarship that makes the larger connections necessary for critique. This knowledge is often interdisciplinary, interactive and time-consuming, which is barely possible within the frantic pace of production speed-ups. In fact, the management of time is central to the containment of critical knowledge in fundamental ways. Randle Nelsen points out that the takeover of computer technology has resulted in cultural notions of time that strip knowledge of any critical or reflective potential.[27] "Computer time" turns knowledge into linear information used for practical (commodity) purposes. Nelsen suggests that this framing of time gives priority to speed, information and the trivial, over reflection, meaning, and connections between knowledge and political contexts. Shelley Park emphasizes that the radical redefinition of concepts, theories, and research and teaching methods that takes place in feminist scholarship clashes with the push for quantity in research production. With production speed-ups, a lack of time and sheer exhaustion keep faculty from sharing common experiences with colleagues and students, including any experiences that reveal oppression and cultivate a larger, more critical view. Educating for critical consciousness becomes all the more difficult as class sizes grow and as education takes place more and more through television or over the Internet.

As Stanley Aronowitz points out, critical knowledge also is managed as it is tolerated at elite undergraduate institutions while being more closely controlled at larger universities, where most research is done. Such knowledge is marginalized with the hiring of "minority" faculty into programs such as Women's Studies, Black Studies and Gay and Lesbian Studies, where pay is minimal and job security is not guaranteed. These programs often are also set up to be in competition with one another for minimal resources.

Structural support for critical knowledge dwindles as the criteria used to hire and reward academics increasingly hinge on the acquisition of grants, which more and more often are reserved for commodity applications. Aronowitz discusses the implications for the social sciences, in which theory is reduced to an unimportant subdiscipline and areas relevant to policy, or "state social science," take priority. He points, for example, to the growing prominence of criminology within sociology. Criminology programs produce labourers for law enforcement and prison systems. This serves state interests, particularly in the United States, where racialized populations are being imprisoned in alarmingly high percentages and inmates are being employed by corporations for below minimum wage. Meanwhile, the number of women in prisons has more than tripled since the 1980s.[28]

Aronowitz gives other examples of how knowledge produced in universities is being used for commodity applications. He notes that funding in physics is being directed primarily to solid-state physics, which serves corporate interests in technology, information and communications. In biology, most grants are being given to studies for bioengineering, and pharmaceutical companies are funding various departments in exchange for patent ownership. And of course, as Aronowitz observes, U.S. universities have been accepting defence contracts from the government to provide technology and information since before World War II. In a recent development that has dramatic implications for the commodity application of academic information, the U.S. Congress approved a 1998 bill that contains a Freedom of Information Act, paving the way for government and corporate access to research data collected in any federally funded institution.[29]

It is particularly significant to note that the commodification of knowledge promotes division among women in academics. Because of downsizing, we are set up to compete with one another for positions, salaries, publications, grants, graduate students, merit awards, teaching awards, and other resources that insure academic job security and success. We are encouraged to distinguish ourselves from one another rather than to recognize the commonalities within our struggles. As we compete to produce knowledge, we are most rewarded not only for allegiance to Western patriarchal standards of knowledge production, but also for forcing those standards on our colleagues and students. And yet it is those very standards that systematically dismiss the work and the careers of faculty and students who promote knowledge from the margins. This is the domain of surveillance and assessment.

GROWING SURVEILLANCE IN ACADEMIA

Many critics have emphasized that, partially because of developments in technology, academics are being subjected to more and more assessment and surveillance. Bill Readings, however, points out that much of this is self-surveillance, similar to what takes place in Michel Foucault's panopticon, a mechanism of state control used in the 18th and 19th centuries.[30]

The panopticon was a prison that was circular in structure, such that all cells were entirely visible to a guard's station in the centre of the structure, and were also entirely visible from each cell. Prisoners could not see into the guard's station, and so did not know when they were and were not being watched. Having to assume that they were always being watched — as well as continuously feeling the eyes of other prisoners on them — prisoners soon engaged in self-surveillance, eliminating the need for the guard altogether.

Readings suggests that the contemporary university, which "understand[s] itself solely in terms of the structure of corporate administration," is not as oriented to visual observation as it is to "exhaustive accounting," but the effect is similar.[31] Thus those of us in higher education continuously engage in self-surveillance and in the surveillance of one another. We do this because we are required to account for every minute of our time; undergo tenure, post-tenure and departmental reviews; serve on various committees (i.e., budget, promotion and tenure, and assessment committees); do teaching evaluations — either our own or those of our colleagues; evaluate others' writing for publication; present or critique at professional meetings; defend theses and dissertations; take exams; get graded on academic work; and engage in countless other activities that require evaluation according to established standards. What is important to remember is that these are the standards of a capitalist, patriarchal structure, a structure that is generated by "a profit economy which needs outsiders as surplus people," in the words of Audre Lorde.[32] Therefore, they are misogynist, racist, heterosexist and elitist standards that work to define both knowledge and personal identities. The implication for those of us who have the privilege of working in academics, and yet in various ways are defined as outsiders, is that such surveillance becomes an exercise in self-loathing and the loathing of "others."

That sounds strong. However, these exercises set us up to feel that our work is never adequate, much less excellent. We are encouraged to work continuously, and yet to feel that we are never quite working hard enough, long enough, efficiently enough or with the right priorities. And we are set up to feel shame for those times when we do resist the status quo. Worse yet, we are positioned to use these same standards against one another. As I have indicated, this situation is especially toxic for academic women who are racialized, do not identify as straight, or are of working-class backgrounds — women who, in our own specific circumstances, are so far from "home" on college and university campuses.

Clearly, one of the most crucial points to be made here is that, to the degree that those of us in academia fail to confront these standards, we are creating one another's oppression — and our own — with our complicity in racism, classism and (hetero)sexism. We work against one another not only through direct acts, but also through allowing our work to be rewarded by the very criteria that are used to marginalize other women's work. This happens when feminist teachers and authors in heterosexual relationships rush to let their audiences know that they are feminists but not lesbians. It happens when there are opportunities to support, hire, reward and promote colleagues whose work fundamentally challenges commodified knowledge, but women not only choose to align themselves with those in positions of power, but also convince themselves of the appropriateness of doing so. It happens when women use implied or stated contrasts between themselves and other women colleagues as leverage for their own promotion. But there are countless possible points of resistance, ones that involve concrete and significant ways of making a difference within higher education.

Directions for Feminist Activism

It is critical that feminists both within and outside academia respond to these trends in higher education, because their consequences are far-reaching. As we have seen, decisions made at universities about such issues as employment and development projects directly impact on local economies in several ways, affecting job opportunities, housing, taxes, labour unions and costs of living. In the larger view, universities not only supply the labourers and technological information that directly affect government and corporate policy, media, medicine, advertising, law enforcement and so on, but also define norms about gender, race, sexuality, ownership, age, desire, authority, nation — in fact all cultural notions, including those central to the oppression of women. Universities are some of the primary locations where history is written and decisions are made about whose realities are spoken and honoured, and whose are buried or exploited. And because higher education also has been one important realm in which the status quo has been critiqued and challenged, and therefore one of the main locations of feminist activism, the erosion of the conditions for such critique makes it vital that all feminists respond.

As Smith, Foucault and many others have suggested, every order has within it contradictions and the potential for disorder. There are various aspects of the present situation in academics that can be used to create change. For example, the university as corporation is more oriented than ever to the demands of students as consumers. Therefore, students can have some effect on courses, their content, and on academic policy, by making demands and using their power as consumers. The fact that teaching is disproportionately done by women at universities has the potential to result in more education for feminist critical consciousness, in spite of the pressures against that. The increasing (although not proportionate) presence of women in administrative roles in academia has the potential to bring more feminist consciousness into decision-making on campuses. Internet access among activists, both within and outside higher education, provides the possibility of heightened communication, support and mobilization among feminists. And the growing presence of people of colour in the U.S. population creates mounting pressure on universities to grapple with issues of race.

However, if these and other potential leverage points are to have actual consequences, it is crucial that feminists commit themselves to seeing and responding to the ways in which higher education operates as a part of global capitalism. Because the relationships between higher education and global capitalism are continually changing and can be very subtle and complex, careful attention to this larger picture must be an ongoing priority. Those of us within higher education can cultivate a critical view of academics within our scholarship, teaching, formal speaking and interactions with colleagues. We can recognize and resist the forces that work to defeat critique, such as the pressure, so consistent with a corporate model, that we become so specialized in our own areas of expertise that we lose all sight of the larger workings of power.

As we closely examine the university as corporation, more specific avenues of response become apparent. Feminists can work for and support the unionization of service workers, graduate students and faculty, for example. We can become aware of university policies in relationship to local communities and act on them. We can fight the tearing down of affirmative action programs. In studying closely the relationships between the state and education, we can respond in many ways. For example, we can organize against legislation such as the Freedom of Information Act that gives the government and corporations massive amounts of information — not only technological information, but also data from research on such things as drug use, sexual practices and undocumented labour. Those of us in higher education can examine closely the connections between how we choose to do research and government and corporate control. When feminists see connections, such as those between the state supplying cheap labour to corporations and women in prisons, we can choose areas of research, majors, careers and so on that reveal and resist these practices. Feminists in academia, especially those in administrative roles, can act in countless ways to defeat trends toward more exploitation and surveillance, and the misogyny, racism and elitism they put into place. For example, cost-cutting measures that see the increasing use of graduate student, part-time and temporary labour can be strongly challenged. Meanwhile, the direction of more and more funding toward "bloated administrations,"[33] highly rewarded research positions, and ever-changing and growing technology also can be challenged.

A central goal of feminist consciousness and activism must be to expose the workings of power that go on in academic processes of defining knowledge. As Mohanty stresses, strategies for change must be based upon continual and vigilant efforts to recognize how power works within academics to define subjective experiences, and this is fundamentally linked to how knowledge gets defined. Mohanty issues one call for response that is specific and urgent — that we resist the management of race and gender that happens when "difference" is reduced to characteristics of individuals, and larger systems and histories of oppression are hidden behind "democratic" claims of "different but equal."[34] There are many specific ways to address this call. Feminists can expose this logic in "diversity" and "multicultural" programs used throughout all levels of education, as well as in many corporations and businesses. Those of us who are involved in education of any type can examine our own ways of thinking and talking about experiences, structures and histories of oppression. Within and outside academia we can look at how this tendency to see "diversity" in individualized terms affects everything from hiring practices to the structuring of workshops, courses, conferences and textbooks. And these are just a few of the potential responses to one method of domination that works through definitions of knowledge and culture. Many more cry out for response. For example, although feminists have long resisted the insistence that knowledge be objective in order to be credible, we must continue to expose the subtle ways in which notions about objectivity, fairness, bias, evidence and democracy hide histories and structures of oppression.

We must expose and challenge the calculative thinking that dominates university interactions and the larger society. As Bin-ky Tan points out, this is the instrumental rationality on campuses that many social theorists have noted.[35] This way of thinking takes for granted that everything and everyone can and must be approached as objects for our use if we are to survive or succeed. This mind-set takes our focus off the present and fixes it on assumed goals that can never be reached. It suggests that our security depends on always achieving more, and that we cannot let down from continuous effort. With this mind-set, we look past the people we encounter to the purposes they serve for our interests. This is especially the case with production speed-ups that convince us we do not have time for any interaction that does not serve taken-for-granted goals. Therefore, as Nelsen explains, our time becomes yet another controlled commodity.[36]

For several reasons, it is essential that feminists challenge this control of time and the calculative thinking behind it. It is this mind-set that turns "others," as well as ourselves, into objects — the fundamental move of oppression. From this perspective, there is no time to step out of the logic of the system to connect with one another and to see and feel experiences of oppression — our own and one another's. Therefore we are divided from one another, from ourselves, and from a larger, more critical view. Transformation depends on feminists supporting one another personally and professionally, and taking the time to make these connections. This is especially the responsibility of those of us who have some of the privileges and rewards in academia, since we will have to forfeit some of these for the sake of this time. There is a great deal to gain, however. Feminists in all levels of education, in social movements, in the arts, in healing services and in many other realms have had, and continue to have, much to gain from one another. We must take back our time in order to reclaim vital connections, out of which comes the very power for our resistance.

ENDNOTES

1. An earlier version of this article was first presented as the Plenary Address at the conference entitled "Toxic Towers: The Impact of Higher Education on Women," University of Akron, Akron, Ohio, August 1997. My thanks go to Dawn Trouard for organizing this conference and inspiring this paper.

2. See, for example: Bill Readings, *The University in Ruins* (Cambridge, MA: Harvard University Press, 1996); Randle W. Nelsen (ed.), *Inside Canadian Universities: Another Day at the*

Plant (Kingston, ON: Cedarcreek, 1997); Cary Nelson, "Between Crisis and Opportunity: The Future of the Academic Workplace," in C. Nelson (ed.), *Will Teach for Food: Academic Labor in Crisis* (Minneapolis: University of Minnesota Press, 1997), pp. 3-31; and Stanley Aronowitz, "Academic Unionism and the Future of Higher Education," in Nelson (1997), pp. 181-214.

3. This is a quote from Janet Pichette, vice-president for business and administration at The Ohio State University, which appeared in: Aruna Jagtiani, "Ford Lends Support to Ohio State," *Ohio State Lantern* (July 14, 1994). This quote is also cited in Readings (1996), p. 21.

4. See: U.S. Department of Education, National Center for Education Statistics, "Integrated Postsecondary Education Data System," Washington, DC, 1995.

5. Robin D.G. Kelley, "The Proletariat Goes to College," in Nelson (1997), pp. 145-46.

6. Dorothy E. Smith, "Women's Perspective as a Radical Critique of Sociology," in S. Harding (ed.), *Feminism and Methodology* (Bloomington: Indiana University Press, 1987), pp. 84-96; and Adrienne Rich, "Toward a Women-Centered University," in J.S. Glaser, E.M. Bensimon & B.K. Townsend (eds.), *Women in Higher Education: A Feminist Perspective* (Needham Heights, MA: Ginn, 1993), pp. 121-134.

7. Jesse L. Jackson, "Civil Rights Gone Wrong," *Nation* 26, 4 (1997), p. 5.

8. Linda Ray Pratt, "Disposable Faculty: Part-time Exploitation as Management Strategy," in Nelson (1997), pp. 264-277.

9. Ibid., p. 265.

10. Nelson (1997).

11. Shelley M. Park, "Research, Teaching and Service: Why Shouldn't Women's Work Count?," *Journal of Higher Education* 67, 1 (1996), pp. 46-84.

12. Leon Anderson & Mara Holt, "The Way We Work Now," *Profession 98*, pp. 131–142.

13. To consider the scholarship that has been done, see: William P. Norris, "Liberal Attitudes and Homophobic Acts: The Paradoxes of Homosexual Experience in a Liberal Institution," in K.M. Harbeck (ed.), *Coming Out of the Classroom Closet: Gay and Lesbian Students, Teachers and Curricula* (New York: Harrington Park, 1992), pp. 81-120; Verta Taylor & Nicole C. Raeburn, "Identity Politics as High-Risk Activism: Career Consequences for Lesbian, Gay and Bisexual Sociologists," *Social Problems* 42 (1995), pp. 252-273; Toni A.H. McNaron, *Poisoned Ivy: Lesbian and Gay Academics Confronting Homophobia* (Philadelphia: Temple University Press, 1997); and Beth Mintz & Esther D. Rothblum (eds.), *Lesbians in Academia: Degrees of Freedom* (New York: Routledge, 1997).

14. Taylor & Raeburn (1995), p. 252.

15. For an extended discussion of discrimination against lesbians, see: Mintz & Rothblum (1997).

16. See, for example: Jake Ryan & Charles Sackrey, *Strangers in Paradise: Academics from the Working Class* (Boston: South End, 1984); and Michelle Tokarczyk & Elizabeth A. Fay, "Introduction," in M. Tokarczyk & E.A. Fay (eds.), *Working-Class Women in the Academy: Laborers in the Knowledge Factory* (Amherst: University of Massachusetts Press, 1993), pp. 3-24.

17. Michelle Tokarczyk & Suzanne Sowinska, "Lesbians, Class and Academia: Some Thoughts about Class-Based Identity and Difference," in Mintz & Rothblum (1997), pp. 221-233; and bell hooks, *Teaching to Transgress: Education as the Practice of Freedom* (New York: Routledge, 1994).

18. bell hooks, *Talking Back: Thinking Feminist, Thinking Black* (Boston: South End, 1989); and Patricia Hill Collins, *Black Feminist Thought: Knowledge, Consciousness, and the Politics of Empowerment* (Boston: Unwin Hyman, 1990).

19. For one of many feminist discussions of objectivity in science and its oppressive implications, see: Sandra Harding, *Whose Science? Whose Knowledge?* (Ithaca, NY: Cornell University Press, 1991).

20. Dorothy E. Smith, "Whistling Women: Reflections on Rage and Rationality," in W.K. Carroll, L. Christiansen-Ruffman, R.F. Currie & D. Harrison (eds.), *Fragile Truths: Twenty-Five Years of Sociology and Anthropology in Canada* (Ottawa: Carleton University Press, 1992), pp. 207-226.

21. Dorothy E. Smith, "Textual Repressions: Hazards for Feminists in the Academy," *Canadian Journal of Women and the Law* 9 (1997), pp. 269-300.

22. Berenice A. Carroll, "The Politics of `Originality': Women and the Class System of the Intellect," *Journal of Women's History* 2, 2 (1990), pp. 136-63.

23. hooks (1989).

24. Chandra Talpade Mohanty, "Under Western Eyes: Feminist Scholarship and Colonial Discourses," in C. T. Mohanty, A. Russo & L. Torres (eds.), *Third World Women and the Politics of Feminism* (Bloomington: Indiana University Press, 1991), pp. 51-80.

25. Chandra Talpade Mohanty, "On Race and Voice: Challenges for Liberal Education in the 1990s," *Cultural Critique* 14 (1990), pp. 179-208.

26. Roxana Ng, "`A Woman Out of Control': Deconstructing Sexism and Racism in the University," in Nelsen (1997), pp. 84-108.

27. Randle Nelsen, "Marking Time in Computopia: The Edubusiness University Revisited," in Nelsen (1997), pp. 26-37.

28. Meda Chesney-Lind, *The Female Offender: Girls, Women and Crime* (Thousand Oaks, CA: Sage, 1997).

29. Information about this bill is available on the Internet at: www.aaup.org/ ombalert.htm#background.

30. Michel Foucault, *Discipline and Punish*, A. Sheridan (trans.), (New York: Vintage, 1979).

31. Readings (1996), p. 29.

32. Audre Lorde, *Sister Outsider* (Freedom, CA: Crossing Press, 1984), p. 115.

33. Barbara R. Bergmann, "Bloated Administration, Blighted Campuses," *Academe* (November-December, 1991), pp. 12-16.

34. Mohanty (1990).

35. Bin-ky Tan, "The Professional Social Scientists and the Technocratic-Administrative System," in Nelsen (1997), pp. 38-50.

36. Nelson (1997), p. 26-37.

PART SIX
THE FUTURE OF ACTIVISM

FEMINIST ANTI-VIOLENCE ACTIVISM
Organizing for Change

Marina Helen Morrow

Introduction

Activism on violence against women is about to enter its fourth decade, and yet women and girls continue to experience physical and sexual abuse at the hands of men. Ending that abuse will require the structural transformation of patriarchal societies. Only a feminist anti-violence movement that reflects the interests and supports the solidarity of diverse groups of women can effectively contribute to this transformation. Much of early grass-roots feminist opposition to violence reflected these beliefs. Activists coming out of the civil-rights, anti-war and socialist movements attempted to develop theories and strategies that drew connections between social inequities and violence against women, and cross-cultural examinations revealed the extent of women's shared vulnerability to male violence. Significantly, feminists from a wide range of political positions converged in their recognition that violence and abuse posed significant barriers to women's equality.[1]

Although feminist activists and service providers have long been convinced of the prevalence of violence and abuse against women, the largest-ever Canadian study on the issue recently confirmed this. The report, released by Statistics Canada in 1994, found that one-half of Canadian women had experienced some form of male violence after the age of 16. Studies in the United States, and in Britain and surveys of women in the global South confirm that violence against women is a serious social concern internationally.[2] This is the single most important reason for feminists to reevaluate the strategies used for political organizing and the analytic frameworks for understanding the role of violence in women's oppression.

Ironically, the broader awareness of these issues by society has contributed to a dilution of feminist political analyses, and to a resurgence of apolitical frameworks for understanding violence — that is, frameworks where violence against women is seen to be rooted in the individual psychology of the women and men involved. This view does not seek to understand underlying causes. The way in which inequities between men and women are socially structured to condone — and tacitly facilitate — the violence of men are not addressed. This in turn allows for a focus on individualized solutions, which do little to change the material and social conditions of women's lives.

At the same time, society's increased attention on the issue of violence has also opened up a space where sociopolitical understandings can be strengthened. Increased international links between feminists, along with the analyses of women of colour, lesbians, immigrant women, women with disabilities, working-class women and First Nations women, have contributed to a more comprehensive understanding of the complexity and diversity of women's experiences. There's also a greater understanding of how different forms of oppression (i.e., based on race, economic class or experiences of colonization) intersect with sexism and violence. For example, it is now much more widely understood that economics often prevents women from leaving abusive men, and that criminal justice strategies may not work well for women who fear racist responses from the police and judiciary.

The challenge for anti-violence activists is to find ways to create transformative visions of what society can be, and to work successfully across women's differences. These two issues are closely linked. Analyses of male violence have to be deep enough to illuminate women's shared interests in change. Likewise, women's shared interests are revealed and structural analyses are developed through interaction among diverse groups.

The next century threatens to bring with it an increased assault on Canada's social-welfare system and on the gains of the women's movement. The decentralization and privatization of essential social services is having a devastating impact, particularly on immigrant, poor, working-class and elderly women. Over the last decade, women's organizations across the board have seen their funding levels decrease. This increased instability makes it difficult for anti-violence activists to provide adequate support services for women, let alone participate in the political advocacy work and coalition-building that is essential for broader social changes.

Weaknesses in some feminist theory and practice also undermine the progressive aims of anti-violence activism. Some forms of feminism, for example, are more committed than others to the development of broad-based women-centred movements that have social transformation as their vision. Further, the failure by some feminists to analyze the interconnectedness of all forms of oppression (i.e., sexism, racism, imperialism, heterosexism, ableism, classism, ageism, fundamentalism) has led to strategies that address only the concerns of a limited group (i.e., white, middle-class women).

These challenges threaten feminism's structural understanding of violence and the solidarity among diverse groups of women. However, research and interviews with Canadian anti-violence activists[3] suggest that new forms of practice and theory are emerging that reflect and sustain these analyses and alliances. These forms of analysis and practice, although diverse, share certain common features, which I have identified as "multicentred."

Drawing on the work of feminist writers who advocate that research be grounded in the lived experiences of women and who propose action-oriented research with emancipatory aims,[4] my own work is intricately linked to the goal of developing a broad-based, feminist anti-violence movement. Over the past decade, my work has allowed me to engage with the issue of violence against women from a variety of vantage points. As a front-line rape crisis and youth hostel worker, I saw with my own eyes the impact that male violence has on the lives of women and girls. The serious physical and psychological effects, as well as the broader social repercussions for women's self-determination, were made apparent to me in the day-to-day counselling and advocacy that I did as part of this work. The struggle to ensure that women's experiences were kept at the forefront of interactions with mental-health professionals, government agencies, the police and the criminal justice system taught me about the ways in which these institutions can work to deny, re-formulate or distort women's perceptions. Later, my work as a researcher, policy analyst and activist in various feminist political organizations gave me insight into the particular difficulties associated with maintaining radical, progressive politics in the face of myriad institutional obstacles, professionalization of services and the backlash against feminism.

Aside from the difficult day-to-day work of advocating for women under these conditions, there is also an ongoing struggle in feminist organizations to implement processes and practices that allow for alternative relationships (i.e., non-hierarchical and cooperative). These processes allow women to grapple in meaningful ways with the power inequities (i.e., sexism, racism, heterosexism, classism, ableism, ageism) that they are attempting to change through their work. The internal politics of feminist organizations thus take on a particular significance because there is an explicit recognition that women are, through their very actions, attempting to forge new social relationships. Feminists have not always been successful in their attempts to develop these new relationships, and some forms of feminism have replicated the exclusionary practices they were set up to challenge. Nevertheless, I am hopeful about the potential for change that a broad-based movement can foster.

Maintaining Structural Analyses

RECOGNIZING THE ROLE OF MALE POWER IN WOMEN'S OPPRESSION
The tension for anti-violence activists is between resisting simplistic calls to universal sisterhood based on women's shared victimization (which prevents us from recognizing women as social actors and from recognizing power inequities between women) and claims that no basis for solidarity among women exists (which obscures institutionalized male power). Unquestionably, the struggle to identify violence as a concern for all women has led to analyses and practices that reify gender or "institutionalize difference." Chandra Mohanty takes issue with Robin Morgan's analysis in her successful collection *Sisterhood Is Global: The International Women's Movement Anthology*. Of Morgan's analysis, Mohanty states:

> "Universal sisterhood, defined as the transcendence of the 'male' world, thus ends up being a middle-class, psychologized notion which effectively erases material and ideological power differences within and among groups of women especially between first and third world women and paradoxically, removes us all as actors from history and politics."[5]

Movement history suggests that some forms of feminist theory have been more successful than others at illustrating the connections between different forms of oppression and the simultaneity with which those oppressions are lived. The work of women of colour, immigrant women and First Nations women has been particularly important. For example, much can be learned from Black feminists who examine Black women's experiences of violence in the context of slavery and the racialization of

Black male and female sexuality, First Nations feminists who analyze violence in the context of colonialism, and the work of women in the South who analyze women's experiences in the context of imperialism and globalization.[6] Work by lesbians, disability-rights and anti-poverty activists has also been critical in this regard.[7]

Conversely, sometimes gender analyses have been displaced in efforts to avoid monolithic overarching theories of oppression and, ironically, in attempts to highlight race and class oppression. For example, the pressure on women to ally themselves with men of their particular race, class or sexual orientation sometimes undermines analyses of male power. For socially privileged women, alliances with privileged men serves to undercut structural analyses in favour of liberal and postmodern forms of feminism, which can obscure race and class privilege. For women whose communities are socially marginalized, identifying male violence may be seen as class or race "treason." Joyce,[8] a health worker in Toronto, described how she and other Black women were sometimes targetted in their communities for their work against sexism:

> "[T]hen of course there is the whole issue of taking up the issue of sexism with Black men in the community, which is something that a few of us are really strong about. And it targets us in the community, but it's something that we know that we can't stop doing because it has to be done. And you know sometimes for Black men it's much easier to say, well you are taking up a white woman's issue, and you have to remind them all the time that women in Africa had strategies for dealing with this before they had any interactions with Europeans."

Fatima, a woman working with assaulted women in the Portuguese community in Toronto, identified similar tensions:

> "There are people and members of the community who don't feel comfortable with having an agency such as ours ... I mentioned we were sponsored or helped along by the Catholic church ... and even then there were certain outspoken people who refused to acknowledge that there was wife assault and that it was a problem in the community. There are other members of the community that feel that the Portuguese community has been labelled in

negative terms and that here we are identifying the problems and making it worse for people, so there has been backlash."

This situation is exacerbated by dominant Euro-Canadian stereotypes of other cultures, classes, races and religious traditions as violent. These stereotypes are often used to excuse violence against women from these groups as culturally acceptable, forcing women to defend their communities against racist attack, while at the same time denouncing the sexism and violence of men in their communities.[9]

First Nations feminists in particular face these pressures as their communities work toward actualizing self-government. In these situations, discussions about internal power imbalances often are not welcome. An example of this can be seen in the long battle that First Nations women fought, and continue to fight, against gender inequities contained in the Indian Act and in disagreements regarding constitutional renewal (i.e., the Charlottetown Accord). In the later instance, the Native Women's Association of Canada (supported by the National Action Committee on the Status of Women [NAC]) opposed the accord because Aboriginal women had not been represented in the constitutional talks.

Analyses that suggest the violence of First Nations men arises directly out of colonization and the imposition of Christian European values have helped to popularize healing frameworks. But women who disagree with some healing frameworks because they do not recognize gender inequities may be reluctant to challenge male power out of concern both for their own safety and for the safety of their communities. On the other hand, these frameworks may be much more consistent with Aboriginal cultures and traditions than the legal and criminal justice systems of Euro-Canadian society. Whichever system is used, First Nations feminists are working both on and off reserves to ensure that male violence is addressed and that women's rights are respected in shifts to self-government.

Feminists must act against pressures to split forms of oppression off from each other, and instead maintain analyses that see violence against women as emerging out of historically and culturally specific practices, values and social relationships (of which sexism, heterosexism, racism, ableism, colonialism, imperialism and classism are integral ingredients).

STATE CO-OPTATION: REJECTING INDIVIDUALISTIC,
APOLITICAL PARADIGMS FOR UNDERSTANDING MALE VIOLENCE

Beyond feminist debates about the role of male power in women's oppression exist demands to adopt the theoretical frameworks, language and organizational structures of the mental-health and legal professions. As part of this process, grass-roots activism by survivors of violence has often been silenced. That is, the voices of women who have experienced male violence are no longer the central axis from which feminist theory and activism was developed, but are now the voices of "clients" with a very limited role in feminist theorizing.

The ways in which the progressive agendas of movements for social changes are gradually contained through interaction with the structures and ideologies of social and state institutions has been widely documented. At the heart of this is the dilemma that faces all social-change movements: that is, how to resist the social institutions that they see as responsible for the inequities they are protesting, and at the same time garner support for their services and influence systemic changes?

The activists I interviewed often identified chronic underfunding as one of the primary ways governments constrain activists from pursuing political advocacy. Brenda, a Toronto activist, indicated:

"[T]he volume of the work, the funding constraints, has also ... created a sort of hopelessness that I think is infecting lots of women in different agencies about our ability to deal with the political problems that exist for women. And I think that without people ever consciously saying it, ... people have just sort of adopted a ... 'I just want to deal with [individual counselling] and sort of retreat into/away from the enormity of the increasing complexity of the political work that needs to be done out there' ... So I think all of those things sort of happen simultaneously to make us more insular, less political, more fearful of politically engaging."

As Brenda suggests, this has led some activists to focus their energies on providing immediate supports for women (such as crisis counselling and shelter placement) and away from broader political projects. With respect to the shelter movement, Virginia, a long-time shelter worker in Toronto, reflected:

"I am quite critical, for example, quite analytically afraid in some ways of whether or not in fact the whole shelter movement didn't just make liberal white men feel even more safe about their privilege and whether in fact it didn't make things harder to change ... Because I think shelters serve this handmaid function for the state, and so the state feels that they have 'fixed' the problem, they have 'handled' the problem by spending money for shelters."

Immigrant women felt this problem most acutely, in part because their organizations often received less than their share of allocated funds, making them even more fearful of challenging government mandates.

Nevertheless, some organizations and coalitions have been able to focus on political work, usually because they do not have the pressures of providing direct services to women (as is the case, for example, with Education Wife Assault in Toronto, the FREDA Centre for Research on Violence against Women and Children in Vancouver, the Canadian Association of Sexual Assault Centres, and provincial transition-house associations) or because they do not accept government funding on an ongoing basis (as with the short-lived Women's Action Committee in Toronto and the more established Aboriginal Women's Action Network in Vancouver).

Feminist political work can also be undermined when funding schemes require collaboration among feminist organizations, state institutions and non-feminist organizations. Many feminists feel that rejecting such alliances is not an option, given the power of state intervention in women's lives; others feel that interaction with the state is the only way to effectively make change. Indeed, a number of collaborative projects have shown some success. One of the most notable is the Duluth Domestic Abuse Intervention Program in Minnesota. This program, which is now recognized internationally, brings together a wide range of community groups and institutions, and has actually had an impact on how the police and the criminal justice system respond to woman assault. Assaulted women are seen as partners with a role to play in designing actions to change institutional responses to violence against women. The program itself works as a collective and conducts extensive consultations with community representatives before it advocates for any type of change within the system. However, as one of the founding members indicated during my interviews, the success of the Duluth model has come not as a result of fundamental institutional changes but through the development of a very comprehensive and extensive monitoring and evaluation system:

> "No, it isn't transformation, it's reformist work. It's like institutional reform work and it's incorporated into people's thinking on one level but on another level you have to kind of be there all the time because they will slip not only back into old practices, but if they take it over they will operate it from their perspective, as managing cases, rather than from our perspective of how it affects women. So that's why we have to always be there."

Other collaborations that have enjoyed relative success include the Aboriginal Family Healing Project, which saw 11 Ontario NDP ministries and agencies work with First Nations communities in the early 1990s to address issues of poverty, housing, substance use and violence. The broad mandate of the committee was to develop a comprehensive strategy that would "promote healing and positive lifestyles for Aboriginal communities across Ontario."[10] Although the healing strategy was not the first time that violence against women had been assessed in Aboriginal communities, it was the most comprehensive community-based consultation ever undertaken with Aboriginal people in Ontario (more than 6,000 Aboriginal people across 250 communities participated). Most significantly, this project has identified its work as integrally connected to the process of self-government, which Aboriginal communities are currently working towards:

> "For both the Government of Ontario and Aboriginal communities, the Aboriginal Family Healing Strategy marks both a new approach to policy development and a tangible commitment to the successful realization of Aboriginal self-government. The Healing Strategy has been developed with the vision of self-government in mind and is in keeping with both the spirit and intent of the 1991 Statement of Political Relationship."[11]

Violet, who worked closely with the committee, did not describe its beginnings in quite the same way: "I mean, I could give it a very glamorous beginning, but it wasn't. The government recognized that it wasn't doing anything for Aboriginal people, and all of its millions of dollars being spent on violence ..."

The preceding examples show that activists have found ways to work in partnerships without severely compromising their feminist structural analyses. Other collaborations have not been as successful. In one instance, five research centres were set up across Canada to study violence against women; government funding was given with the condition that academics and community workers work collaboratively. The government gave control of the money to universities, which set up a power imbalance that was not always easily negotiated. Jan Barnsley offers some guidelines for how feminists can better evaluate and more cautiously approach such partnerships.[12] She suggests that more analysis and discussion are needed about the partnerships and their impact on feminist political agendas. Groups need to continually evaluate how partnerships will affect the lives of abused women, and when participating in partnerships should establish short-term specific goals (therefore avoiding the entrenchment of relationships between women's groups and institutions). It is equally important that groups that are drawn into partnerships advocate for a wide range of women's concerns to be represented.

The erosion of the welfare state means that activists now more than at any other time face cutbacks and loss of services. This is forcing new levels of self-reliance (i.e., intensified fundraising) and new alliances with private-sector companies (where a percentage of the profits made are contributed to feminist projects such as shelters). The state's disengagement — or, alternatively, its selective engagement — has shaped, and will continue to shape, feminist anti-violence work.

It has been argued that feminist service organizations will be able to maintain their radical goals only if they are able to incorporate and prioritize the voices of the women who use their services. Professionalization reinforces class divisions (working-class and poor women are most often the clients of agencies that employ primarily middle-class women). The adoption by many agencies of professional standards and middle-class values makes the systematic integration of issues related to class and poverty difficult.

For the full participation of poor and working-class women to occur, feminists must first commit themselves to working actively on issues related to poverty, such as welfare rights and housing. The 1996 Women's March against Poverty, sponsored by the NAC, is one example of how these issues are being addressed. Coalitions or exchanges with anti-poverty activists, as well as an inclusion of these issues in groups' current agendas, are necessary. Feminists must also be willing to look at the ways in which their organizations preclude the participation of working-class women, including critiquing how professionalization works against poor women's interests.

There is evidence that some groups are implementing "client-centred" models that allow survivors to participate more fully in decision-making bodies (i.e., opening up board positions to service recipients) and encourage women to act as their own political advocates. Groups in Vancouver and Toronto have adopted these models include Mothers on Trial (which brought together women who have lost custody of their children), Women of Courage (which developed out of immigrant and refugee women's experiences in shelters) and the Downtown Eastside Women's Centre in Vancouver. Another example can be seen in the activism of a woman in Toronto, who upon leaving her abusive husband initiated Project Esperance, a housing co-op for assaulted women. Stella, the woman who initiated this project, spoke about how her credibility was initially challenged because of her working-class and survivor identification:

> "[T]he fact that I was not acknowledged, a known feminist at the time that I began the housing project, I was just some battered woman looking to do — a do-gooder who really didn't understand the dogma, the ideology of feminism — well, my goodness, do we call that classist or what do you call that? Wherever it was it precluded my immediate participation and it slowed down the building of that housing project."

The Transition House Association of Nova Scotia has also been active in fighting for the participation of ex-shelter residents. In 1994 the association organized a conference, "Strong Women United for Change: Avoiding Revictimization." The move back to "self-advocacy" models that actively engage survivors is crucial to the project of social change. As Marilyn Struthers maintains, allowing space for the voices of battered women through formal structural mechanisms makes it possible to "reclaim the early radical feminist vision of social change."[13]

Working Across Differences

THE IMPORTANCE OF AUTONOMOUS ORGANIZING AND
RECOGNIZING MANY "CENTRES" OF THEORIZING AND ACTIVISM
Multicentred political models allow for many "centres" of activity within
the anti-violence movement. That is, they support communities of
women autonomously working on issues that are of importance to them.
In Angela Miles' terms, these autonomous processes are essential
because they allow women to "create themselves as the centres of their
own politics."[14]

The women I interviewed cited many things that they believed acted
against the recognition of many centres and the development of
constructive interactions among different groups of women. Oppressive
practices such as racism, classism, heterosexism and ableism, for
example, have had a dramatic impact on organizations and their ability
to provide services that are responsive to a wide range of women. These
practices have also prevented important political alliances (i.e., between
the anti-violence movement and anti-racist activists) or have mitigated
against the effectiveness of those alliances. Brenda, a Toronto activist, and
Eryn, who has worked in both Canada and the United States, felt that
white women needed to see the links between violence against women
and violence against other oppressed groups. As Brenda put it:

> "We [white feminists] can't any more ignore the oppression that
> [is] being experienced by people of colour in this city; we have to
> be part of it and that may cause us to reassess our so-called
> mandates in our agencies. There will be people here who will say,
> 'Racism? Why are you forming a coalition about police racism or
> police brutality? What has that got to do with violence against
> women?' And I think we have to be continually redefining that to
> broaden ourselves, take us into those avenues and to not allow
> compartmentalization any more of what issues of violence are ..."

Over time, these constraints have meant that particular feminist
standpoints have come to dominate, and some groups within the anti-
violence movement (i.e., survivors of violence, women of colour) have
been structurally hindered from participating fully in the discourses used
to understand violence against women and the strategies used to address
it. Nancy Fraser suggests that groups in this position can do one or both

of two things. They can adopt the dominant forms of, in this case, thinking and organizing, or they can develop what she terms "ideolects" that allow them to voice their own experiences. Neither of these positions, in and of itself, is sufficient for transformative multicentred politics. Instead what is needed is a "movement which, through dialogue and collective struggle, forges *new vocabularies and narrative forms* capable of giving voice to many kinds of women."[15]

Women who have been "working from the margins" of society are often seen to have special insights into the nature of their own oppression and the ways in which the dominant society functions.[16] Although the extent and form of this knowledge is debated, certain practices must be established to foster it more consciously. bell hooks, for example, speaks about how "much feminist theory emerges from privileged women who live at the center, whose perspectives on reality rarely include knowledge and awareness of the lives of women and men who live in the margin." She argues that the most visionary politics "will emerge from those who have knowledge of both margin and center."[17]

Communication among diverse groups of women who may not always agree on the same political strategies must begin with the acknowledgement of the power inequities among groups. Rather than seeing sharing power as a loss, privileged women must think of it as an opportunity to adopt new ways of looking at the world and their relationship to other women. Uma Narayan argues that the "goodwill" to learn about each other is not enough to bridge gaps of mistrust that are a result of social and political inequities. She suggests that "outsiders" (i.e. privileged groups) must exercise "methodological humility" and "methodological caution" in challenging "insiders" (i.e. oppressed groups) and their knowledge of oppression.[18]

Clearly, the ability of different groups to link with one another requires Euro-Canadian activists to recognize the importance of supporting political issues that are central to the survival of communities other than their own. Supporting the leadership of women of colour, First Nations women, women with disabilities, lesbians and immigrant women is key to changing the composition of feminist organizations and to shifting the policies and practices that have been built up around the experiences of only certain groups of women. NAC is one organization that has made a commitment to supporting the leadership of women of colour; the International Women's Day committee in Toronto is another. Many other organizations have gone through anti-racist reviews, which look at hiring practices, how incidents of racism are dealt with in the organization, and how to make their services more accessible to a broader range of women. The Toronto Rape Crisis Centre, for example, changed its name to Multicultural Women against Rape to reflect its new focus. A number of women I interviewed described how their contact with activists, particularly women in the global South, had influenced their understanding of violence against women. Anna, a counsellor for battered women in Toronto, described her changing awareness this way:

> "[W]hen I looked into how they [women in the third world] were framing it, I realized that they may in fact be doing something fundamentally different, whereby they are linking up issues of violence against women with economic issues and with the whole value of women in terms of ... every aspect of women's lives, and [making] those connections between access to birth control or access to any kind of health care and access to financial resources. I think it became clear that the issues are very interconnected."

Increased international linkages have bolstered the knowledge coming from women from different immigrant groups, working-class women, women of colour and First Nations women who have challenged the predominant strategies used to address violence.

Some feminists have tried to develop a "politics of difference" by designing collectives that attempt to allow for the participation of all members of the group, or by having a structure that allows for the formation of caucuses that meet separately and bring their concerns to the larger group. One group that has worked successfully with this latter model is Toronto Multicultural Women against Rape. Although sometimes effective, these structures do not always allow for incidents of exclusion to be adequately addressed. This is primarily because of assumptions that each group within a collective has equal power to bring its concerns forward, which ignores the structures of hidden power that exist in any group.

Other anti-violence activists support the idea of formal organizational methods for dealing with exclusions. For example, Sonya Boyce proposes a "Right to Refuse to Work Policy" to address incidents of racism. Her proposal includes: (1) a racial-harassment policy; (2) an advocate for those lodging a complaint, paid for by the organization; (3) an individual responsible for investigating complaints who has the power to institute changes; (4) an appeal process; and (5) ongoing anti-racism training.[19]

Although formal policies (i.e., sexual-harassment policies) are often limited in their ability to adequately address structured inequities, they can signify that members of an organization are willing to recognize the issues seriously. Ideally, policies and formal mechanisms work to ensure that racism, for example, is not construed as "a personality conflict" or "bad group dynamics." These procedures must be informed and bolstered by ongoing anti-racist education and the development of new and better methods of communication.

It is necessary to implement specific strategies for specific forms of exclusionary practices; however, finding concrete ways of addressing inequities should not overshadow the importance of using women's different experiences of oppression to shift our political and analytical frameworks. It is through repeated contact with different communities of women that these practices will emerge. In this respect, broad forums that attempt to struggle with these issues are also useful. The 1993 conference "Making the Links: Feminism and Anti-Racism," sponsored by CRIAW (Canadian Research Institute for the Advancement of Women) and attended by international feminists, is an example of such a forum.

BUILDING COALITIONS, FOSTERING ALLIANCES AND EXCHANGES
The women I interviewed differed as to whether they felt that coalition-building was useful for bridging gaps between women and for working toward social change. Some women suggested that the coalitions they had been part of "wasted" valuable time in debates about what the group should focus on (i.e., reaching a common agenda) or disintegrated because of incidents of racism.

Because coalitions can serve a number of purposes (i.e., information-sharing, development of political strategies, a means to ensure different groups' accountability to one another), it is important at the outset to be clear about what is to be accomplished. For disparate groups of women to support coalition-building, each must have a sense of what it can gain from its participation in the short term and what the possible long-term gains might be. Some activists suggested the use of short-term, goal-oriented coalitions might work better than long-term ones. At times, these ventures may not even be formalized, but rather may arise organically out of political need.

Perhaps the most powerful recent example of this is the widespread and varied efforts of Canadian anti-violence activists to protect the counselling records of women whose cases of sexual assault have been taken to court. Bonnie Agnew documents how defence counsels in criminal and civil cases, and even in tribunals, have increasingly been issuing subpoenas requiring therapists, doctors, shelter and rape crisis workers to hand over women's counselling records.[20] This issue first gained public attention in the case of Bishop Hubert O'Connor, whom four First Nations women testified sexually abused them in a residential school. During the trial, requests for the women's counselling and medical records were upheld by the court. This case and many similar ones sparked activism across the country — shelter and rape crisis workers shredded records rather than give them over to legal authorities. For their actions, many of these centres faced heavy legal fines and charges of civil disobedience. Lee Lakeman, a Vancouver activist, describes how the work of a broad range of feminists (i.e., including many individual workers, the National Action Committee on the Status of Women, the DisAbled Women's Network, the Legal Education and Action Fund, the Canadian Association of Sexual Assault Centres and the Aboriginal Women's Action Network), in conjunction with feminist academics, media personalities, lawyers, policy-makers and the Canadian Auto Workers' Union, managed to force the implementation of a bill that restricts the use of these records in court.[21]

Coalitions can be particularly powerful when they form to protest a particular court judgement or political decision. For example, a large number of Aboriginal and non-Aboriginal women protested against the ruling in the aforementioned O'Connor case (the guilty bishop was sentenced to participate in an Aboriginal healing circle, rather than serve jail time for his offences).

Apart from coalitions, many other creative exchanges allow groups to share their knowledge. In one example told to me, a well-established anti-violence organization used its credibility with the police to arrange a meeting between officers and women in the Tamil community. The Tamil women used the opportunity to teach police how to better handle domestic-violence cases. Another successful alliance saw the Cowichan Valley Independent Living Resource Centre Society and the Cowichan Rape/Assault Society in British Columbia team up to develop a participatory workshop and a facilitator's manual.[22] This partnership was designed so that women from both organizations could pool their skills to better address the needs of women with disabilities who had experienced sexual assault. The alliance continued beyond the duration of this initial project, and both agencies continue to work at increasing support and access to services.

These types of local projects are bolstered by broad-based international coalitions (including the New York-based Center for Women's Global Leadership, the regionally based International Network against Female Sexual Slavery and Traffic in Women, the International Solidarity Network of Women Living under Muslim Laws, the Global Alliance Against Trafficking in Women, and the International Commission for the Abolition of Sexual Mutilations). The increasing dialogue among feminists globally is helping to shift the parochialism and ethnocentrism of Northern feminists.

Although there are valid concerns that broad-based coalitions sometimes serve to "water down" feminist demands, connections with other social-justice activists can often be key to developing more comprehensive analyses of oppression. These alliances can also serve as important political strategies. Coalitions to protest the polices and actions of the G-7 (now the G-8) and the APEC (Asia Pacific Economic Cooperation) leaders' summits, for example, or to defeat the MAI (Multilateral Agreement on Investments), are critical. Examples of such coalitions include the People's Summit (or P-7) held in Halifax, Nova Scotia, in June 1995; anti-APEC organizing in Vancouver during the 1997 APEC leaders' summit; and widespread activism against the MAI.

Conclusion

The development of a broad-based feminist anti-violence movement requires multicentred analyses and practices, and these in turn require concrete interaction among diverse groups of women. Shared interest in change, shared visions and cooperative practice will emerge only from an understanding of the many and varied ways in which women are abused and controlled by men. Only with this understanding will analyses of the ways in which violence is used to maintain male power be strengthened and the critical importance of women working across differences in political solidarity be fully realized.

The pressures and challenges that seek to threaten feminist anti-violence activism have given rise to new forms of theorizing and new strategies. It was clear in my interviews, for example, that activists were strongly resisting individual, apolitical frameworks for understanding violence. Structural analyses of violence against women were being fostered in three ways: (1) by ensuring the participation of a broad range of diverse groups of women in anti-violence organizations; (2) by ensuring the equal participation of women who are survivors in anti-violence work; and (3) by broad coalition-building, which brings anti-violence activists into contact with a wide range of feminist and other social-justice activists.

That groups were becoming more diverse was evident. This diversity was forcing activists to recognize power differences in the movement and to implement mechanisms for dealing with exclusionary practices. Having women represent, as Brenda puts it, "each piece of a larger puzzle" was allowing for the emergence of a critical awareness of the ways in which women's needs differ. In fact, many activists were employing practices that allowed them to better respond to broader groups of women (i.e., by providing services in multiple languages and recognizing that certain strategies many not be equally useful for all women). There was evidence, too, that women of colour, immigrant women and First Nations women were becoming increasingly visible both within and outside of their own communities (i.e., in the National Action Committee on the Status of Women, Women's Health in Women's Hands, the Aboriginal Family Healing Strategy). This was displacing the dominance of Euro-Canadian women in the movement.

Exchanges with activists in other countries and international networks also appeared to play a critical role in the incorporation of a wider range of women's experiences into frameworks for understanding violence. Canadian activists who participated in the international campaign for women's rights encountered a wide range of women working to understand the role of imperialist economic globalization in their oppression. As each woman strives to see beyond her own vantage point, the possibility of supporting diverse strategies without sacrificing individual needs becomes possible.

The majority of feminist organizations receive funding from the government and their work requires ongoing interaction with institutions of the state. These interactions constrain the ability of feminists to analyze how state institutions work to reinforce the social inequities that foster men's violence against women. Many activists fear that their organizations will lose their funding if they actively challenge institutional and state structures. Further, the fact that feminist service organizations are only minimally and inequitably funded gives rise to competition between groups and maintains a crisis-ridden work environment, where political advocacy work and coalition-building is inhibited by the struggle of groups to survive financially. This has led, in some instances, to creative alliances and exchanges of resources.

Individually, many activists have already identified the importance of coalitions and exchanges among diverse groups of women. To build such coalitions, activists must draw on and strengthen strategies which resist traditional political paradigms that reinforce contestatory, oppositional approaches. The affirmation of the early feminist assertion that the "personal is political," and the use of identity politics as a critical form of consciousness-raising (as advocated by bell hooks), should help to ensure that political strategies do not get reduced to debates between two polarities.

The fragility of these newly emerging elements of multicentred theory and practice was evident in activists' reflections about the fragmentation of the movement and the predominance of apolitical frameworks for understanding violence. The ability of feminists to maintain and strengthen multicentred activism is, in part, dependent on their ability to see the ways in which women's lives are interconnected while still supporting one another's autonomous activism. A strong, broad-based movement should lead to deeper, more radical political practices and analytic frameworks — which, in turn, will contribute to the transformation of society so that women and girls can live free of male violence.

ENDNOTES

1. I want to thank the women who originally agreed to be interviewed in 1993 for the project from which this paper arises, as well as the many other survivors and anti-violence activists I have met over the years. Their strength and dedication to ending violence against women and girls is the foundation of this work.

2. See, for example: Martin Schwartz, *Researching Sexual Violence against Women: Methodological and Personal Perspectives* (Newbury Park, CA: Sage, 1997); Russell Dobash & Rebecca Dobash, *Women, Violence and Social Change* (New York: Routledge, 1992); and MATCH International Centre, *Linking Women's Global Struggles to End Violence* (Ottawa: MATCH, 1990).

3. The interviews on which this article is based were first conducted in Toronto in 1993 as part of my doctoral research, which was completed in 1997. In the ensuing years, my analysis has been supplemented through further research and participation in anti-violence activism in Halifax and Vancouver.

4. See, for example: Sandra Kirby & Kate McKenna, *Experience, Research, Social Change: Methods from the Margins* (Toronto: Garamond Press, 1989).

5. Chandra Mohanty, "Feminist Encounters: Locating the Politics of Experience," in Michelle

Barrett & Ann Phillips (eds.), *Destabilizing Theory, Contemporary Feminist Debates* (Cambridge: Polity, 1992), p. 83.

6. See, for example: Gloria Anzaldúa & Cherríe Moraga, *This Bridge Called My Back: Writings by Radical Women of Color* (New York: Kitchen Table Press, 1981); Gloria Anzaldúa, *Making Face, Making Soul/Haceindo Caras: Creative and Critical Perspectives by Women of Color* (San Francisco: Aunt Lute, 1990); Linda Carty, "Combining Our Efforts: Making Feminism Relevant to the Changing Sociality," in Linda Carty (ed.), *And Still We Rise: Feminist Political Mobilizing in Contemporary Canada* (Toronto: Women's Press, 1993); Karen Flynn & Charmaine Crawford, "Committing ` Race Treason': Battered Women and Mandatory Arrest in Toronto's Caribbean Community," in Kevin Bonnycastle & George Rigakos (eds.), *Unsettling Truths: Battered Women, Policy, Politics and Contemporary Research in Canada* (Vancouver: Collective Press, 1998); Anne McGillvray and Brenda Comaskey, ` everybody had black eyes ... nobody don't say nothing': Intimate Violence, Aboriginal Women, and Justice System Response," in Bonnycastle & Rigakos (1998); N. Gupta & Makeda Silvera, *The Issue Is 'Ism: Women of Colour Speak Out* (Toronto: Sister Vision, 1989); Angela Davis, *Women, Race and Class* (New York: Random House, 1981); Gerda Lerner, *Black Women in White America: A Documentary History* (New York: Pantheon, 1972); Paula Giddings, *When and Where I Enter: The Impact of Black Women on Race and Sex in America* (New York: Morrow, 1984); Patricia Hill Collins, "The Sexual Politics of Black Womanhood," in Pauline Bart & Eileen Geil Moran (eds.), *Violence against Women: The Bloody Footprints* (Newbury Park, CA: Sage, 1993); Toni Morrison, *Race-ing Justice, En-gendering Power: Essays on Anita Hill, Clarence Thomas and the Construction of Social Reality* (New York: Pantheon, 1992); Sharon McIvor & Teresa Nahanee, "Aboriginal Women: Invisible Victims of Abuse," in Bonnycastle & Rigakos (1998); Ontario Native Women's Association, *Breaking Free: A Proposal for Change to Aboriginal Family Violence* (Toronto: Ontario Native Women's Association, 1989); and Chandra Mohanty, Ann Russo & Lourdes Torres, *Third World Women and the Politics of Feminism* (Bloomington: Indiana University Press, 1991).

7. Consider the work of: Sharon Stone & JoAnn Doucette, "Organizing the Marginalized: The DisAbled Women's Network," in Sue Findlay, Frank Cunningham, Marlene Kadar, Amita Lennon & Ed Silva (eds.), *Social Movements/Social Change: The Politics and Practice of Organizing* (Toronto: Between the Lines, 1988), pp. 20-47; DisAbled Women's Network, "An Open Letter from the DisAbled Women's Network (DAWN), Toronto, to the Women's Movement," in Ruth Roach Pierson, Marjorie Griffin Cohen, Paula Bourne & Philinda Masters (eds.), *Canadian Women's Issues, Vol. 1: Strong Voices, Twenty Five Years of Women's Activism in English Canada* (Toronto: Lorimer, 1993), p. 225; Cathy Stevens, "Stopping Violence against Women with Disabilities," in Leslie Timmins (ed.), *Listening to the Thunder: Advocates Speak about the Battered Women's Movement* (Vancouver: Women's Research Centre, 1995), pp. 223-234; and Charlotte Bunch, "Lesbian-Feminist Theory," in Charlotte Bunch (ed.), *Passionate Politics: Feminist Theory in Action* (New York: St. Martin's Press, 1987), pp. 196-202.

8. The names used in this paper are pseudonyms.

9. A prime example of this was the treatment by the Canadian media of the murders of Rajwar Gakhal, a South Asian Sikh woman, and eight of her family members by her husband, Mark Chahal, in Vernon, British Columbia, in 1996. The media consistently attributed Chahal's violence to his culture and in particular to the constraints they saw as inherent to arranged marriages. The same "culture" talk does not appear in parallel situations in Euro-Canadian communities. For a discussion of the media treatment of these murders see: Yasmin Jiwani, "Violence Against Women Is Bigger Than ...," *Vancouver Sun* (April 13, 1996), p. A1.

10. Aboriginal Family Healing Joint Steering Committee (AFHJSC), *For Generations to Come, The Time Is Now: A Strategy for Aboriginal Family Healing* (Toronto, ON: AFHJSC, 1993), p. ii.

11. Ibid.

12. Jan Barnsley, "Co-operation or Co-optation? The Partnership Trend of the Nineties," in Timmins (1995), pp. 215-222.

13. Marilyn Struthers, "Structuring in the Voice of Experience: Creating Organizational Space for Women's Experience in Anti-Violence Organizations," Ph.D thesis (University of Toronto, 1995), p. 3.

14. Angela Miles, *Integrative Feminisms: Building Global Visions, 1960s-1990s* (New York: Routledge, 1996).

15. Nancy Fraser, "Toward a Discourse Ethic of Solidarity," *Praxis International* 5, 4 (1986), p. 429 [emphasis added].

16. bell hooks (*Feminist Theory: From Margin to Centre* {Boston: South End, 1984}) and Patricia Hill Collins (1993) are concerned with the development of Black feminist identities, while Naomi Scheman ("On Waking Up One Morning and Discovering We Are Them: Problems in Negotiating Positions of Power and Privilege," talk given at Philosophy and Women's Studies, Dalhousie University, Halifax, NS, 1994) is concerned with the development of Jewish women's identities (what she terms a "diasporic identity").

17. hooks (1984).

18. Uma Narayan, "Working Together Across Difference: Some Considerations on Emotions and Political Practice," *Hypatia* 3, 2 (1988), pp. 31-47.

19. Sonya Boyce, "Wanted Women: Women of Colour Encouraged to Apply-We Are an Equal Opportunity Employer," in Timmins (1995), pp. 235-246.

20. Bonnie Agnew, "Why Are Rape Crisis Centres and Transition Houses Engaged in Civil Disobedience?" (available from the Vancouver Rape Relief and Women's Shelter).

21. Bill C-46 requires the accused to prove the relevancy of a woman's records to the judge presiding over the case.

22. Stevens (1995).

FEMINISM

The Antidote to the Global Capitalist Economic Agenda

Joan Grant-Cummings

The globalization of the capitalist economic system through structural adjustment programs in the South (Asia, Africa, Latin America, the Caribbean), as well as economic restructuring in the North, have wreaked havoc on the lives of most women and destroyed our communities. Its proponents — largely the business and corporate elite, supportive governments and right-wing followers — have in the last two and a half decades sought to eradicate all other economic systems and devastate the social economy.[1]

As a consequence, the human rights of women and workers — including migrant workers and the unemployed, people living in poverty, indigenous peoples, people with disabilities and people of colour — have been violated in some way, shape or form. In every category, women's rights and conditions have been the most adversely impacted. This globalized capitalism relies increasingly on the exploitation of women's unpaid work for its survival.

This is the most important indicator of the inherent anti-woman, anti-feminist, discriminatory principles along which capitalism is constructed. For women, feminism is, therefore, an important antidote to this global capitalist beast.

Feminism is a women-led revolutionary imperative to make changes from an equality-seeking framework, changes that will reframe the "global family" from a human-rights perspective, ensuring that women, men and children are equal in all societies. Of course, women as a group are not homogeneous. Some groups of women who clearly identify themselves as part of the feminist movement have to consider not only the context of their own lived experiences within their communities and globally, and within movements of liberation such as feminism, but also the fact of their oppression within other arenas. Specifically, the lives of Aboriginal women, women of colour, lesbians, women with disabilities, women living in poverty, immigrant women, refugee women and women who work at the bottom of the corporate heap differ greatly from the "average" Canadian woman, whoever she may be. This leads many women to frame feminism within the context of their complete identities and the different revolutionary struggles they may simultaneously engage in and experience. Their knowledge base and full experiences challenge feminism to incorporate an integrated analysis of equality.

It is important to enunciate our definition of feminism, as it will inform the actions we will or must take to ensure that our society is a place where human rights and equality rights are guaranteed and protected. While human rights are our birthright and it is the responsibility of our governments to ensure that they are not violated, feminists know that they are violated daily. Male violence against women and other forms of sexism; racism; lesbophobia and homophobia; ableism; ageism; lack of access to health care; bias in the justice system; xenophobia; bias in the educational system; poverty; forced migration; inequity in our work places and our homes; sexist media portrayals; and so on — all are ways that the rights of women are impacted upon daily. On top of this, the new economic world order has rapidly created the greatest economic apartheid we have ever seen.

The globalization of the capitalist economic system is not an accidental phenomenon or a natural course of events. This is a well-thought-out and orchestrated plan by the corporate capitalist business elite. In 1976, the Business Council on National Issues (BCNI) was formed in Canada, with a membership of 150 corporate giants. It developed a long-range plan of how Canada (along with its G-7 partners) could actively support corporations largely from the G-7 nations, with the aim of fully integrating them nationally, and thus internationalizing capitalism. In other words, destroy or discredit any other economic systems, control all markets and control the agenda.

One major component of the BCNI's plan was to silence, isolate and discredit the voices of those social-justice movements that they saw as "too influential" on government. Of course, this included the feminist movement. The other "culprits" in their books are the labour movement, environmentalists, human-rights activists, anti-racist groups and other anti-discriminatory movements.

Some Feminist History

To adequately understand this issue, some global feminist history is necessary. The 1960s and the 1970s were different for feminists in the South than for feminists in the North. The restructuring of the capitalist economy had already been implemented in the South, through structural adjustment programs (SAPs), by the time feminists in the North caught up in the 1980s and 1990s. The analyses of SAPs by feminists in the South has thus been instructive for many feminists in the North, and has furthered our understanding of the latest make-over of the capitalist beast.[2]

Simply put, SAPs are the economic and political processes used by governments in the North to pressure countries in the South to adopt a capitalist economic system. G-7 countries like Canada, thinking about how to maximize profits with little cost, saw the South as a source of cheap labour. Using the power of the International Monetary Fund (IMF) and the World Bank (WB), they pressed the countries of the South to "develop" and liberalize their economies. They influenced governments by offering them major loans and encouraging them to build factories and to aggressively mine, log and farm the land. But the loans from the IMF and the WB were given at high interest rates and with many strings attached. With debt payments undermining the economies of the South, governments ended up cutting social programs and other progressive means of development.

Let us look at the results through Southern women's eyes: the destruction of women's own markets; the destruction of women's own economic systems; reduced or no land ownership; the loss of indigenous lands without compensation or restitution; the destruction of traditional farming practices and their subsequent replacement with cash crops; the underdevelopment of health, education and social-service systems; the disappearance of traditional social and cultural ways of community development; the disappearance of traditional diets and eating patterns; an increase in women's poverty; under- and unemployment; trafficking in women and girls; the phenomenon of the feminization of migration, when women leave their communities to seek work as domestics, migrant workers and so on, in the "rich nations" of the North; increased civil-rights violations and a loss of democratic structures within societies; widespread abuses and inequities in workplaces; the phenomenon of the urban poor and the homeless, who were indigenous peoples displaced from their lands; the feminization of poverty.[3]

I grew up in Kingston, Jamaica, when all of this was occurring. The profits made by the higglers (street vendors) within their own markets literally paid off Jamaica's IMF loans when the elite and the business barons diverted their profits from the suffering of the poor — largely women — into American, Canadian and other foreign banks. There are always those who reap benefits from the suffering of the people, especially under the auspices of the IMF and the WB. You see, the terms of the IMF and the WB loans demanded that none of the money borrowed be put toward indigenous farming practices. All food produced as a result of these loans must be put toward export markets.[4] Still today, in many countries of the South, two-thirds of the goods sold in the marketplaces hail from the North, and are not indigenous to the land.

In the face of this, how then can governments in the South truly develop health, education and social-development systems? It is a testament to the tenacity, resistance and abilities of the people of the South that there still remain today any traditional cultural practices, foods, social systems, identities, and so on, and that resistance to global capitalism is actually growing.

In the North, in the 1970s and 1980s, feminists, armed with recommendations from the Royal Commission on the Status of Women, were pushing and pressuring governments to make: changes for employment rights; state-funded daycare; anti-violence programs; changes to the justice system; a women's equality fund; changes in economic policies; changes to the Immigration Act; and so on. Word had started to spread about the SAPs and their impact on the political, economic and social life of countries in the South. Yet Northern feminists did not for the most part see or understand the threat to the North. It was not until the end of the 1980s and the beginning of the 1990s that Northern feminists realized we needed to look at what was transpiring in our own backyard.

Simultaneously within the feminist movement, the work to deal with racism was also beginning to take root. Women of colour and Aboriginal women had started to openly and publicly challenge their white sisters in the movement; within the National Action Committee on the Status of Women (NAC), the challenge and struggle was public, vocal and instructive in terms of organizational change. NAC's ultimate adoption of anti-racist feminism had a major impact on its international work and its understanding of the capitalist economic restructuring process.

In fact, a feminist analysis, in the North, of the capitalist economic restructuring process eventually included an anti-racist analysis of globalization, exposing the racism implicit in globalization.

Additionally, work with women from the South changed from a patronizing, prescriptive feminism to an anti-racist, equality-seeking perspective, and the analysis of women from the South was valued and fully integrated in the economic analyses of women in the North. In developing its analysis of the federal government's policies and programs from an anti-racist, feminist perspective, NAC broadened, not narrowed, its ability to communicate with women nationally and globally, and to have an understanding of the government's and the corporate elites' agenda that was inclusive of a more broadly based population of women.

The Alphabetization of Oppression

The marker most activists use to denote Canada's active involvement with the make-over of the capitalist beast is the negotiation and signing of the Free Trade Agreement (FTA). The FTA was ratified despite a major public outcry, and it foretold what could be expected from subsequent governments — despite public opposition, the corporate agenda will prevail.

The new economic world order involved a re-regulation (some say de-regulation) that favoured the business elite, the right wing and the political elites. In order to actualize this new economic world order, some things had to happen: money had to be found to fuel it; it had to be sold to the public; and opposition had to be dimmed or squelched.

The government, for its part, came up with the deficit dragon. Trade agreements and international investments along the lines that capitalists dreamed of meant the lowering of corporate taxes and tariffs to "allow the free flow of capital and goods."[5] What our government and corporations neglected to tell us was that by lowering corporate taxes and tariffs (taxes on goods for export and import), the government loses revenue. What Canada really had was a revenue-generating problem, not a deficit problem!

The creation of the deficit dragon and the making of the deficit slayer had begun. The federal Finance minister would prove to be the noble knight designated for this adventure. He would take us into the black.

But how did he choose to take us into the black? Well, he cut social spending; destroyed the social economy; cut health care, welfare, education, public and social services. Welfare bums, power-hungry feminists, greedy union bosses, irresponsible students, single mothers, those pesky immigrants and refugees, gays and lesbians, and "lying" environmentalists became the scapegoats for the revenue shortfall. But not to worry. "The women will pick up the slack" became the refrain of our governments and the capitalist giants. After all, women love volunteering in our communities.

Public- and private-sector downsizing — massive layoffs that disproportionately affected women, people of colour, indigenous peoples and people with disabilities — also became the order of the day, to maximize profits and to pay for the new global economy. The 80 or so right-wing think-tanks employed by the business elite and the corporate media in North America were used to sell the message that globalization is here to stay and that it is good for us.

In the meantime, countless treaties and trade agreements were being put in place. To date, the treaty with the greatest threat to people's rights, and therefore women's rights, is the Multilateral Agreement on Investments (MAI). The MAI is a new international treaty proposed by the 29 countries of the Organization of Economic Co-operation and Development (OECD), the rich nations, to give unprecedented rights to investors to enter foreign countries and operate freely in all sectors. These multinationals will not be accountable to national laws, and in fact a country could be held liable if the corporation deems that it or its citizens have acted in any way that undermines their profit-making capacity. For the Government of Canada to sit in a room with other rich nations and literally conspire to violate Canadians' rights and the rights of our allies in the South — none of whom is represented within the OECD — signals to us the depth of the control of the political and economic elites in our country and globally.

Once again, it has been the actions of women's, labour, environmental and peoples' rights groups in Canada and globally that have stalled this Charter of Corporate Rights for now. The fact that many elected officials in our federal, provincial and municipal governments were totally unaware of the MAI and its implications is indicative of the anti-democratic nature of global corporate capitalism.

The value principles of the MAI loudly discount the role of governments, and therefore peoples, in deciding on how we access, distribute or share the planet's resources and wealth. The MAI does not take into account the tradition of inequality inherent in capitalism, including its tendency toward sexism, classism and racism. The MAI undermines any movement to protect and guarantee the health of peoples and our environment for future generations. Women must denounce it as anti-woman, anti-equality and anti-sustainable development.

Women understand the benefit of trade and investment in our communities. We also know very clearly that trade must have goals that relate directly to building and ensuring equality in the home and the rest of the community; food security for all; environmental protection; progressive social and political development and participation; economic rights for all; and eradication of poverty and violence against women. Feminists must call for the renegotiation of all trade agreements to ensure that they guarantee, not violate, the security of peoples as it applies to food, housing, access to clean water and clean air, economic and political equality, social rights and the eradication of poverty and violence.

The Effect on Women

For women specifically, the cost of globalization has been great. Through the eyes of Canadian women, this is a snapshot of the price we are still paying:

- Increased poverty for women of all ages — the feminization of poverty;
- Increased migration of women: from the South to the North; within the South; within the North (as migrant workers, temp workers, domestic workers, refugees, immigrants);
- An increase in the wage gap between men and women;
- backward steps regarding pay and employment equity;
- Reduced access to post-secondary institutions owing to rising tuition costs;
- An increase in labour-intensive and part-time jobs;
- Destruction of social services, public services, health and education systems;
- Loss of employment, and underemployment;
- Increased trafficking in women and girls;
- A whopping increase in women's unpaid work — in the home, community and paid workforce;

✤ An attack on public pensions, which women rely on more than do men;

✤ An increase in racism, lesbophobia, xenophobia and the ever-present feminist backlash; and

✤ The de-funding and increased underfunding of equality-seeking women's groups and women's service organizations.

The extent of the feminist backlash is broad and far-reaching, as is the erosion of some of the gains made. The de-funding and underfunding of feminist organizations has resulted in the silencing of women's voices in many places, and affects our ability to do feminist research, advocacy, lobbying, and to have an impact on government policies and programs.

In 1997, Canadian women annually earned an average $30,700, as compared with $41,800 for men.[6] This "wage gap" is growing for women of colour, women with disabilities and Aboriginal women. Health care, education and public- and social-service sectors have received government cuts that have had a disproportionate and adverse impact on women, compared with men. One in three women works in these sectors, where some of the "better-paying" jobs with benefits could once be found. These jobs no longer exist.

Women, now more than ever, work in temporary jobs, low-paid, labour-intensive jobs and part-time jobs. Forty percent of women's positions are "non-standard" (part-time, temporary, self-employment or multiple jobs). On average, women earn 72 percent of what men earn (though for some groups of women, such as Aboriginals, immigrants and women with disabilities, it is as low as 50 percent). Young women are worse off than they were 10 years ago; 71.2 percent of women aged 18-24 earn less than $24,000 per year.[7]

Canada in 1996 had the second-highest incidence of low-paid employment for women among OECD countries, trailing only Japan. By December 1996, women in Canada made up 70.4 percent of part-timers.[8] This makes it even more difficult for women to access the new Employment Insurance.[9]

Of course, multinational corporations and governments tout globalization as a way to liberate the masses from poverty and discrimination. They advance the notion that globalization is genderless, raceless, classless, and so on, and that it is up to us as individuals to make it work. Women globally know this to be a lie. The economy and economic policy are based within the same framework as colonization.

Patriarchy, racism, white supremacy and other elements of oppression inform the goals of globalization. Neither Canada nor any other country has effectively dealt with these issues as yet.

Meanwhile, in Canada, as in many countries, women report that sexual harassment and other forms of sexism are alive and well in the workplace. In Canada, a study by the Canadian Auto Workers' Union reveals that, within the last decade, 90 percent of female workers report being sexually harassed on the job at least once,[10] and 18 percent say their employers have demanded they consent to sex or lose their jobs.

The most recent *United Nations Human Index Report* concluded that women performed $11 trillion worth of unpaid household work within the global economy. This does not include many other areas of unpaid work. Globally and within Canada, women perform two-thirds of all unpaid work. In Canada this is worth between $133 billion and $218 billion per year.[11]

This situation is even worse for women with disabilities, women of colour, Aboriginal women, women who are students, and older women. Women with disabilities earn 17 percent less than other women workers and face an unemployment rate of more than 50 percent for those who can work.[12]

Women of colour have an unemployment rate of 13.4 percent and earn 16 percent less than other women workers. Additionally, they are forced into accepting the bulk of the cheap labour positions (in factories, domestic work, hotels, restaurants, clerical). Migrant workers who are women of colour work without the protection of labour laws, since Canada refuses to sign the U.N. Convention on the Rights of All Migrant Workers and Their Families. Even though they pay taxes and make Canada Pension Plan (CPP) and Employment Insurance (EI) contributions, they are not guaranteed basic employment standards.[13]

Aboriginal women have unemployment rates of between 20 to 80 percent, depending whether they live on or off reserves. They earn 15 percent less than the average for other women workers.

More than 54 percent of Canada student-loan borrowers are women, and female students drop out at a higher rate than males, owing to economic barriers.[14]

Older single women are twice as poor as their male counterparts, and older women in general have a poverty rate of 22.1 percent. With the proposed changes to the CPP and the old-age pension, this will increase.[15]

For women's groups in particular, the fact that the federal government spends only $8.1 million on the Women's Program is very telling. This works out to 53 cents for every woman and girl child in Canada — less than the price of a cup of coffee! Yet the big banks, which made a profit of $7.4 billion in 1997, get more than $130 million to develop programs and new technologies, with the government giving tax breaks and other concessions for any liabilities incurred.

What kind of society are we building?

Capitalism is not a sustainable economic or development policy. It exploits, rather than protects, the guaranteed human rights of the population. It guarantees the wealth of only 20 percent of the population. It is rooted in racism, white supremacy, sexism and other oppressions. Why do we continue to support a system that is biased towards and exploitive of, at least 80 percent of the world's population?

whoa!

nice to hear an opinion other than pro-capitalism, let's Americanize the world

Challenging the Capitalist Beast

Globally, most of us form the opposition. This is why building a globalized resistance and creating alternatives has taken root in the international feminist movement.

Women around the world are challenging trade agreements, trading blocs and the "alphabets": the World Trade Organization (WTO), the General Agreement on Tariffs and Trades (GATT), the Multilateral Agreement on Investments (MAI), the Asia Pacific Economic Cooperation (APEC), the Association of South-East Asian Nations (ASEAN), the Free Trade Agreements of the Americas (FTAA), and so on. These acronyms stand for trading and economic systems that are biased against women, and are definitely not gender-neutral, especially when one considers that women control only 10 percent of the world economy, own only 1 percent of the world's land, yet perform more than 66 percent of the world's work![16] Women are 52 percent of the world's population.

It is important for us to challenge our governments to divest from these trade agreements and blocs in as many public fora as we can, and to put forward alternatives rooted in a people-first, before-economics framework. We must form our own think-tanks and reclaim our own markets. Women's groups, by teaming up with labour movements, environmentalists, human-rights activists, anti-poverty groups, peasant farmers, health-care workers, educators, gay and lesbian organizations, and grass-roots anti-violence movements, can challenge this new corporate, global beast. A more international activist movement is taking root. The women's movement in Canada has to increasingly solidify its own activism at a global level.

To achieve this, there are some key proposals being put forward by NAC and other women's groups here in Canada and globally. There are also some strategic points of pressure that women can apply to push our governments into acting on our behalf.

The stalling of the MAI, for example, gives us some breathing space to develop a Peoples' Alternative, an alternative that takes into account our social, political and economic rights. In Canada, NAC and other women's groups are participating in a broad coalition that is attempting to stop the MAI and develop a people-first, before-profits charter instead. This is happening all over the world. The fact that the MAI discussions will supposedly be taken away from the OECD and become the concern of the WTO, which has a broader membership and includes North, South, "rich" and "poor" nations, increases the likelihood that the most regressive and destructive components of the MAI will die.

Women of the world, with our meagre resources, have researched to some extent, and analyzed to a greater degree, the real impact of corporate global capitalism, trade and investment treaties, and the impact of international financial institutions such as the IMF and the WB in our lives and on our communities. It is NAC's belief, and that of many of our international partners, that the time has come for the world's economic structures to be reframed and remade from an equality standpoint. To this end, our call is for the abolition of the IMF and the WB, and their replacement with an International Economic and Social Council. This new council would be constructed using the principles outlined in the United Nations Economic and Social Protocol, the Beijing Platform for Action, and the World Summit on Social and Economic Rights.

This body must have enforcement powers and must be developed along democratic lines (i.e., with elected members, and a provision for all decisions affecting the economic, social and political development of countries to be voted on by these representatives before adoption). Mechanisms and funds that are slated to assist countries must do just that, not what has transpired so far with the SAPs.

In 1999, the United Nations will start a series of sessions with member states to assess their progress on the implementation of the Beijing Platform for Action and the U.N. Covenant on Economic and Social Rights, among others. In June 2000, the United Nations will host a special assembly comprising of women's groups that were accredited for the 1995 Fourth World Conference on Women in Beijing. We can choose to be "conference tourists" or "conference activists." We have the potential to influence and impact women's equality rights internationally and we must be prepared. Our ability to discern how our local conditions are tied up with global conditions is essential to any strategy we intend to employ in the next millennium.

In that year too, women in Canada and globally will be participating in the World March 2000 for the Eradication of Women's Poverty and Violence against Women.[17] This march builds on the work of the Quebec Women's March of 1995 and the NAC/Canadian Labour Congress March of 1996. The idea for the World 2000 March came from women in Beijing, who heard of the Quebec Women's March. This is an example of resistance and charting an agenda in action.

This agenda requires the women's movement in this country to challenge our solidarity partners locally, nationally and internationally not to see this as only a nationalistic issue, or an issue of sovereignty, or an issue of number of jobs. Our strategy must be to create a charter for peoples' rights and equality now. We must have clear non-negotiables. Race equality is a non-negotiable; women's equality is a non-negotiable; disability rights are a non-negotiable; anti-ageism is a non-negotiable; lesbian and gay rights are a non-negotiable; protection of the environment is a non-negotiable; protection of health, education and social programs is a non-negotiable; poverty eradication is non-negotiable; violence eradication is a non-negotiable; workers rights are a non-negotiable; valuing and including unpaid work in any economic or political strategy is a non-negotiable; Aboriginal self-government is a non-negotiable.

This basket of non-negotiables contains key tools that must be applied to all of our strategies in the third millennium that purport to advance peoples' rights and progressive social, economic and political development of all societies.

Human rights, democracy, sustainable development and peace make up the bottom line of the feminist agenda. Women's rights are human rights.

ENDNOTES

1. This article arises from a speech given at the University of Toronto for International Women's Day, March 8, 1998, and is based on an article published in *Canadian Woman Studies* 18, 1 (1998), pp. 6-10.

2. Development Alternatives for Women, "Women Reclaim the Market," paper presented at NGO Forum, World Summit for Social Development, Copenhagen, Denmark, March 8, 1995.

3. Ibid.

4. Michael Witter, "Higglering/Sidewalk Vending: Informal Commercial Trading in the Jamaican Economy," proceedings of a conference at the University of West Indies, Jamaica, June 1989.

5. Asia Pacific Economic Co-operation (APEC) Business Committee, *The Report of the Asia Pacific Economic Co-operation Business Committee* (APEC Business Committee, 1996).

6. Statistics Canada, *Labour Force Annual Averages* (Ottawa: Statistics Canada, 1998).

7. Canadian Labour Congress (CLC), *Women's Work: A Report* (Ottawa: CLC, 1997); and Canadian Auto Workers (CAW), *The Status of Women in Canada: Some Facts* (Toronto: CAW, 1997).

8. CLC (1997).

9. CAW (1997).

10. Ibid.

11. Statistics Canada, *Census* (Ottawa: Statistics Canada, 1996).

12. CAW (1997)

13. Toronto Organization for Domestic Workers, *Annual Report of INTERCEDE* (Toronto: INTERCEDE, 1996).

14. Canadian Federation of Students (CFS), *Strategy for Change* (Ottawa: CFS, 1997).

15. Older Women's Network, *Report on Pensions and Older Women's Poverty* (Toronto: Older Women's Network, no date).

16. United Nations, *1996 United Nations Human Index Report* (New York: 1996).

17. Fédération des femmes du Québec, "2000 Good Reasons to March" (see pages 273-283 in this book).

2000 GOOD REASONS TO MARCH

Fédération des femmes du Québec

The idea to hold a world march of women in the year 2000 was born out of the experience of the Women's March Against Poverty that took place in Québec in 1995. This march, initiated by the Fédération des femmes du Québec (FFQ), was hugely successful. Fifteen thousand people greeted the 850 women who marched for ten days to win nine demands related to economic justice. The entire Québec women's movement mobilized for the march as did many other segments of the population. The presence of women from countries of the South in that march reminded us of the importance of global solidarity-building.

The Beijing Conference later that year proved that women everywhere are struggling for equality, development and peace more than ever before. It was in Beijing that we made our first proposal to organize an international women's march. The International Preparatory Meeting for the World March was held in Montréal, Québec, Canada, on October 16-18, 1998; 140 delegates from 65 countries adopted the platform of world demands stated here and developed a plan of action for the World March of Women in the Year 2000.

The World March of Women in the Year 2000 is an action to improve women's living conditions. More precisely, the specific demands centre on the issues of poverty and violence against women. The international meeting held in October 1998 was only one of countless initiatives from civil society where women reaffirmed their determination to eradicate poverty and violence against women, with the conviction that this change must come from a large-scale mobilization of women around the world.

We Are Counting on the Presence of Thousands, Hopefully Millions, of Women in the Streets in the Year 2000!

We, the women of the world, are marching against the poverty that crushes four billion people on our planet, most of whom are women.

We are also marching to protest violence against women because this is a fundamental negation of human rights.

Against neoliberal capitalism that turns human beings, especially women, into an increasingly disposable, interchangeable and exploitable commodity. Against the subordination of individual and collective rights to the dictates of financial markets. Against the progressive disappearance of political power in the face of rising economic power.

Against the complicit silence of international financial institutions that sprang up after the Second World War (International Monetary Fund, World Bank, World Trade Organization) and other international and regional institutions: they perpetuate the exploitation of peoples by imposing structural adjustment programs in the South, deficit fighting and social program cutbacks in the North, and by concocting trade and other kinds of agreements such as the Multinational Agreement on Investment.

Against patriarchal ideology, still largely dominant today, under which violence against women continues to be a universal fact of life: spousal violence, sexual abuse, genital mutilation, homophobic and racist attacks, systematic rape in wartime, etc.

Against all wars. Against threats to the planet's survival and to a healthy environment.

Against all forms of violence against women, adolescent girls and children. Against all forms of violence perpetrated against the most vulnerable women in society.

We are marching against poverty and for sharing of wealth, against violence against women, and for the control and respect of our bodies.

What Kind of a World Do We Live In?

We live in a world where, at the turn of the millennium, profound disparities still exist between North and South, rich and poor, women and men, human beings and Nature.

We live in a world where unrestricted globalization of markets coupled with unbridled speculation are giving rise to extreme poverty. A total of 1.3 billion people, of whom 70 percent are women and children, live in abject poverty. It is a world that is hungry, a world where the richest 20 percent possess 83 percent of the planets revenue.

We live in a world where the State is neglecting its responsibilities and obligations due to the dictatorship of the market. It is a world where institutions such as the World Bank and the International Monetary Fund impose their rules on governments through structural adjustment policies.

We live in a world where discrimination against women is the main source of gender inequality. It is a world where, since time immemorial, women have contributed to humanity's development without their work being truly acknowledged. Thus, although women actually supply two-thirds of work hours, they only receive one-tenth of world revenue. Since the earliest times, the economy, no matter what kind, has been largely based on women's work, whether paid or unpaid, visible or invisible.

We live in a world where violence against women continues to be a universal reality. Conjugal violence, sexual aggression, genital mutilation, rape in wartime are the plight of thousands of women. Racism and homophobia add to the bleak picture.

What Kind of World Do We Want to Live In?

Women from all over the world are marching so that in the third millennium, their fundamental freedoms, indissociable from their human rights and undeniably universal in nature, are implemented once and for all. They are determined in their belief that all human rights are interdependent and that the values of equality, justice, peace, and solidarity will predominate.

Women from all over the world are marching in the knowledge that they have a responsibility to participate in political, economic, cultural and social life.

Women from all over the world are marching against all forms of violence and discrimination to which they are subjected.

Women from all over the world are marching to consolidate actions, based on principles of cooperation and sharing, aimed at instituting crucial changes.

Women are marching in affirmation of their desire to live in a better world.

Our Demands

Central to the purpose of the World March are the demands to end poverty and violence against women (drafted at the International Preparatory Meeting in October, 1998).

TO ELIMINATE POVERTY, WE DEMAND:

1. That all States adopt a legal framework and strategies aimed at eliminating poverty.

    States must implement national anti-poverty policies, programs, action plans and projects including specific measures to eliminate women's poverty and to ensure their economic and social independence through the exercise of their right to:

    o   Education;
    o   Employment, with statutory protection for work in the home and in the informal sectors of the economy;
    o   Pay equity and equality at the national and international levels;
    o   Association and unionization;
    o   Property and control of safe water;
    o   Decent housing;
    o   Health care and social protection;
    o   Culture;
    o   Life-long income security;
    o   Natural and economic resources (credit, property, vocational training, technologies);
    o   Full citizenship, including in particular recognition of civil identity and access to relevant documents (identity card); and
    o   Minimum social wage.

    States must guarantee, as a fundamental right, the production and distribution of food to ensure food security for their populations.

    States must develop incentives to promote the sharing of family respon-sibilities (education and care of children and domestic tasks) and provide concrete support to families such as daycare adapted to parents' work schedules, community kitchens, programs to assist children with their school work, etc.

    States must promote women's access to decision-making positions. They must make provisions to ensure women's equal participation in decision-making political bodies.

    States must ratify and observe the labour standards of the International

Labour Office (ILO). They must enforce observance of national labour standards in free trade zones.

States and international organizations should take measures to counter and prevent corruption.

All acts, pieces of legislation, regulations and positions taken by governments will be assessed in the light of indicators such as the human poverty index (HPI), introduced in the Human Development Report 1997; the human development index (HDI), put forth by the United Nations Development Program; the gender-related development index (including an indicator on the representation of women in positions of power) discussed in the Human Development Report 1995, and Convention 169 of the International Labour Organization particularly as it concerns Indigenous and tribal peoples' rights.

2. The urgent implementation of measures such as:
    o The Tobin tax. [In 1972, to stem rising speculation, James Tobin, economist and advisor to President Kennedy of the USA, proposed that a small tax of 0.1 percent to 0.5 percent be imposed on each speculative transaction. The World March has chosen to target the Tobin Tax in particular for its immediate impact on speculation, because this tax would generate a significant world fund, and because it is an attainable objective in the short term.] Revenue from the tax would be paid into a special fund:
        ❏ Earmarked for social development;
        ❏ Managed democratically by the international community as a whole;
        ❏ According to criteria respecting fundamental human rights and democracy;
        ❏ With equal representation of women and men; and
        ❏ To which women (who represent 70 percent of the 1.3 billion people living in extreme poverty) would have preferred access;
    o Investment of 0.7 percent of the rich countries' Gross National Product (GNP) in aid for developing countries;
    o Adequate financing and democratization of United Nations programs that are essential to defend women's and children's fundamental rights; for example, UNIFEM (UN women's program), UNDP (United Nations Development Program) and UNICEF (program for children);
    o An end to structural adjustment programs;
    o An end to cutbacks in social budgets and public services; and
    o Rejection of the proposed Multilateral Agreement on Investment (MAI).

3. Cancellation of the debt of all Third World countries, taking into account the principles of responsibility, transparency of information and accountability.

    We demand the immediate cancellation of the debt of the 53 poorest countries on the planet, in support of the objectives of the Jubilee 2000 campaign.

    In the longer term, we demand cancellation of the debt of all Third World countries and the setting up of a mechanism to monitor debt write-off, ensuring that this money is employed to eliminate poverty and further the well-being of people most affected by structural adjustment programs, the majority of whom are women and girls.

4. The implementation of the 20/20 formula between donor countries and the recipients of international aid. (In this scheme, 20 percent of the sum contributed by the donor country must be allocated to social development and 20 percent of the receiving government's spending must be used for social programs.)

5. A non-monolithic world political organization, with authority over the economy and egalitarian and democratic representation of all countries on earth and equal representation of women and men. This organization must have real decision-making power and authority to act in order to implement a world economic system that is fair, participatory and where solidarity plays a key role. The following measures must be instituted immediately:

    o   A World Council for Economic and Financial Security, which would be in charge of redefining the rules for a new international financial system based on the fair and equitable distribution of the planet's wealth. It would also focus on increasing the well-being, based on social justice, of the world population, particularly women, who make up over half that population. Gender parity should be observed in the composition of the Council's membership. Membership should also be comprised of representatives of the civil society (for example NGO's, unions, etc.), and should reflect parity of representation between countries from the North and South;

    o   Any ratification of trade conventions and agreements should be subordinated to individual and collective fundamental human rights. Trade should be subordinated to human rights, not the other way around;

    o   The elimination of tax havens;

[handwritten note at top: article seems to imply that all women want all of these things]

- ○ The end of banking secrecy;
- ○ Redistribution of wealth by the seven richest countries; and
- ○ A protocol to ensure application of the International Covenant on Economic, Social and Cultural Rights.

6. That the embargoes and blockades — principally affecting women and children — imposed by the major powers on many countries, be lifted.

TO ELIMINATE ALL FORMS OF VIOLENCE AGAINST WOMEN, WE DEMAND:

1. That governments claiming to be defenders of human rights condemn any authority — political, religious, economic or cultural — that controls women and girls, and denounce any regime that violates their fundamental rights.

2. That States recognize, in their statutes and actions, that all forms of violence against women are violations of fundamental human rights and cannot be justified by any custom, religion, cultural practice or political power. Therefore, all states must recognize a woman's right to determine her own destiny, and to exercise control over her body and reproductive functions.

3. That States implement action plans, effective policies and programs equipped with adequate financial and other means to end all forms of violence against women. States should take all possible steps to end patriarchal values and sensitize the society towards democratization of the family structure.

   These action plans must include the following elements in particular: prevention; public education; punishment; "treatment" for attackers; research and statistics on all forms of violence against women; assistance and protection for victims; campaigns against pornography, procuring, and sexual assault, including child rape; non-sexist education; end to the process of homogenization of culture and the commodification of women in media to suit the needs of the market; easier access to the criminal justice system; and training programs for judges and police.

4. That the United Nations bring extraordinary pressure to bear on member states to ratify without reservation and implement the conventions and covenants relating to the rights of women and children, in particular, the

International Covenant on Civil and Political Rights, the Convention on the Elimination of All Forms of Discrimination Against Women, the Convention on the Rights of the Child, the International Convention on the Elimination of All Forms of Racial Discrimination, the International Convention on the Protection of the Rights of All Migrant Workers and their Families.

That the United Nations pressure governments to respect human rights and resolve conflicts.

That States harmonize their national laws with these international human rights instruments as well as the Universal Declaration of Human Rights, the Declaration on the Elimination of Violence against Women, the Cairo and Vienna Declarations, and the Beijing Declaration and Platform for Action.

5. That, as soon as possible, protocols be adopted (and implementation mechanisms be established):
    o   To the International Convention on the Elimination of All Forms of Discrimination Against Women; and
    o   To the Convention on the Rights of the Child.
    These protocols will enable individuals and groups to bring complaints against their governments. They are a means to apply international pressure on governments to force them to implement the rights set out in these covenants and conventions. Provision must be made for appropriate sanctions against non-compliant States.

6. That mechanisms be established to implement the 1949 Convention for the Suppression of the Traffic in Persons and of the Exploitation of the Prostitution of Others, taking into account recent relevant documents such as the two resolutions of the United Nations General Assembly (1996) concerning trafficking in women and girls and violence against migrant women.

7. That States recognize the jurisdiction of the International Criminal Court and conform in particular to the provisions defining rape and sexual abuse as war crimes and crimes against humanity.

    That the United Nations end all forms of intervention, aggression and military occupation.

8. That all States adopt and implement disarmament policies with respect to conventional, nuclear, and biological weapons. That all countries ratify the Convention Against Land Mines.

9. That the right to asylum for women victims of sexist discrimination and persecution and sexual violence be adopted as soon possible. Also, that the United Nations assure the right of refugees to return to their homeland.

The next two demands were supported by the majority of women present at the meeting on the condition of a country-by-country adoption process. Some delegates were not in a position to be able to commit to defending publicly these demands in their country. They remain an integral part of the World March of Women in the year 2000.

10. That, based on the principle of equality of all persons, the United Nations and States of the international community recognize formally that a person's sexual orientation should not bar them from the full exercise of the rights set out in the following international instruments: the Universal Declaration of Human Rights, the International Covenant on Civil and Political Rights, the International Covenant on Economic, Social and Cultural Rights and the International Convention on the Elimination of All Forms of Discrimination Against Women.

11. That the right to asylum for victims of discrimination and persecution based on sexual orientation be adopted as soon as possible.

The Next Steps

The World March of Women in the Year 2000 is about women gathering from around the globe to fight poverty and violence against women. Since the very beginning, women from many countries have helped to organize the World March and many more are taking part in their own countries. There will be as many ways of mobilizing on the national scale as there are countries participating in the March. Each will bear the stamp of its own traditions and day-to-day reality, the richness of its own history and culture, and the array of its own concerns.

Three levels of action have been proposed for the March. First, there will be an action demonstrating women's mass support of the overall demands, signified by signing support cards. On March 8, 2000, the awareness and support card campaigns will be launched.

Secondly, women's movements in each country will organize national actions that will present demands reflecting their realities and priorities. National coalitions made up of different groups in the women's movement in each country will coordinate the local and national activities having to do with their priorities. Some coalitions may decide to take up as national demands some of the world demands that are most important in their context. Other coalitions will concentrate on existing demands of the women's movement in their country in relation to poverty and violence against women.

Finally, a world demonstration or rally will be held. On October 17, 2000, International Day for the Eradication of Poverty, women from the participating countries will meet in front of the United Nations after having marched, rallied or demonstrated in their respective country. In some countries, women will choose to have a big national rally. Others will organize a relay march from one end of the country to the other, or simultaneous one-day marches in many cities and towns. Together with marches and rallies, others will hold awareness-raising workshops, popular theatre, training sessions, school contests, photo or art exhibitions, or activities in streets and markets. Women's imagination and creativity know no bounds!

What we want is to stimulate a vast movement of grassroots women's groups so that the march becomes a gesture of affirmation by the women of the world. What we want is to promote equality between men and women. What we want is to highlight the common demands and initiatives issuing from the global women's movement relating to the issues of poverty and violence against women. What we want is to force governments, decision-makers and individuals the world over to institute the changes necessary for improving the status of women and women's quality of life. And what we want is to enter the new millennium by demonstrating women's ongoing determination to change the world.

We are certain that our international mobilization and pooling of ideas and analyses will generate world political pressure that cannot be ignored. It will be strong enough to initiate radical changes that are indispensable to the well-being of the world's population. This is how women will march forth into the new millennium: They will put the world back on track through sharing, peace and formal equality and they will proclaim that women more than ever will be players in fostering major change.

ENDNOTES

For further information or to get involved, contact: Marche mondiale des femmes en l'an 2000 / World March of Women in the Year 2000 / Marcha mundial de las mujeres en el año 2000, 110 rue Ste-Thérèse, #307, Montréal, Québec, Canada H2Y 1E6; phone: 514-395-1196; fax: 514-395-1224; e-mail: marche2000@ffq.qc.ca; website: http://www.ffq.qc.ca.

CONCLUSION

Some Like Indians Endure

Paula Gunn Allen

dykes remind me of Indians
like Indians dykes
are supposed to die out
or forget
or drink all the time
or shatter
or go away
to nowhere
to remember
what will happen
if they don't

they don't
anyway
even though it
happens
and they remember
they don't

because the moon remembers
because so does the sun
because so do the stars
remember
and the persistent stubborn
grass
of the earth

ABOUT THE CONTRIBUTORS

Paula Gunn Allen is an Aboriginal woman of Laguna Pueblo, Sioux, Lebanese and Scottish descent. She is a poet, novelist, literary critic and Professor Emerita of English at UCLA. She is the author of numerous books including *Off the Reservation: Reflections on Boundary Busting, Border Crossing, Loose Cannons* (Beacon, 1998) and *Life is a Fatal Disease: Collected Poems 1962-1995* (University of New Mexico Press, 1996), the novel *The Woman Who Owned the Shadows* (Aunt Lute, 1986) and edited several anthologies including *Voice of the Turtle: American Indian Literature 1900-1970* (Ballantine, 1995) and *Spider Woman's Granddaughters: Traditional Tales and Contemporary Writing by Native American Women* (Fawcett, 1990), which won a 1990 American Book Award.

Mary Ann Beavis was senior research associate at the Institute of Urban Studies, the University of Winnipeg for nine years, where she developed and taught the course "Women and Urban Environments." She is the founder of the Canadian Urban Research Network, and founder and principal editor of the *Canadian Journal of Urban Research*. She is currently assistant professor of religious studies at St. Thomas More College, the University of Saskatchewan. Her research interests include feminist biblical interpretation, ecofeminism and feminist eutopian literature.

Annette Burfoot, Ph.D, is associate professor of sociology and is cross appointed with the Institute of Women's Studies at Queen's University, Kingston, Ontario. Her areas of teaching and research include feminism and reproductive technologies, popular culture of the body, and the sociology of science and technology. In addition to *The Encyclopedia of Reproductive Technologies* (Westview, 1999) she has published widely on feminist perspectives of reproduction, the popular representation of women in science fiction film, and the social impact of biotechnology.

Kate Campbell is a doctoral student in the graduate program in women's studies at York University. Her dissertation research is on child custody decisions in Canada, with a focus on the legal and cultural impact of the current debates over "father's rights." The research for this article was completed as part of her MA thesis on the representation of lesbians in Canadian print media, undertaken at the School of Canadian Studies, Carleton University.

The **Fédération des femmes du Québec** (FFQ) is a non-partisan pressure group founded in 1966 whose aim is to promote and protect the interests and rights of women. The FFQ defines itself as a pluralistic, feminist organization. The FFQ encourages political activism, debate, education, coalition building and collective action. It is open to all women, without distinction as to colour, sexual orientation, civil status, religion, political conviction, language, ethnic origin or nationality, social, physical or mental condition. In addition to organizing and co-ordinating the international World March of Women 2000, the FFQ is very active in the struggle for social justice. The FFQ has been involved in many campaigns, including: social programs cutbacks; pay equity legislation; an increase in the minimum wage; and women's access to work, regardless of the sector.

Kathryn M. Feltey is an associate professor of sociology and former director of women's studies at the University of Akron. She is currently serving as vice-president of Sociologists for Women in Society. Her research focuses on the experience of homelessness in women's lives and programs designed to transition women and their children into stable housing. In addition, she has explored the ways that groups of individuals can effect change within their communities through activism and political participation. She is committed to the possibility of women reclaiming the future and creating a world in which homelessness and poverty are left behind in the 20th century.

Joan Grant-Cummings is the 13th president of Canada's National Action Committee on the Status of Women (NAC). She came to office in 1996 after being voted in by 90 percent of the delegates. Her appointment was the culmination of extensive community activism on women's issues. An African-Caribbean woman, she has also worked as an anti-racist pro-choice health activist and as an advocate for women's training and education programs. She is a founding member of the Ontario Black Women's coalition, was the executive director of Women's Health in Women's Hands Community Health Centre and has developed and facilitated anti-racist organizational development. She continues to promote the benefits of an anti-racist health system, provincially and nationally. She chaired Working Skills Centre for Women, was a board member of New Experiences for Refugee Women and was a board member of Intercede (the Toronto organization for Domestic Workers' Rights). She was a reproductive health counselor/administrative coordinator at the Immigrant Women's Health Centre and settlement counselor/administrator at the Jamaican Canadian Association (JCA). She continues to be a member of the JCA's women's committee. She has served as an appointed member of the Ontario Council of Regents — the body that appoints Governors to the 25 Ontario Community College Boards — and actively participated in many of its committees. She firmly believes that the struggle for equality rights rest heavily with the organizing of our movement as a cohesive anti-racist and anti-discriminatory force. She holds a BSc in Biology from the University of Ottawa and lives with her partner Everton and child Khiry.

Mary Beth Krouse is an assistant professor of sociology at Ohio University in Athens, Ohio, where she teaches courses in sociological theory, feminist theory and women's studies. She received her Ph.D from The Ohio State University in 1993. Her doctoral dissertation involved an indepth study of the AIDS Memorial Quilt and its beginnings as a cultural expression of gay activism in the late 1980s. She has published articles on the AIDS Memorial Quilt, on adaptations to feminist standpoint theory and on feminist pedagogy. In her scholarship and teaching, she focuses on the intersections of race, class and gender, and social movements and activism.

Marina Morrow is a community psychologist who currently teaches in women's studies at the University of British Columbia in Vancouver. She is also a research associate with the B.C. Centre of Excellence for Women's Health, where she has recently completed a project on women and mental health reform. She has been involved in feminist anti-violence activism and research for over ten years. In particular, her work focuses on the interactions between women's experiences, feminist movements, social policy and systemic change. Her other research interests include women and mental health and critical feminist and anti-racist pedagogy.

Laura Nichols is a graduate student in sociology at the University of Akron and has just completed a research fellowship at the Institute for Women's Policy Research in Washington, D.C. She has volunteered and worked in homeless shelters and has conducted research with people in the United States who have experienced homelessness and who are affected by welfare reform. She is especially concerned about the impact of homelessness and poverty on children. She has also had the opportunity to learn from women in El Salvador about poverty, community, hope and social change. Her other areas of interest include the impact of children on women's economic well-being, alternative economies, and work and family policies.

m.c. schraefel has an interdisciplinary background and Ph.D. Her research has ranged from feminist literary theory to digital document systems design. A musician and recording artist, schraefel has also taught in computer science, English and fine arts at University of Victoria, where she developed and taught the first interdisciplinary multimedia design courses for artists and engineers. She is currently an assistant professor in the computer science department at the University of Toronto, and consults for industry on issues of user experience and interface design.

Sunera Thobani is the immediate past-president of the National Action Committee on the Status of Women (NAC), Canada's largest feminist organization. The first woman of colour president of NAC, her tenure marked a milestone in building an anti-racist feminist movement in Canada. Prominent among the campaigns organized by NAC under her leadership are: the campaign for women's economic and social rights; participation in the United Nations Fourth World Conference on Women in Beijing, China; and the cross-Canada Women's March Against Poverty, the biggest women's march in Canadian history. She is currently serving as the Ruth Wynn Woodward Endowed Professor in women's studies at

Simon Fraser University, and was one of the key organizers of the Women's Conference Against APEC, held in Vancouver in November, 1997.

Margaret E. Thompson, who holds a Ph.D from the University of Wisconsin-Madison, is an associate professor in the School of Communication at the University of Denver. She teaches international and intercultural communication, and her research focuses on globalization and media issues in Central America and China, as well as international feminist media, and media processes and effects. She has published a number of articles in such journals as *Journal of Communication*, *Journal of Broadcasting & Electronic Media*, *Journalism & Mass Communication Quarterly* and *Mass Communication Review*.

María Suárez Toro is a Puerto Rican and Costa Rican feminist, teacher and women's human rights activist. She holds her teaching accreditation in the State of New York and in Costa Rica and a Masters Degree from The State University of New York at Albany. From 1988 to 1991, she was coordinator of the human rights popular education secretariat at the Central American Human Rights Commission (CODEHUCA), during which time she initiated the Women's Human Rights Project. She has taught adult literacy in Honduras, Costa Rica, Nicaragua and El Salvador; was a professor at the University of Costa Rica School of Education; and was an organizing member of the Latin American and Caribbean Linking Committee. She was also a member of the coalition that organized the Global Tribunal on Violations of Women's Human Rights at the NGO Forum in Vienna. She is currently involved in the Women's Human Rights Education Campaign, member of the board of directors of the Latin American and Caribbean Women's Health Network, of the Asociación de Mujeres en Salud, of the Advisory Board of the Global Fund for Women, and President of the Asociación de Comunicaciones Feminist Interactive Radio Endeavour. At present, she is co-producer of Feminist International Radio Endeavour (FIRE) at Radio for Peace International. She is author of many articles and chapters in books about international communities, women's rights are human rights, women's rights in Central America and adult literacy for refugees.

Vera M. Wabegijig is Anishnawbe:kwe from Mississauga First Nation in Ontario. She is a member of the Bear Clan and a Jingle Dress Dancer. She is a single parent of her beautiful two-year-old daughter, Storm. Currently, she is committed to a degree in fine arts with her major in creative writing and a minor in women's studies at the University of Victoria. Vera's poetry can be found in various anthologies such as *Gatherings VIII* and *IX* and *Native Women In the Arts*.

Allison Whitney holds an MA from the graduate program in communications at McGill University and an Honours BA in cinema studies from the University of Toronto. Her research interests include gender and technology, experimental Canadian cinema, immersive art installations and digital semiotics. In the fall of 1999, she began doctoral work in Cinema and Media Studies at the University of Chicago.

ABOUT THE EDITOR

Somer Brodribb is the author of *Nothing Mat(t)ers*, a feminist critique of postmodernism published by Spinifex, a feminist press in Australia. She earned a "plucky wench of the year award" for this book from *Ms. Magazine*. She has been active in issues of violence against women and poverty, and established a shelter with the Yukon Indian Women's Association. She has worked with international networks to stop reproductive and genetic engineering. With other feminists across campuses and in the community she has worked to raise awareness of systemic discrimination and harassment in universitites. She has been an editor with *Resources for Feminist Research* and *Women's Studies International Forum* and a guest editor with *Canadian Woman Studies*. Currently, she is an associate professor in the department of women's studies at the University of Victoria.

Best of gynergy books

Sweeping the Earth: Women Taking Action for a Healthy Planet, **Miriam Wyman** (ed.). "... a large and long-overdue contribution to our knowledge of how human-generated pollutants are affecting our health, our bodies and ourselves. Woven in among the science are the stories of women as activists, not only in Canada, but globally. We should feel the rising tide of anger at losing so many of our mothers and sisters and daughters to the 'down-side' of the Industrial Revolution. We must launch our new revolution to detoxify the planet. *Sweeping the Earth* provides the spark." Elizabeth May, Executive Director, Sierra Club of Canada

ISBN 0-921881-48-7   **$24.95**

Fragment by Fragment: Feminist Perspectives on Memory and Child Sexual Abuse, **Margo Rivera** (ed.). "The powerful threads of social, political and philosophical contexts that have informed the feminist discussion on memory and trauma are brilliantly illuminated here. A genuine addition to the library of anyone who takes this topic seriously." Laura Brown, Ph.D, psychologist in private practice

ISBN 0-921881-50-9   **$24.95**

Consciousness Rising: Women's Stories of Connection and Transformation, **Cheryl Malmo & Toni Suzuki Laidlaw** (eds.). "By focusing on the deep connections that women have forged with themselves and others, editors Malmo and Laidlaw have created a collection that seamlessly weaves the personal and the political into a vision of feminism that will flourish into the next century." Jeri Wine, Ph.D, psychologist in private practice

ISBN 0-92188-52-5   **$19.95**

---

gynergy books titles are available in quality bookstores everywhere. Ask for our books at your favourite local bookstore. Individual prepaid orders may be sent to: **gynergy books**, P.O. Box 2023, Charlottetown, PEI Canada C1A 7N7. Please add postage and handling ($4 for first book and $1 for each additional book) to your order. Payment may be made in U.S. or Canadian dollars. Canadian residents add 7% GST to the total amount. GST registration number R104383120.